APR. 07

U.S. Department of Justice
Office of Justice Programs
National Institute of Justice

NIJ

Special **REPORT**

Test Results for Digital Data Acquisition Tool: IXimager
(Version 2.0, Feb-01 2006)

www.ojp.usdoj.gov/nij

Office of Justice Programs
Innovation • Partnerships • Safer Neighborhoods
www.ojp.usdoj.gov

U.S. Department of Justice
Office of Justice Programs
810 Seventh Street N.W.
Washington, DC 20531

Alberto R. Gonzales
Attorney General

Regina B. Schofield
Assistant Attorney General

David W. Hagy, Ph.D.
*Deputy Assistant Attorney General, Office of Justice Programs
and Acting Principal Deputy Director, National Institute of Justice*

This and other publications and products of the National Institute
of Justice can be found at:

National Institute of Justice
www.ojp.usdoj.gov/nij

Office of Justice Programs
Innovation • Partnerships • Safer Neighborhoods
www.ojp.usdoj.gov

APR. 07

Test Results for Digital Data Acquisition
Tool: IXimager (Version 2.0, Feb-01 2006)

NCJ 217678

David W. Hagy, Ph.D.
*Deputy Assistant Attorney General, Office of Justice Programs
and Acting Principal Deputy Director, National Institute of Justice*

This report was prepared for the National Institute of Justice, U.S. Department of Justice, by the Office of Law Enforcement Standards of the National Institute of Standards and Technology under Interagency Agreement 2003–IJ–R–029.

The National Institute of Justice is a component of the Office of Justice Programs, which also includes the Bureau of Justice Assistance, the Bureau of Justice Statistics, the Office of Juvenile Justice and Delinquency Prevention, and the Office for Victims of Crime.

Test Results for Digital Data Acquisition Tool: IXimager (Version 2.0, Feb-01 2006)

April 2007

National Institute of Standards and Technology
Technology Administration, U.S. Department of Commerce

Contents

Introduction 4

Test Results for Digital Data Acquisition Tool 5

1 Results Summary 5
2 Test Case Selection 5
3 Results by Test Assertion 7
4 Testing Environment 9
    4.1   Test Computers 9
    4.2   Support Software 10
5 Test Results 10
    5.1   Test Results Report Key 10
    5.2   Test Details 11
        5.2.1   DA-01-ATA28 11
        5.2.2   DA-01-ATA48 12
        5.2.3   DA-01-FIREWIRE 14
        5.2.4   DA-01-SATA28 15
        5.2.5   DA-01-SATA48 17
        5.2.6   DA-01-SCSI 18
        5.2.7   DA-01-USB 19
        5.2.8   DA-02-CF 21
        5.2.9   DA-02-F12 22
        5.2.10   DA-02-F16 23
        5.2.11   DA-02-F32 25
        5.2.12   DA-02-F32X 26
        5.2.13   DA-02-HIDDEN 28
        5.2.14   DA-02-LX 30
        5.2.15   DA-02-NT 31
        5.2.16   DA-02-SWAP 33
        5.2.17   DA-02-THUMB 34
        5.2.18   DA-02-ZIP 36
        5.2.19   DA-04 37
        5.2.20   DA-06-ATA28 38
        5.2.21   DA-06-ATA48 40
        5.2.22   DA-06-FIREWIRE 41
        5.2.23   DA-06-SATA28 42
        5.2.24   DA-06-SATA48 44
        5.2.25   DA-06-SCSI 45
        5.2.26   DA-06-USB 46
        5.2.27   DA-07-CF 47
        5.2.28   DA-07-F12 48
        5.2.29   DA-07-F16 50
        5.2.30   DA-07-F32 51
        5.2.31   DA-07-F32X 53
        5.2.32   DA-07-FLOPPY 54
        5.2.33   DA-07-HIDDEN 55

5.2.34	DA-07-NT	57
5.2.35	DA-07-R1	58
5.2.36	DA-07-R5	59
5.2.37	DA-07-SWAP	60
5.2.38	DA-07-X2	62
5.2.39	DA-08-ATA28	63
5.2.40	DA-08-ATA48	65
5.2.41	DA-08-DCO	66
5.2.42	DA-09	68
5.2.43	DA-10-ENCRYPTED	70
5.2.44	DA-10-RAW	71
5.2.45	DA-12	73
5.2.46	DA-13	74
5.2.47	DA-14-ATA28	76
5.2.48	DA-14-ATA48	77
5.2.49	DA-14-CF	79
5.2.50	DA-14-ENCRYPTED	80
5.2.51	DA-14-F12	81
5.2.52	DA-14-F16	82
5.2.53	DA-14-F32	84
5.2.54	DA-14-F32X	85
5.2.55	DA-14-FIREWIRE	86
5.2.56	DA-14-FLOPPY	87
5.2.57	DA-14-HIDDEN	88
5.2.58	DA-14-HOT	89
5.2.59	DA-14-NT	91
5.2.60	DA-14-RAW	92
5.2.61	DA-14-SATA28	94
5.2.62	DA-14-SATA48	95
5.2.63	DA-14-SCSI	97
5.2.64	DA-14-SWAP	98
5.2.65	DA-14-THUMB	99
5.2.66	DA-14-USB	100
5.2.67	DA-14-X2	102
5.2.68	DA-14-ZIP	103
5.2.69	DA-17	104
5.2.70	DA-24	105
5.2.71	DA-25	106
5.2.72	DA-26-d2dd	107
5.2.73	DA-26-D2E	109
5.2.74	DA-26-D2R	110
5.2.75	DA-26-e2d	113
5.2.76	DA-26-r2d	114

Introduction

The Computer Forensics Tool Testing (CFTT) program is a joint project of the National Institute of Justice (NIJ), the research and development organization of the U.S. Department of Justice, and the National Institute of Standards and Technology's (NIST's) Office of Law Enforcement Standards (OLES) and Information Technology Laboratory (ITL). CFTT is supported by other organizations, including the Federal Bureau of Investigation, the U.S. Department of Defense Cyber Crime Center, U.S. Internal Revenue Service Criminal Investigation Division Electronic Crimes Program, and the U.S. Department of Homeland Security's Bureau of Immigration and Customs Enforcement and U.S. Secret Service. The objective of the CFTT program is to provide measurable assurance to practitioners, researchers, and other applicable users that the tools used in computer forensics investigations provide accurate results. Accomplishing this requires the development of specifications and test methods for computer forensics tools and subsequent testing of specific tools against those specifications.

Test results provide the information necessary for developers to improve tools, users to make informed choices, and the legal community and others to understand the tools' capabilities. This approach to testing computer forensic tools is based on well-recognized methodologies for conformance and quality testing. The specifications and test methods are posted on the CFTT Web site (http://www.cftt.nist.gov/) for review and comment by the computer forensics community.

This document reports the results from testing the **IXimager**—a noncommercial, restricted-use, law-enforcement-only, evidence production tool—against the *Digital Data Acquisition Tool Assertions and Test Plan Version 1.0*, available at the CFTT Web site (http://www.cftt.nist.gov/DA-ATP-pc-01.pdf).

Test results from other software packages and the CFTT tool methodology can be found on NIJ's computer forensics tool testing Web page, http://www.ojp.usdoj.gov/nij/topics/ecrime/cftt.htm.

Test Results for Digital Data Acquisition Tool

Tool Tested: ILook IXimager
Version: 2.0, Feb-01 2006
Run Environment: Custom (Linux version 2.4.32-erik)

Supplier: U.S. Internal Revenue Service, Criminal Investigation Division,
                   Electronic Crimes Program

Address: IRS CI Electronic Crimes—Springfield Facility
                       6359 Walker Lane, Suite 210
                       Alexandria, VA 22310
                       703-822-8411

                   http://www.ilook-forensics.org/homepage.html
                   ecilookproject@ilook-forensics.org

1 Results Summary

The tested tool acquired all visible and hidden sectors completely and accurately from the test media. In the case of a hard drive with 22 defective sectors, the sectors of the image corresponding to the defective sectors were replaced with forensically benign content.

2 Test Case Selection

Not all test cases or test assertions are appropriate for all tools. Each test case is assigned to a selection criterion based on optional tool features needed for the test case. If a given tool implements a given feature listed below then test cases assigned to the associated criterion are executed. In addition, the availability of a test support tool to generate device I/O errors is required for execution of some test cases.

Two test assertions only apply in special circumstances. The assertion AO–22 is checked only for tools that create block hashes. This assertion does not apply for the IXimager. The assertion AO–24 is only checked if the tool is executed in a run time environment that does not modify attached storage devices, such as MS–DOS. In normal operation an imaging tool is used in conjunction with a write block device to protect the source drive, however a blocker was not used during the tests so that assertion AO–24 could be checked.

Test cases DA–06, DA–07, DA–08, and DA–12 were selected because they are basic to all tools.

The other test cases are either selected or not selected based on tool features and capabilities.

The tool does not create cylinder-aligned clones: omit DA–03, DA–15, DA–21, and DA–23.

The tool creates image files in more than one format: include DA–10.

The tool converts image files from one format to another: include DA–26.

The tool can create a clone during acquisition: include DA–01, DA–02, and DA–04.

The tool implements destination device switching: include DA–13.

A device I/O error generator is available (but only for source drives): include DA–09; omit DA–05, DA–11, and DA–18.

The tool does not fill excess sectors on a clone device: omit DA–19, DA–20, DA–21, DA–22, and DA–23.

The tool can create a clone from an image file: include DA–14 and DA–17, but omit DA–22 (no fill feature).

The tool does not create a clone from a subset of an image file: omit DA–16.

The tool can detect a corrupted (or changed) image file: include DA–24 and DA–25.

Some test cases have variant forms to accomadate parameters within test assertions AM–01, AM–02, AM–03, AM–05, and AO–13. For an acquisition the tool must execute in an execution environment, XE. In addition, a digital source, DS, defines the type of object acquired. The access interface for the source, SRC–AI, must be specified. Additional test parameters include the file system type, FS, for creation of the image file and the access interface used to write to a clone, DST–AI. Variations were also created for AO–02 image file format and AO–09, image format conversion.

The IXimager only executes in a custom environment: Linux version 2.4.32-erik.

The following source interfaces (SRC–AI) were tested: ATA28, ATA48, SATA28, SATA48, SCSI, USB, and FireWire.

The following digital sources were tested: partitions (FAT12, FAT16, FAT32, FAT32X, EXT2, hidden FAT, NTFS, and Linux Swap), RAID–1, RAID–5, flash card, thumb drive, floppy, and ZIP.

The image files were created, FS, on FAT32X partitions.

The following interfaces (DST–AI) were used for clone creation: ATA28, ATA48, SATA28, SATA48, SCSI, USB, and FireWire.

Tested image formats include the ILook default (compressed), ILook encrypted, and raw.

Format conversion variations include: default to unformatted (as would be produced by the Unix command **dd**), default to ILook encrypted, default to ILook raw, ILook encrypted to default, and ILook raw to default.

3 Results by Test Assertion

Table 1 summarizes the test results by assertion. The column labeled **Assertion** gives the text of each assertion. The column labeled **Tests** gives the number of test cases that use the given assertion. The column labeled **Anomalies** gives the number of observed anomalies for the given assertion. Note that no anomalies were observed for any assertion.

Table 1 Results Summary by Assertion

Assertion	Tests	Anomalies
AM-01 The tool uses access interface SRC-AI to access the digital source.	46	0
AM-02 The tool acquires digital source, DS.	46	0
AM-03 The tool executes in execution environment, XE.	76	0
AM-04 If clone creation is specified, the tool creates a clone of the digital source.	19	0
AM-05 If image file creation is specified, the tool creates an image file on file system type, FS.	27	0
AM-06 All visible sectors are acquired from the digital source.	45	0
AM-07 All hidden sectors are acquired from the digital source.	3	0
AM-08 All sectors acquired from the digital source are acquired accurately.	45	0
AM-09 If unresolved errors occur while reading from the selected digital source, the tool notifies the user of the error type and location within the digital source.	1	0
AM-10 If unresolved errors occur while reading from the selected digital source, the tool uses a benign fill in the destination object in place of the inaccessible data.	1	0
AO-01 If the tool creates an image file, the data represented by the image file is the same as the data acquired by the tool.	26	0
AO-02 If an image file format is specified, the tool creates an image file in the specified format.	2	0
AO-03 If there is an error while writing the image file, the tool notifies the user.	0	0
AO-04 If the tool is creating an image file and there is insufficient space on the image destination device to contain the image file, the tool shall notify the user.	2	0
AO-05 If the tool creates a multifile image of a requested size then all the individual files shall be no larger than the requested size.	26	0
AO-06 If the tool performs an image file integrity check on an image file that has not been changed since the file was created, the tool shall notify the user that the image file has not been changed.	1	0
AO-07 If the tool performs an image file integrity check on an image file that has been changed since the file was created, the tool shall notify the user that the image file has been changed.	1	0
AO-08 If the tool performs an image file integrity check on an image file that has been changed since the file was created, the tool shall notify the user of	1	0

Assertion	Tests	Anomalies
the affected locations.		
AO-09 If the tool converts a source image file from one format to a target image file in another format, the acquired data represented in the target image file is the same as the acquired data in the source image file.	5	0
AO-10 If there is insufficient space to contain all files of a multifile image and if destination device switching is supported, the image is continued on another device.	1	0
AO-11 If requested, a clone is created during an acquisition of a digital source.	19	0
AO-12 If requested, a clone is created from an image file.	23	0
AO-13 A clone is created using access interface DST-AI to write to the clone device.	42	0
AO-14 If an unaligned clone is created, each sector written to the clone is accurately written to the same disk address on the clone that the sector occupied on the digital source.	41	0
AO-15 If an aligned clone is created, each sector within a contiguous span of sectors from the source is accurately written to the same disk address on the clone device relative to the start of the span as the sector occupied on the original digital source. A span of sectors is defined to be either a mountable partition or a contiguous sequence of sectors not part of a mountable partition. Extended partitions, which may contain both mountable partitions and unallocated sectors, are not mountable partitions.	0	0
AO-16 If a subset of an image or acquisition is specified, all the subset is cloned.	0	0
AO-17 If requested, any excess sectors on a clone destination device are not modified.	40	0
AO-18 If requested, a benign fill is written to excess sectors of a clone.	0	0
AO-19 If there is insufficient space to create a complete clone, a truncated clone is created using all available sectors of the clone device.	2	0
AO-20 If a truncated clone is created, the tool notifies the user.	2	0
AO-21 If there is a write error during clone creation, the tool notifies the user.	0	0
AO-22 If requested, the tool calculates block hashes for a specified block size during an acquisition for each block acquired from the digital source.	0	0
AO-23 If the tool logs any log significant information, the information is accurately recorded in the log file.	76	0
AO-24 If the tool executes in a forensically safe execution environment, the digital source is unchanged by the acquisition process.	46	0

4 Testing Environment

The tests were run in the NIST CFTT lab. This section describes the test computers available for testing.

4.1 Test Computers

Eight test computers were used.

Freddy, **Frank**, **Joe**, and **Max** have the following configuration:

Intel® Desktop Motherboard D865GB/D865PERC (with ATA–6 IDE on board controller)
BIOS Version BF86510A.86A.0053.P13
Adaptec SCSI BIOS V3.10.0
Intel® Pentium® 4 CPU
SONY DVD RW DRU–530A, ATAPI CD/DVD-ROM drive
1.44MB floppy drive
Two slots for removable IDE hard disk drives
Two slots for removable SATA hard disk drives
Two slots for removable SCSI hard disk drives

JohnSteed has the following configuration:

FIC IC–VL67 (865G; S478; 800MHz) Intel® Desktop Motherboard
Phoenix-Award BIOS version v6.00PG
Intel® Pentium® 4 CPU
Plextor DVDR PX–716A, ATAPI CD/DVD-ROM drive
WDC WD800JB–00JJC0, 80 GB ATA disk drive
1.44MB floppy drive
Three IEEE 1394 ports
Four USB ports

Nick has the following configuration:

Dell Optiplex GX260 Series
Intel® Pentium® 4 CPU 2GHz
Phoenix ROM BIOS PLUS version 1.10 revision A06
2048 MB DDR SDRAM
80 GB IC35L090AUV207–0 Hitachi IDE hard drive
NEC DVD+RW ND–1100A Drive
Lite-On LTN486S 48x CD-ROM drive
ZIP 250 Drive
Floppy Drive
6 USB ports
Firestorm 6D906 IEEE 1394a PCI Adapter

Paladin has the following configuration:

Intel® D845WNL Motherboard

BIOS: HV84510A.86A.0022.P05
Intel® Pentium® IV 2.0Ghz
512672k Memory
Adaptec 29160 SCSI Adapter card
Tekram DC–390U3W SCSI Adapter card
Plextor CR–RW PX–W124TS Rev: 1.06
LG 52X CDROM
floppy drive
Three slots for removable IDE hard disk drives
Two slots for removable SCSI hard disk drive

SamSpade has the following configuration:

Intel® D865PERL Motherboard
Intel® Pentium® 4 CPU 2.4GHz
BE7X 1.08.00.048 BIOS
FE7X 1.05.00.063 Firmware
2048 MB RAM
ABIT R9200SE–T APG graphics adapter
3ware ATA RAID Contoller: Escalade 7506–4LP
Lite-On DVDRW SHOW–1234 Drive
Floppy Drive
4 USB ports
4 slots for IDE RAID drives

4.2 Support Software

A package of programs to support test analysis, FS–TST Release 2.0, was used. The software can be obtained from: http://www.cftt.nist.gov/diskimaging/fs-tst20.zip.

5 Test Results

The main item of interest for interpreting the test results is determining the conformance of the device with the test assertions. Conformance with each assertion tested by a given test case is evaluated by examining **Log Highlights** box of the test report summary.

5.1 Test Results Report Key

A summary of the actual test results is presented in this report. The following table presents a description of each section of the test report summary.

Heading	Description
First Line	Test case ID, name and version of tool tested.
Case Summary	Test case summary from *Digital Data Acquisition Tool Assertions and Test Plan Version 1.0*.
Assertions	The test assertions applicable to the test case, selected from *Digital Data Acquisition Tool Assertions and Test Plan Version 1.0*.
Tester Name	Name or initials of person executing test procedure.
Test Host	Host computer executing the test.
Test Date	Time and date that test was started.
Drives	Source drive (the drive acquired), destination drive (if a clone is created) and media drive (to contain a created image).
Source Setup	Layout of partitions on the source drive and the expected hash of the drive.
Log Highlights	Information extracted from various log files to illustrate conformance or non-conformance to the test assertions.
Results	Expected and actual results for each assertion tested.
Analysis	Whether or not the expected results were achieved.

5.2 Test Details

5.2.1 DA-01-ATA28

```
Test Case DA-01-ATA28 ILook IXimager Version 2.0, Feb 01 2006
```

Description:	DA-01 Acquire a physical device using access interface AI to an unaligned clone.
Assertions:	AM-01 The tool uses access interface SRC-AI to access the digital source. AM-02 The tool acquires digital source DS. AM-03 The tool executes in execution environment XE. AM-04 If clone creation is specified, the tool creates a clone of the digital source. AM-06 All visible sectors are acquired from the digital source. AM-08 All sectors acquired from the digital source are acquired accurately. AO-11 If requested, a clone is created during an acquisition of a digital source. AO-13 A clone is created using access interface DST-AI to write to the clone device. AO-14 If an unaligned clone is created, each sector written to the clone is accurately written to the same disk address on the clone that the sector occupied on the digital source. AO-17 If requested, any excess sectors on a clone destination device are not modified. AO-22 If requested, the tool calculates block hashes for a specified block size during an acquisition for each block acquired from the digital source. AO-23 If the tool logs any log significant information, the information is accurately recorded in the log file. AO-24 If the tool executes in a forensically safe execution environment, the digital source is unchanged by the acquisition process.
Tester Name:	brl
Test Host:	Max
Test Date:	Tue Mar 21 16:58:41 2006
Drives:	src(41) dst (42) other (none)
Source Setup:	src hash: < 15CAA1A307271160D8372668BF8A03FC45A51CC9 > 78125000 total sectors (40000000000 bytes)

	Test Case DA-01-ATA28 ILook IXimager Version 2.0, Feb 01 2006

	65534/015/63 (max cyl/hd values)
	65535/016/63 (number of cyl/hd)
	IDE disk: Model (WDC WD400BB-75JHC0) serial # (WD-WMAMC4658355)
	  N Start LBA Length Start C/H/S End C/H/S boot Partition type
	  1 P 000000063 078107967 0000/001/01 1023/254/63 Boot 07 NTFS
	  2 P 000000000 000000000 0000/000/00 0000/000/00 00 empty entry
	  3 P 000000000 000000000 0000/000/00 0000/000/00 00 empty entry
	  4 P 000000000 000000000 0000/000/00 0000/000/00 00 empty entry
	1 078107967 sectors 39991279104 bytes

Log Highlights:	Comparision of original to clone Sectors compared: 78125000 Sectors match: 78125000 Sectors differ: 0 Bytes differ: 0 Diffs range 0 source read errors, 0 destination read errors IXImager Log file hda: 78125000 sectors (40000 MB) w/2048KiB Cache, CHS=65535/16/63, UDMA(100) hdb: 78125000 sectors (40000 MB) w/2048KiB Cache, CHS=65535/16/63, UDMA(100) Initializing... Opened input device '/dev/hdb' Opened output device '/dev/hda' Beginning Clone operation for 40000000000 bytes Beginning Clone operation Beginning Clone operation Clone Complete Clone was completed successfully. Read : 40.00 GB (40000000000 bytes) Written : 40.00 GB (40000000000 bytes) Total Processed: 40.00 GB (40000000000 bytes) Clone Speed : 31.45 MB/sec Elapsed Time : 0h 21m 12s Bad Sectors : 0 Clearing computer memory... Source SHA1 Hash: 15CAA1A307271160D8372668BF8A03FC45A51CC9
Results:	

Assertion & Expected Result	Actual Result
AM-01 Source acquired using interface AI.	as expected
AM-02 Source is type DS.	as expected
AM-03 Execution environment is XE.	as expected
AM-04 A clone is created.	as expected
AM-06 All visible sectors acquired.	as expected
AM-08 All sectors accurately acquired.	as expected
AO-11 A clone is created during acquisition.	as expected
AO-13 Clone created using interface AI.	as expected
AO-14 An unaligned clone is created.	as expected
AO-17 Excess sectors are unchanged.	as expected
AO-22 Tool calculates hashes by block.	option not available
AO-23 Logged information is correct.	as expected
AO-24 Source is unchanged by acquisition.	as expected

Analysis:	Expected results achieved

5.2.2 DA-01-ATA48

	Test Case DA-01-ATA48 ILook IXimager Version 2.0, Feb 01 2006
Description:	DA-01 Acquire a physical device using access interface AI to an unaligned clone.
Assertions:	AM-01 The tool uses access interface SRC-AI to access the digital source. AM-02 The tool acquires digital source DS. AM-03 The tool executes in execution environment XE.

Test Case DA-01-ATA48 ILook IXimager Version 2.0, Feb 01 2006

	AM-04 If clone creation is specified, the tool creates a clone of the digital source. AM-06 All visible sectors are acquired from the digital source. AM-08 All sectors acquired from the digital source are acquired accurately. AO-11 If requested, a clone is created during an acquisition of a digital source. AO-13 A clone is created using access interface DST-AI to write to the clone device. AO-14 If an unaligned clone is created, each sector written to the clone is accurately written to the same disk address on the clone that the sector occupied on the digital source. AO-17 If requested, any excess sectors on a clone destination device are not modified. AO-22 If requested, the tool calculates block hashes for a specified block size during an acquisition for each block acquired from the digital source. AO-23 If the tool logs any log significant information, the information is accurately recorded in the log file. AO-24 If the tool executes in a forensically safe execution environment, the digital source is unchanged by the acquisition process.
Tester Name:	brl
Test Host:	Freddy
Test Date:	Wed Mar 22 15:46:50 2006
Drives:	src(4F) dst (4D) other (none)

Source Setup:	src hash: < 51FE53FD6BF7B7B69A875EDBD9AC01D41194C78C >
	488397168 total sectors (250059350016 bytes)
	30400/254/63 (max cyl/hd values)
	30401/255/63 (number of cyl/hd)
	IDE disk: Model (WDC WD2500JB-00EVA0) serial # (WD-WMAEH2681554)
	  N Start LBA Length Start C/H/S End C/H/S boot Partition type
	  1 P 000000063 268413957 0000/001/01 1023/254/63 Boot 07 NTFS
	  2 P 000000000 000000000 0000/000/00 0000/000/00 00 empty entry
	  3 P 000000000 000000000 0000/000/00 0000/000/00 00 empty entry
	  4 P 000000000 000000000 0000/000/00 0000/000/00 00 empty entry
	1 268413957 sectors 137427945984 bytes

Log Highlights:	Comparision of original to clone Sectors compared: 488397168 Sectors match: 488397168 Sectors differ: 0 Bytes differ: 0 Diffs range 0 source read errors, 0 destination read errors IXImager Log file hda: 488397168 sectors (250059 MB) w/8192KiB Cache, CHS=30401/255/63, UDMA(33) hdb: 488397168 sectors (250059 MB) w/8192KiB Cache, CHS=30401/255/63, UDMA(33) Initializing... Opened input device '/dev/hdb' Opened output device '/dev/hda' Beginning Clone operation for 250059350016 bytes Beginning Clone operation Beginning Clone operation Clone Complete Clone was completed successfully. Read : 250.1 GB (250059350016 bytes) Written : 250.1 GB (250059350016 bytes) Total Processed: 250.1 GB (250059350016 bytes) Clone Speed : 14.71 MB/sec Elapsed Time : 4h 43m 19s Bad Sectors : 0 Clearing computer memory... Source SHA1 Hash: 51FE53FD6BF7B7B69A875EDBD9AC01D41194C78C
Results:	

Assertion & Expected Result	Actual Result
AM-01 Source acquired using interface AI.	as expected

Test Case DA-01-ATA48 ILook IXimager Version 2.0, Feb 01 2006		
	AM-02 Source is type DS.	as expected
	AM-03 Execution environment is XE.	as expected
	AM-04 A clone is created.	as expected
	AM-06 All visible sectors acquired.	as expected
	AM-08 All sectors accurately acquired.	as expected
	AO-11 A clone is created during acquisition.	as expected
	AO-13 Clone created using interface AI.	as expected
	AO-14 An unaligned clone is created.	as expected
	AO-17 Excess sectors are unchanged.	as expected
	AO-22 Tool calculates hashes by block.	option not available
	AO-23 Logged information is correct.	as expected
	AO-24 Source is unchanged by acquisition.	as expected
Analysis:	Expected results achieved	

5.2.3 DA-01-FIREWIRE

Test Case DA-01-FIREWIRE ILook IXimager Version 2.0, Feb 01 2006	
Description:	DA-01 Acquire a physical device using access interface AI to an unaligned clone.
Assertions:	AM-01 The tool uses access interface SRC-AI to access the digital source. AM-02 The tool acquires digital source DS. AM-03 The tool executes in execution environment XE. AM-04 If clone creation is specified, the tool creates a clone of the digital source. AM-06 All visible sectors are acquired from the digital source. AM-08 All sectors acquired from the digital source are acquired accurately. AO-11 If requested, a clone is created during an acquisition of a digital source. AO-13 A clone is created using access interface DST-AI to write to the clone device. AO-14 If an unaligned clone is created, each sector written to the clone is accurately written to the same disk address on the clone that the sector occupied on the digital source. AO-17 If requested, any excess sectors on a clone destination device are not modified. AO-22 If requested, the tool calculates block hashes for a specified block size during an acquisition for each block acquired from the digital source. AO-23 If the tool logs any log significant information, the information is accurately recorded in the log file. AO-24 If the tool executes in a forensically safe execution environment, the digital source is unchanged by the acquisition process.
Tester Name:	brl
Test Host:	Joe
Test Date:	Fri Mar 24 16:09:33 2006
Drives:	src(24-FU2) dst (61-FU2) other (none)
Source Setup:	src hash: < A78EDB5E90298D0CDF199B4B62119F81208A252A > 39070080 total sectors (20003880960 bytes) 19076/063/32 (max cyl/hd values) 19077/064/32 (number of cyl/hd) Model (ATCS04-0) serial # (CSH206D9DSEL)
Log Highlights:	Comparision of original to clone Sectors compared: 39070080 Sectors match: 39070080 Sectors differ: 0 Bytes differ: 0 Diffs range Source (39070080) has 78234912 fewer sectors than destination (117304992) Zero fill: 0 Src Byte fill (24): 0 Dst Byte fill (61): 78234912 Other fill: 0 Other no fill: 0 Zero fill range: Src fill range: Dst fill range: 39070080-117304991

	Test Case DA-01-FIREWIRE ILook IXimager Version 2.0, Feb 01 2006
	Other fill range: Other not filled range: 0 source read errors, 0 destination read errors IXImager Log file SCSI device sdb: 117304992 512-byte hdwr sectors (60060 MB) SCSI device sdc: 39070080 512-byte hdwr sectors (20004 MB) SCSI device sdb: 117304992 512-byte hdwr sectors (60060 MB) Initializing... Opened input device '/dev/sdc' Opened output device '/dev/sdb' Beginning Clone operation for 20003880960 bytes Beginning Clone operation Beginning Clone operation Clone Complete Clone was completed successfully. Read : 20.00 GB (20003880960 bytes) Written : 20.00 GB (20003880960 bytes) Total Processed: 20.00 GB (20003880960 bytes) Clone Speed : 6.428 MB/sec Elapsed Time : 0h 51m 52s Bad Sectors : 0 Clearing computer memory... Source SHA1 Hash: A78EDB5E90298D0CDF199B4B62119F81208A252A
Results:	

Assertion & Expected Result	Actual Result
AM-01 Source acquired using interface AI.	as expected
AM-02 Source is type DS.	as expected
AM-03 Execution environment is XE.	as expected
AM-04 A clone is created.	as expected
AM-06 All visible sectors acquired.	as expected
AM-08 All sectors accurately acquired.	as expected
AO-11 A clone is created during acquisition.	as expected
AO-13 Clone created using interface AI.	as expected
AO-14 An unaligned clone is created.	as expected
AO-17 Excess sectors are unchanged.	as expected
AO-22 Tool calculates hashes by block.	option not available
AO-23 Logged information is correct.	as expected
AO-24 Source is unchanged by acquisition.	as expected

Analysis:	Expected results achieved

5.2.4 DA-01-SATA28

Test Case DA-01-SATA28 ILook IXimager Version 2.0, Feb 01 2006	
Description:	DA-01 Acquire a physical device using access interface AI to an unaligned clone.
Assertions:	AM-01 The tool uses access interface SRC-AI to access the digital source. AM-02 The tool acquires digital source DS. AM-03 The tool executes in execution environment XE. AM-04 If clone creation is specified, the tool creates a clone of the digital source. AM-06 All visible sectors are acquired from the digital source. AM-08 All sectors acquired from the digital source are acquired accurately. AO-11 If requested, a clone is created during an acquisition of a digital source. AO-13 A clone is created using access interface DST-AI to write to the clone device. AO-14 If an unaligned clone is created, each sector written to the clone is accurately written to the same disk address on the clone that the sector occupied on the digital source. AO-17 If requested, any excess sectors on a clone destination device are not modified. AO-22 If requested, the tool calculates block hashes for a specified block size during an acquisition for each block acquired from the digital source. AO-23 If the tool logs any log significant information, the information is

Test Case DA-01-SATA28 ILook IXimager Version 2.0, Feb 01 2006

	accurately recorded in the log file. AO-24 If the tool executes in a forensically safe execution environment, the digital source is unchanged by the acquisition process.
Tester Name:	brl
Test Host:	Joe
Test Date:	Wed Mar 22 10:41:20 2006
Drives:	src(07) dst (06) other (none)
Source Setup:	src hash: < 655E9BDDB36A3F9C5C4CC8BF32B8C5B41AF9F52E> 156301488 total sectors (80026361856 bytes) Model (WDC WD800JD-32HK) serial # (WD-WMAJ91510044) N Start LBA Length Start C/H/S End C/H/S boot Partition type 1 P 000000063 156280257 0000/001/01 1023/254/63 Boot 07 NTFS 2 P 000000000 000000000 0000/000/00 0000/000/00 00 empty entry 3 P 000000000 000000000 0000/000/00 0000/000/00 00 empty entry 4 P 000000000 000000000 0000/000/00 0000/000/00 00 empty entry 1 156280257 sectors 80015491584 bytes
Log Highlights:	Comparision of original to clone Sectors compared: 156301488 Sectors match: 156301488 Sectors differ: 0 Bytes differ: 0 Diffs range 0 source read errors, 0 destination read errors IXImager Log file ata1: dev 0 ATA-6, max UDMA/133, 156301488 sectors: LBA ata2: dev 0 ATA-6, max UDMA/133, 156301488 sectors: LBA SCSI device sdb: 156301488 512-byte hdwr sectors (80026 MB) SCSI device sdc: 156301488 512-byte hdwr sectors (80026 MB) SCSI device sdc: 156301488 512-byte hdwr sectors (80026 MB) Initializing... Opened input device '/dev/sdb' Opened output device '/dev/sdc' Beginning Clone operation for 80026361856 bytes Beginning Clone operation Beginning Clone operation Clone Complete Clone was completed successfully. Read : 80.03 GB (80026361856 bytes) Written : 80.03 GB (80026361856 bytes) Total Processed: 80.03 GB (80026361856 bytes) Clone Speed : 48.01 MB/sec Elapsed Time : 0h 27m 47s Bad Sectors : 0 Clearing computer memory... Source SHA1 Hash: 655E9BDDB36A3F9C5C4CC8BF32B8C5B41AF9F52E
Results:	

Assertion & Expected Result	Actual Result
AM-01 Source acquired using interface AI.	as expected
AM-02 Source is type DS.	as expected
AM-03 Execution environment is XE.	as expected
AM-04 A clone is created.	as expected
AM-06 All visible sectors acquired.	as expected
AM-08 All sectors accurately acquired.	as expected
AO-11 A clone is created during acquisition.	as expected
AO-13 Clone created using interface AI.	as expected
AO-14 An unaligned clone is created.	as expected
AO-17 Excess sectors are unchanged.	as expected
AO-22 Tool calculates hashes by block.	option not available
AO-23 Logged information is correct.	as expected
AO-24 Source is unchanged by acquisition.	as expected

Analysis:	Expected results achieved

5.2.5 DA-01-SATA48

Test Case DA-01-SATA48 ILook IXimager Version 2.0, Feb 01 2006	
Description:	DA-01 Acquire a physical device using access interface AI to an unaligned clone.
Assertions:	AM-01 The tool uses access interface SRC-AI to access the digital source. AM-02 The tool acquires digital source DS. AM-03 The tool executes in execution environment XE. AM-04 If clone creation is specified, the tool creates a clone of the digital source. AM-06 All visible sectors are acquired from the digital source. AM-08 All sectors acquired from the digital source are acquired accurately. AO-11 If requested, a clone is created during an acquisition of a digital source. AO-13 A clone is created using access interface DST-AI to write to the clone device. AO-14 If an unaligned clone is created, each sector written to the clone is accurately written to the same disk address on the clone that the sector occupied on the digital source. AO-17 If requested, any excess sectors on a clone destination device are not modified. AO-22 If requested, the tool calculates block hashes for a specified block size during an acquisition for each block acquired from the digital source. AO-23 If the tool logs any log significant information, the information is accurately recorded in the log file. AO-24 If the tool executes in a forensically safe execution environment, the digital source is unchanged by the acquisition process.
Tester Name:	brl
Test Host:	Joe
Test Date:	Wed Mar 22 16:46:04 2006
Drives:	src(0D) dst (0E) other (none)
Source Setup:	src hash: < BAAD80E8781E55F2E3EF528CA73BD41D228C1377 > 488397168 total sectors (250059350016 bytes) 30400/254/63 (max cyl/hd values) 30401/255/63 (number of cyl/hd) Model (WDC WD2500JD-22F) serial # (WD-WMAEH2678216) N Start LBA Length Start C/H/S End C/H/S boot Partition type 1 P 000000063 488375937 0000/001/01 1023/254/63 Boot 07 NTFS 2 P 000000000 000000000 0000/000/00 0000/000/00 00 empty entry 3 P 000000000 000000000 0000/000/00 0000/000/00 00 empty entry 4 P 000000000 000000000 0000/000/00 0000/000/00 00 empty entry 1 488375937 sectors 250048479744 bytes
Log Highlights:	Comparision of original to clone Sectors compared: 488397168 Sectors match: 488397168 Sectors differ: 0 Bytes differ: 0 Diffs range 0 source read errors, 0 destination read errors IXImager Log file ata1: dev 0 ATA-6, max UDMA/100, 488397168 sectors: LBA48 ata2: dev 0 ATA-6, max UDMA/100, 488397168 sectors: LBA48 SCSI device sdb: 488397168 512-byte hdwr sectors (250059 MB) SCSI device sdc: 488397168 512-byte hdwr sectors (250059 MB) SCSI device sdb: 488397168 512-byte hdwr sectors (250059 MB) Initializing... Opened input device '/dev/sdc' Opened output device '/dev/sdb' Beginning Clone operation for 250059350016 bytes Beginning Clone operation Beginning Clone operation Clone Complete Clone was completed successfully. Read : 250.1 GB (250059350016 bytes) Written : 250.1 GB (250059350016 bytes) Total Processed: 250.1 GB (250059350016 bytes) Clone Speed : 45.25 MB/sec

Test Case DA-01-SATA48 ILook IXimager Version 2.0, Feb 01 2006	
	Elapsed Time : 1h 32m 6s Bad Sectors : 0 Clearing computer memory... Source SHA1 Hash: BAAD80E8781E55F2E3EF528CA73BD41D228C1377
Results:	

Assertion & Expected Result	Actual Result
AM-01 Source acquired using interface AI.	as expected
AM-02 Source is type DS.	as expected
AM-03 Execution environment is XE.	as expected
AM-04 A clone is created.	as expected
AM-06 All visible sectors acquired.	as expected
AM-08 All sectors accurately acquired.	as expected
AO-11 A clone is created during acquisition.	as expected
AO-13 Clone created using interface AI.	as expected
AO-14 An unaligned clone is created.	as expected
AO-17 Excess sectors are unchanged.	as expected
AO-22 Tool calculates hashes by block.	option not available
AO-23 Logged information is correct.	as expected
AO-24 Source is unchanged by acquisition.	as expected

Analysis:	Expected results achieved

5.2.6 DA-01-SCSI

Test Case DA-01-SCSI ILook IXimager Version 2.0, Feb 01 2006	
Description:	DA-01 Acquire a physical device using access interface AI to an unaligned clone.
Assertions:	AM-01 The tool uses access interface SRC-AI to access the digital source. AM-02 The tool acquires digital source DS. AM-03 The tool executes in execution environment XE. AM-04 If clone creation is specified, the tool creates a clone of the digital source. AM-06 All visible sectors are acquired from the digital source. AM-08 All sectors acquired from the digital source are acquired accurately. AO-11 If requested, a clone is created during an acquisition of a digital source. AO-13 A clone is created using access interface DST-AI to write to the clone device. AO-14 If an unaligned clone is created, each sector written to the clone is accurately written to the same disk address on the clone that the sector occupied on the digital source. AO-17 If requested, any excess sectors on a clone destination device are not modified. AO-22 If requested, the tool calculates block hashes for a specified block size during an acquisition for each block acquired from the digital source. AO-23 If the tool logs any log significant information, the information is accurately recorded in the log file. AO-24 If the tool executes in a forensically safe execution environment, the digital source is unchanged by the acquisition process.
Tester Name:	brl
Test Host:	Freddy
Test Date:	Wed Mar 22 10:59:15 2006
Drives:	src(2A) dst (2C) other (none)
Source Setup:	src hash: < F5F9F2903DCAB895F36E270FB22A722E27918125 > 17783249 total sectors (9105023488 bytes) Model (QM39100TD-SCA) serial # (PCB=20-116711-06 HDAQM39100TD-SCA) N Start LBA Length Start C/H/S End C/H/S boot Partition type 1 P 000000063 017751762 0000/001/01 1023/254/63 Boot 07 NTFS 2 P 000000000 000000000 0000/000/00 0000/000/00 00 empty entry 3 P 000000000 000000000 0000/000/00 0000/000/00 00 empty entry 4 P 000000000 000000000 0000/000/00 0000/000/00 00 empty entry 1 017751762 sectors 9088902144 bytes
Log Highlights:	Comparision of original to clone Sectors compared: 17783249

	Test Case DA-01-SCSI ILook IXimager Version 2.0, Feb 01 2006
	Sectors match: 17783249 Sectors differ: 0 Bytes differ: 0 Diffs range 0 source read errors, 0 destination read errors IXImager Log file SCSI device sdb: 17783249 512-byte hdwr sectors (9105 MB) SCSI device sdc: 17783249 512-byte hdwr sectors (9105 MB) SCSI device sdb: 17783249 512-byte hdwr sectors (9105 MB) Initializing... Opened input device '/dev/sdc' Opened output device '/dev/sdb' Beginning Clone operation for 9105023488 bytes Beginning Clone operation Beginning Clone operation Clone Complete Clone was completed successfully. Read : 9.105 GB (9105023488 bytes) Written : 9.105 GB (9105023488 bytes) Total Processed: 9.105 GB (9105023488 bytes) Clone Speed : 11.66 MB/sec Elapsed Time : 0h 13m 1s Bad Sectors : 0 Clearing computer memory... Source SHA1 Hash: F5F9F2903DCAB895F36E270FB22A722E27918125
Results:	<table><tr><th>Assertion & Expected Result</th><th>Actual Result</th></tr><tr><td>AM-01 Source acquired using interface AI.</td><td>as expected</td></tr><tr><td>AM-02 Source is type DS.</td><td>as expected</td></tr><tr><td>AM-03 Execution environment is XE.</td><td>as expected</td></tr><tr><td>AM-04 A clone is created.</td><td>as expected</td></tr><tr><td>AM-06 All visible sectors acquired.</td><td>as expected</td></tr><tr><td>AM-08 All sectors accurately acquired.</td><td>as expected</td></tr><tr><td>AO-11 A clone is created during acquisition.</td><td>as expected</td></tr><tr><td>AO-13 Clone created using interface AI.</td><td>as expected</td></tr><tr><td>AO-14 An unaligned clone is created.</td><td>as expected</td></tr><tr><td>AO-17 Excess sectors are unchanged.</td><td>as expected</td></tr><tr><td>AO-22 Tool calculates hashes by block.</td><td>option not available</td></tr><tr><td>AO-23 Logged information is correct.</td><td>as expected</td></tr><tr><td>AO-24 Source is unchanged by acquisition.</td><td>as expected</td></tr></table>
Analysis:	Expected results achieved

5.2.7 DA-01-USB

	Test Case DA-01-USB ILook IXimager Version 2.0, Feb 01 2006
Description:	DA-01 Acquire a physical device using access interface AI to an unaligned clone.
Assertions:	AM-01 The tool uses access interface SRC-AI to access the digital source. AM-02 The tool acquires digital source DS. AM-03 The tool executes in execution environment XE. AM-04 If clone creation is specified, the tool creates a clone of the digital source. AM-06 All visible sectors are acquired from the digital source. AM-08 All sectors acquired from the digital source are acquired accurately. AO-11 If requested, a clone is created during an acquisition of a digital source. AO-13 A clone is created using access interface DST-AI to write to the clone device. AO-14 If an unaligned clone is created, each sector written to the clone is accurately written to the same disk address on the clone that the sector occupied on the digital source. AO-17 If requested, any excess sectors on a clone destination device are not modified. AO-22 If requested, the tool calculates block hashes for a specified block

Test Case DA-01-USB ILook IXimager Version 2.0, Feb 01 2006

	size during an acquisition for each block acquired from the digital source. AO-23 If the tool logs any log significant information, the information is accurately recorded in the log file. AO-24 If the tool executes in a forensically safe execution environment, the digital source is unchanged by the acquisition process.
Tester Name:	brl
Test Host:	JohnSteed
Test Date:	Sun Mar 26 14:50:02 2006
Drives:	src(63-FU2) dst (61-FU2) other (none)
Source Setup:	src hash: < F7069EDCBEAC863C88DECED82159F22DA96BE99B > 117304992 total sectors (60060155904 bytes) Model (SP0612N) serial # () N Start LBA Length Start C/H/S End C/H/S boot Partition type 1 P 000000063 004192902 0000/001/01 0260/254/63 Boot 06 Fat16 2 X 004192965 113097600 0261/000/01 1023/254/63 0F extended 3 S 000000063 113097537 0261/001/01 1023/254/63 0B Fat32 4 S 000000000 000000000 0000/000/00 0000/000/00 00 empty entry 5 P 000000000 000000000 0000/000/00 0000/000/00 00 empty entry 6 P 000000000 000000000 0000/000/00 0000/000/00 00 empty entry 1 004192902 sectors 2146765824 bytes 3 113097537 sectors 57905938944 bytes
Log Highlights:	Comparision of original to clone Sectors compared: 117304992 Sectors match: 117304992 Sectors differ: 0 Bytes differ: 0 Diffs range 0 source read errors, 0 destination read errors IXImager Log file hda: 156301488 sectors (80026 MB) w/8192KiB Cache, CHS=9729/255/63, UDMA(100) SCSI device sda: 117304992 512-byte hdwr sectors (60060 MB) SCSI device sdb: 117304992 512-byte hdwr sectors (60060 MB) SCSI device sdb: 117304992 512-byte hdwr sectors (60060 MB) Initializing... Opened input device '/dev/sda' Opened output device '/dev/sdb' Beginning Clone operation for 60060155904 bytes Beginning Clone operation Beginning Clone operation Clone Complete Clone was completed successfully. Read : 60.06 GB (60060155904 bytes) Written : 60.06 GB (60060155904 bytes) Total Processed: 60.06 GB (60060155904 bytes) Clone Speed : 13.88 MB/sec Elapsed Time : 1h 12m 6s Bad Sectors : 0 Clearing computer memory... Source SHA1 Hash: F7069EDCBEAC863C88DECED82159F22DA96BE99B
Results:	

Assertion & Expected Result	Actual Result
AM-01 Source acquired using interface AI.	as expected
AM-02 Source is type DS.	as expected
AM-03 Execution environment is XE.	as expected
AM-04 A clone is created.	as expected
AM-06 All visible sectors acquired.	as expected
AM-08 All sectors accurately acquired.	as expected
AO-11 A clone is created during acquisition.	as expected
AO-13 Clone created using interface AI.	as expected
AO-14 An unaligned clone is created.	as expected
AO-17 Excess sectors are unchanged.	as expected
AO-22 Tool calculates hashes by block.	option not available
AO-23 Logged information is correct.	as expected
AO-24 Source is unchanged by acquisition.	as expected

Test Case DA-01-USB ILook IXimager Version 2.0, Feb 01 2006	
Analysis:	Expected results achieved

5.2.8 DA-02-CF

Test Case DA-02-CF ILook IXimager Version 2.0, Feb 01 2006	
Description:	DA-02 Acquire a digital source of type DS to an unaligned clone.
Assertions:	AM-01 The tool uses access interface SRC-AI to access the digital source. AM-02 The tool acquires digital source DS. AM-03 The tool executes in execution environment XE. AM-04 If clone creation is specified, the tool creates a clone of the digital source. AM-06 All visible sectors are acquired from the digital source. AM-08 All sectors acquired from the digital source are acquired accurately. AO-11 If requested, a clone is created during an acquisition of a digital source. AO-13 A clone is created using access interface DST-AI to write to the clone device. AO-14 If an unaligned clone is created, each sector written to the clone is accurately written to the same disk address on the clone that the sector occupied on the digital source. AO-17 If requested, any excess sectors on a clone destination device are not modified. AO-22 If requested, the tool calculates block hashes for a specified block size during an acquisition for each block acquired from the digital source. AO-23 If the tool logs any log significant information, the information is accurately recorded in the log file. AO-24 If the tool executes in a forensically safe execution environment, the digital source is unchanged by the acquisition process.
Tester Name:	brl
Test Host:	JohnSteed
Test Date:	Wed May 10 15:41:28 2006
Drives:	src(C1-CF) dst (C2-CF) other (none)
Source Setup:	src hash: < 5B8235178DF99FA307430C088F81746606638A0B > 503808 total sectors (257949696 bytes) Removable media, no partition table.
Log Highlights:	Comparision of original to clone Sectors compared: 503808 Sectors match: 503808 Sectors differ: 0 Bytes differ: 0 Diffs range 0 source read errors, 0 destination read errors IXImager Log file hda: 156301488 sectors (80026 MB) w/8192KiB Cache, CHS=9729/255/63, UDMA(100) SCSI device sda: 503808 512-byte hdwr sectors (258 MB) SCSI device sdb: 503808 512-byte hdwr sectors (258 MB) SCSI device sdb: 503808 512-byte hdwr sectors (258 MB) Initializing... Opened input device '/dev/sda' Opened output device '/dev/sdb' Beginning Clone operation for 257949696 bytes Beginning Clone operation Beginning Clone operation Clone Complete Clone was completed successfully. Read : 257.9 MB (257949696 bytes) Written : 257.9 MB (257949696 bytes) Total Processed: 257.9 MB (257949696 bytes) Clone Speed : 5.862 MB/sec Elapsed Time : 0h 0m 44s Bad Sectors : 0 Clearing computer memory...

Test Case DA-02-CF ILook IXimager Version 2.0, Feb 01 2006		
Results:	Assertion & Expected Result	Actual Result
	AM-01 Source acquired using interface AI.	as expected
	AM-02 Source is type DS.	as expected
	AM-03 Execution environment is XE.	as expected
	AM-04 A clone is created.	as expected
	AM-06 All visible sectors acquired.	as expected
	AM-08 All sectors accurately acquired.	as expected
	AO-11 A clone is created during acquisition.	as expected
	AO-13 Clone created using interface AI.	as expected
	AO-14 An unaligned clone is created.	as expected
	AO-17 Excess sectors are unchanged.	as expected
	AO-22 Tool calculates hashes by block.	option not available
	AO-23 Logged information is correct.	as expected
	AO-24 Source is unchanged by acquisition.	as expected
Analysis:	Expected results achieved	

5.2.9 DA-02-F12

Test Case DA-02-F12 ILook IXimager Version 2.0, Feb 01 2006	
Description:	DA-02 Acquire a digital source of type DS to an unaligned clone.
Assertions:	AM-01 The tool uses access interface SRC-AI to access the digital source. AM-02 The tool acquires digital source DS. AM-03 The tool executes in execution environment XE. AM-04 If clone creation is specified, the tool creates a clone of the digital source. AM-06 All visible sectors are acquired from the digital source. AM-08 All sectors acquired from the digital source are acquired accurately. AO-11 If requested, a clone is created during an acquisition of a digital source. AO-13 A clone is created using access interface DST-AI to write to the clone device. AO-14 If an unaligned clone is created, each sector written to the clone is accurately written to the same disk address on the clone that the sector occupied on the digital source. AO-17 If requested, any excess sectors on a clone destination device are not modified. AO-22 If requested, the tool calculates block hashes for a specified block size during an acquisition for each block acquired from the digital source. AO-23 If the tool logs any log significant information, the information is accurately recorded in the log file. AO-24 If the tool executes in a forensically safe execution environment, the digital source is unchanged by the acquisition process.
Tester Name:	brl
Test Host:	Joe
Test Date:	Wed Apr 19 14:12:39 2006
Drives:	src(43) dst (A7) other (none)
Source Setup:	src hash: < 888E2E7F7AD237DC7A732281DD93F325065E5871 > 78125000 total sectors (40000000000 bytes) Model (0BB-75JHC0) serial # (WD-WMAMC46588) N Start LBA Length Start C/H/S End C/H/S boot Partition type 1 P 000000063 020980827 0000/001/01 1023/254/63 0C Fat32X 2 X 020980890 057143205 1023/000/01 1023/254/63 0F extended 3 S 000000063 000032067 1023/001/01 1023/254/63 01 Fat12 4 x 000032130 002104515 1023/000/01 1023/254/63 05 extended 5 S 000000063 002104452 1023/001/01 1023/254/63 06 Fat16 6 x 002136645 004192965 1023/000/01 1023/254/63 05 extended 7 S 000000063 004192902 1023/001/01 1023/254/63 16 other 8 x 006329610 008401995 1023/000/01 1023/254/63 05 extended 9 S 000000063 008401932 1023/001/01 1023/254/63 0B Fat32 10 x 014731605 010490445 1023/000/01 1023/254/63 05 extended 11 S 000000063 010490382 1023/001/01 1023/254/63 83 Linux 12 x 025222050 004209030 1023/000/01 1023/254/63 05 extended 13 S 000000063 004208967 1023/001/01 1023/254/63 82 Linux swap 14 x 029431080 027712125 1023/000/01 1023/254/63 05 extended

```
Test Case DA-02-F12 ILook IXimager Version 2.0, Feb 01 2006
                  15 S 000000063 027712062 1023/001/01 1023/254/63    07 NTFS
                  16 S 000000000 000000000 0000/000/00 0000/000/00    00 empty entry
                  17 P 000000000 000000000 0000/000/00 0000/000/00    00 empty entry
                  18 P 000000000 000000000 0000/000/00 0000/000/00    00 empty entry
                   1 020980827 sectors 10742183424 bytes
                   3 000032067 sectors    16418304 bytes
                   5 002104452 sectors  1077479424 bytes
                   7 004192902 sectors  2146765824 bytes
                   9 008401932 sectors  4301789184 bytes
                  11 010490382 sectors  5371075584 bytes
                  13 004208967 sectors  2154991104 bytes
                  15 027712062 sectors 14188575744 bytes
```

Log Highlights:	IXImager Log file SCSI device sdb: 39102336 512-byte hdwr sectors (20020 MB) SCSI device sdc: 78125000 512-byte hdwr sectors (40000 MB) SCSI device sdb: 39102336 512-byte hdwr sectors (20020 MB) Initializing... Opened input device '/dev/sdc5' Opened output device '/dev/sdb' Beginning Clone operation for 16418304 bytes Beginning Clone operation Beginning Clone operation Clone Complete Clone was completed successfully. Read : 16.42 MB (16418304 bytes) Written : 16.42 MB (16418304 bytes) Total Processed : 16.42 MB (16418304 bytes) Clone Speed : 8.209 MB/sec Elapsed Time : 0h 0m 2s Bad Sectors : 0 Clearing computer memory... Hashes of src and dst partitions Src SHA1 Hash: 6853B517F50BF3CCADED3DB5FEAE08C18C62FCA0 - Dst SHA1 Hash: 6853B517F50BF3CCADED3DB5FEAE08C18C62FCA0 - Source SHA1 Hash: 888E2E7F7AD237DC7A732281DD93F325065E5871
Results:	

Assertion & Expected Result	Actual Result
AM-01 Source acquired using interface AI.	as expected
AM-02 Source is type DS.	as expected
AM-03 Execution environment is XE.	as expected
AM-04 A clone is created.	as expected
AM-06 All visible sectors acquired.	as expected
AM-08 All sectors accurately acquired.	as expected
AO-11 A clone is created during acquisition.	as expected
AO-13 Clone created using interface AI.	as expected
AO-14 An unaligned clone is created.	as expected
AO-17 Excess sectors are unchanged.	as expected
AO-22 Tool calculates hashes by block.	option not available
AO-23 Logged information is correct.	as expected
AO-24 Source is unchanged by acquisition.	as expected

Analysis:	Expected results achieved

5.2.10 DA-02-F16

Test Case DA-02-F16 ILook IXimager Version 2.0, Feb 01 2006	
Description:	DA-02 Acquire a digital source of type DS to an unaligned clone.
Assertions:	AM-01 The tool uses access interface SRC-AI to access the digital source. AM-02 The tool acquires digital source DS. AM-03 The tool executes in execution environment XE. AM-04 If clone creation is specified, the tool creates a clone of the digital source. AM-06 All visible sectors are acquired from the digital source.

Test Case DA-02-F16 ILook IXimager Version 2.0, Feb 01 2006

	AM-08 All sectors acquired from the digital source are acquired accurately. AO-11 If requested, a clone is created during an acquisition of a digital source. AO-13 A clone is created using access interface DST-AI to write to the clone device. AO-14 If an unaligned clone is created, each sector written to the clone is accurately written to the same disk address on the clone that the sector occupied on the digital source. AO-17 If requested, any excess sectors on a clone destination device are not modified. AO-22 If requested, the tool calculates block hashes for a specified block size during an acquisition for each block acquired from the digital source. AO-23 If the tool logs any log significant information, the information is accurately recorded in the log file. AO-24 If the tool executes in a forensically safe execution environment, the digital source is unchanged by the acquisition process.
Tester Name:	brl
Test Host:	Joe
Test Date:	Thu Apr 20 09:24:03 2006
Drives:	src(43) dst (A7) other (none)
Source Setup:	src hash: < 888E2E7F7AD237DC7A732281DD93F325065E5871 > 78125000 total sectors (40000000000 bytes) Model (0BB-75JHC0) serial # (WD-WMAMC46588) N Start LBA Length Start C/H/S End C/H/S boot Partition type 1 P 000000063 020980827 0000/001/01 1023/254/63 0C Fat32X 2 X 020980890 057143205 1023/000/01 1023/254/63 0F extended 3 S 000000063 000032067 1023/001/01 1023/254/63 01 Fat12 4 x 000032130 002104515 1023/000/01 1023/254/63 05 extended 5 S 000000063 002104452 1023/001/01 1023/254/63 06 Fat16 6 x 002136645 004192965 1023/000/01 1023/254/63 05 extended 7 S 000000063 004192902 1023/001/01 1023/254/63 16 other 8 x 006329610 008401995 1023/000/01 1023/254/63 05 extended 9 S 000000063 008401932 1023/001/01 1023/254/63 0B Fat32 10 x 014731605 010490445 1023/000/01 1023/254/63 05 extended 11 S 000000063 010490382 1023/001/01 1023/254/63 83 Linux 12 x 025222050 004209030 1023/000/01 1023/254/63 05 extended 13 S 000000063 004208967 1023/001/01 1023/254/63 82 Linux swap 14 x 029431080 027712125 1023/000/01 1023/254/63 05 extended 15 S 000000063 027712062 1023/001/01 1023/254/63 07 NTFS 16 S 000000000 000000000 0000/000/00 0000/000/00 00 empty entry 17 P 000000000 000000000 0000/000/00 0000/000/00 00 empty entry 18 P 000000000 000000000 0000/000/00 0000/000/00 00 empty entry 1 020980827 sectors 10742183424 bytes 3 000032067 sectors 16418304 bytes 5 002104452 sectors 1077479424 bytes 7 004192902 sectors 2146765824 bytes 9 008401932 sectors 4301789184 bytes 11 010490382 sectors 5371075584 bytes 13 004208967 sectors 2154991104 bytes 15 027712062 sectors 14188575744 bytes
Log Highlights:	IXImager Log file SCSI device sdb: 78125000 512-byte hdwr sectors (40000 MB) SCSI device sdc: 39102336 512-byte hdwr sectors (20020 MB) SCSI device sdc: 39102336 512-byte hdwr sectors (20020 MB) Initializing... Opened input device '/dev/sdb6' Opened output device '/dev/sdc' Beginning Clone operation for 1077479424 bytes Beginning Clone operation Beginning Clone operation Clone Complete Clone was completed successfully. Read : 1.077 GB (1077479424 bytes) Written : 1.077 GB (1077479424 bytes) Total Processed: 1.077 GB (1077479424 bytes) Clone Speed : 10.67 MB/sec Elapsed Time : 0h 1m 41s Bad Sectors : 0 Clearing computer memory...

```
Test Case DA-02-F16 ILook IXimager Version 2.0, Feb 01 2006
```

	Hashes of src and dst partitions Src SHA1 Hash: 443CCEC9A22F726DAF6CE384817151C83B3EBC8B - Dst SHA1 Hash: 443CCEC9A22F726DAF6CE384817151C83B3EBC8B - Source SHA1 Hash: 888E2E7F7AD237DC7A732281DD93F325065E5871	
Results:		

Assertion & Expected Result	Actual Result
AM-01 Source acquired using interface AI.	as expected
AM-02 Source is type DS.	as expected
AM-03 Execution environment is XE.	as expected
AM-04 A clone is created.	as expected
AM-06 All visible sectors acquired.	as expected
AM-08 All sectors accurately acquired.	as expected
AO-11 A clone is created during acquisition.	as expected
AO-13 Clone created using interface AI.	as expected
AO-14 An unaligned clone is created.	as expected
AO-17 Excess sectors are unchanged.	as expected
AO-22 Tool calculates hashes by block.	option not available
AO-23 Logged information is correct.	as expected
AO-24 Source is unchanged by acquisition.	as expected

Analysis:	Expected results achieved

5.2.11 DA-02-F32

```
Test Case DA-02-F32 ILook IXimager Version 2.0, Feb 01 2006
```

Description:	DA-02 Acquire a digital source of type DS to an unaligned clone.
Assertions:	AM-01 The tool uses access interface SRC-AI to access the digital source. AM-02 The tool acquires digital source DS. AM-03 The tool executes in execution environment XE. AM-04 If clone creation is specified, the tool creates a clone of the digital source. AM-06 All visible sectors are acquired from the digital source. AM-08 All sectors acquired from the digital source are acquired accurately. AO-11 If requested, a clone is created during an acquisition of a digital source. AO-13 A clone is created using access interface DST-AI to write to the clone device. AO-14 If an unaligned clone is created, each sector written to the clone is accurately written to the same disk address on the clone that the sector occupied on the digital source. AO-17 If requested, any excess sectors on a clone destination device are not modified. AO-22 If requested, the tool calculates block hashes for a specified block size during an acquisition for each block acquired from the digital source. AO-23 If the tool logs any log significant information, the information is accurately recorded in the log file. AO-24 If the tool executes in a forensically safe execution environment, the digital source is unchanged by the acquisition process.
Tester Name:	brl
Test Host:	Joe
Test Date:	Thu Apr 20 11:23:27 2006
Drives:	src(43) dst (A7) other (none)
Source Setup:	src hash: < 888E2E7F7AD237DC7A732281DD93F325065E5871 > 78125000 total sectors (40000000000 bytes) Model (0BB-75JHC0) serial # (WD-WMAMC46588) N Start LBA Length Start C/H/S End C/H/S boot Partition type 1 P 000000063 020980827 0000/001/01 1023/254/63 0C Fat32X 2 X 020980890 057143205 1023/000/01 1023/254/63 0F extended 3 S 000000063 000032067 1023/001/01 1023/254/63 01 Fat12 4 x 000032130 002104515 1023/000/01 1023/254/63 05 extended 5 S 000000063 002104452 1023/001/01 1023/254/63 06 Fat16 6 x 002136645 004192965 1023/000/01 1023/254/63 05 extended 7 S 000000063 004192902 1023/001/01 1023/254/63 16 other 8 x 006329610 008401995 1023/000/01 1023/254/63 05 extended 9 S 000000063 008401932 1023/001/01 1023/254/63 0B Fat32

| | ```
         10 x 014731605 010490445 1023/000/01 1023/254/63    05 extended
         11 S 000000063 010490382 1023/001/01 1023/254/63    83 Linux
         12 x 025222050 004209030 1023/000/01 1023/254/63    05 extended
         13 S 000000063 004208967 1023/001/01 1023/254/63    82 Linux swap
         14 x 029431080 027712125 1023/000/01 1023/254/63    05 extended
         15 S 000000063 027712062 1023/001/01 1023/254/63    07 NTFS
         16 S 000000000 000000000 0000/000/00 0000/000/00    00 empty entry
         17 P 000000000 000000000 0000/000/00 0000/000/00    00 empty entry
         18 P 000000000 000000000 0000/000/00 0000/000/00    00 empty entry
       1 020980827 sectors 10742183424 bytes
       3 000032067 sectors    16418304 bytes
       5 002104452 sectors  1077479424 bytes
       7 004192902 sectors  2146765824 bytes
       9 008401932 sectors  4301789184 bytes
      11 010490382 sectors  5371075584 bytes
      13 004208967 sectors  2154991104 bytes
      15 027712062 sectors 14188575744 bytes
``` | |
| Log Highlights: | ```
IXImager Log file
SCSI device sdb: 78125000 512-byte hdwr sectors (40000 MB)
SCSI device sdc: 39102336 512-byte hdwr sectors (20020 MB)
SCSI device sdc: 39102336 512-byte hdwr sectors (20020 MB)
Initializing...
Opened input device '/dev/sdb8'
Opened output device '/dev/sdc'
Beginning Clone operation for 4301789184 bytes
Beginning Clone operation
Beginning Clone operation
Clone Complete
Clone was completed successfully.

Read             : 4.302 GB (4301789184 bytes)
Written          : 4.302 GB (4301789184 bytes)
Total Processed: 4.302 GB (4301789184 bytes)
Clone Speed      : 10.70 MB/sec
Elapsed Time     : 0h  6m 42s
Bad Sectors      : 0
Clearing computer memory...

Hashes of src and dst partitions
Src SHA1 Hash: 72462489BCF79A98B59B6A8CD938FEB46FA2A781  -
Dst SHA1 Hash: 72462489BCF79A98B59B6A8CD938FEB46FA2A781  -

Source SHA1 Hash: 888E2E7F7AD237DC7A732281DD93F325065E5871
``` | |
Results:	Assertion & Expected Result	Actual Result
	AM-01 Source acquired using interface AI.	as expected
	AM-02 Source is type DS.	as expected
	AM-03 Execution environment is XE.	as expected
	AM-04 A clone is created.	as expected
	AM-06 All visible sectors acquired.	as expected
	AM-08 All sectors accurately acquired.	as expected
	AO-11 A clone is created during acquisition.	as expected
	AO-13 Clone created using interface AI.	as expected
	AO-14 An unaligned clone is created.	as expected
	AO-17 Excess sectors are unchanged.	as expected
	AO-22 Tool calculates hashes by block.	option not available
	AO-23 Logged information is correct.	as expected
	AO-24 Source is unchanged by acquisition.	as expected
Analysis:	Expected results achieved	

5.2.12 DA-02-F32X

Test Case DA-02-F32X ILook IXimager Version 2.0, Feb 01 2006	
Description:	DA-02 Acquire a digital source of type DS to an unaligned clone.
Assertions:	AM-01 The tool uses access interface SRC-AI to access the digital source.

Test Case DA-02-F32X ILook IXimager Version 2.0, Feb 01 2006

	AM-02 The tool acquires digital source DS. AM-03 The tool executes in execution environment XE. AM-04 If clone creation is specified, the tool creates a clone of the digital source. AM-06 All visible sectors are acquired from the digital source. AM-08 All sectors acquired from the digital source are acquired accurately. AO-11 If requested, a clone is created during an acquisition of a digital source. AO-13 A clone is created using access interface DST-AI to write to the clone device. AO-14 If an unaligned clone is created, each sector written to the clone is accurately written to the same disk address on the clone that the sector occupied on the digital source. AO-17 If requested, any excess sectors on a clone destination device are not modified. AO-22 If requested, the tool calculates block hashes for a specified block size during an acquisition for each block acquired from the digital source. AO-23 If the tool logs any log significant information, the information is accurately recorded in the log file. AO-24 If the tool executes in a forensically safe execution environment, the digital source is unchanged by the acquisition process.
Tester Name:	brl
Test Host:	Max
Test Date:	Wed Apr 19 09:01:16 2006
Drives:	src(44) dst (23-FU2) other (none)
Source Setup:	src hash: < E196D36E7B322C0EF83923112AD1800581742B6E > 78165360 total sectors (40020664320 bytes) 65534/015/63 (max cyl/hd values) 65535/016/63 (number of cyl/hd) IDE disk: Model (WDC WD400JB-00FMA0) serial # (WD-WMAJC1011319) N Start LBA Length Start C/H/S End C/H/S boot Partition type 1 P 000000063 020980827 0000/001/01 1023/254/63 0C Fat32X 2 X 020980890 057175335 1023/000/01 1023/254/63 0F extended 3 S 000000063 000032067 1023/001/01 1023/254/63 01 Fat12 4 x 000032130 002104515 1023/000/01 1023/254/63 05 extended 5 S 000000063 002104452 1023/001/01 1023/254/63 06 Fat16 6 x 002136645 004192965 1023/000/01 1023/254/63 05 extended 7 S 000000063 004192902 1023/001/01 1023/254/63 16 other 8 x 006329610 008401995 1023/000/01 1023/254/63 05 extended 9 S 000000063 008401932 1023/001/01 1023/254/63 0B Fat32 10 x 014731605 010490445 1023/000/01 1023/254/63 05 extended 11 S 000000063 010490382 1023/001/01 1023/254/63 83 Linux 12 x 025222050 004209030 1023/000/01 1023/254/63 05 extended 13 S 000000063 004208967 1023/001/01 1023/254/63 82 Linux swap 14 x 029431080 027744255 1023/000/01 1023/254/63 05 extended 15 S 000000063 027744192 1023/001/01 1023/254/63 07 NTFS 16 S 000000000 000000000 0000/000/00 0000/000/00 00 empty entry 17 P 000000000 000000000 0000/000/00 0000/000/00 00 empty entry 18 P 000000000 000000000 0000/000/00 0000/000/00 00 empty entry 1 020980827 sectors 10742183424 bytes 3 000032067 sectors 16418304 bytes 5 002104452 sectors 1077479424 bytes 7 004192902 sectors 2146765824 bytes 9 008401932 sectors 4301789184 bytes 11 010490382 sectors 5371075584 bytes 13 004208967 sectors 2154991104 bytes 15 027744192 sectors 14205026304 bytes
Log Highlights:	IXImager Log file SCSI device sdb: 39070080 512-byte hdwr sectors (20004 MB) SCSI device sdc: 78165360 512-byte hdwr sectors (40021 MB) SCSI device sdb: 39070080 512-byte hdwr sectors (20004 MB) Initializing... Opened input device '/dev/sdc1' Opened output device '/dev/sdb' Beginning Clone operation for 10742183424 bytes Beginning Clone operation Beginning Clone operation Clone Complete Clone was completed successfully.

```
Test Case DA-02-F32X ILook IXimager Version 2.0, Feb 01 2006
                   Read              : 10.74 GB (10742183424 bytes)
                   Written           : 10.74 GB (10742183424 bytes)
                   Total Processed:   10.74 GB (10742183424 bytes)
                   Clone Speed       : 7.987 MB/sec
                   Elapsed Time      : 0h 22m 25s
                   Bad Sectors       : 0
                   Clearing computer memory...

                   Hashes of src and dst partitions
                   Src SHA1 Hash: D190A47B60A17FE6912CA26BE237E923AD592FAE  -
                   Dst SHA1 Hash: D190A47B60A17FE6912CA26BE237E923AD592FAE  -

                   Source SHA1 Hash: E196D36E7B322C0EF83923112AD1800581742B6E
```

Results:	Assertion & Expected Result	Actual Result
	AM-01 Source acquired using interface AI.	as expected
	AM-02 Source is type DS.	as expected
	AM-03 Execution environment is XE.	as expected
	AM-04 A clone is created.	as expected
	AM-06 All visible sectors acquired.	as expected
	AM-08 All sectors accurately acquired.	as expected
	AO-11 A clone is created during acquisition.	as expected
	AO-13 Clone created using interface AI.	as expected
	AO-14 An unaligned clone is created.	as expected
	AO-17 Excess sectors are unchanged.	as expected
	AO-22 Tool calculates hashes by block.	option not available
	AO-23 Logged information is correct.	as expected
	AO-24 Source is unchanged by acquisition.	as expected

Analysis:	Expected results achieved

5.2.13 DA-02-HIDDEN

Test Case DA-02-HIDDEN ILook IXimager Version 2.0, Feb 01 2006	
Description:	DA-02 Acquire a digital source of type DS to an unaligned clone.
Assertions:	AM-01 The tool uses access interface SRC-AI to access the digital source. AM-02 The tool acquires digital source DS. AM-03 The tool executes in execution environment XE. AM-04 If clone creation is specified, the tool creates a clone of the digital source. AM-06 All visible sectors are acquired from the digital source. AM-08 All sectors acquired from the digital source are acquired accurately. AO-11 If requested, a clone is created during an acquisition of a digital source. AO-13 A clone is created using access interface DST-AI to write to the clone device. AO-14 If an unaligned clone is created, each sector written to the clone is accurately written to the same disk address on the clone that the sector occupied on the digital source. AO-17 If requested, any excess sectors on a clone destination device are not modified. AO-22 If requested, the tool calculates block hashes for a specified block size during an acquisition for each block acquired from the digital source. AO-23 If the tool logs any log significant information, the information is accurately recorded in the log file. AO-24 If the tool executes in a forensically safe execution environment, the digital source is unchanged by the acquisition process.
Tester Name:	brl
Test Host:	Joe
Test Date:	Fri Apr 21 09:35:20 2006
Drives:	src(43) dst (2F) other (none)
Source Setup:	src hash: < 888E2E7F7AD237DC7A732281DD93F325065E5871 > 78125000 total sectors (40000000000 bytes) Model (0BB-75JHC0) serial # (WD-WMAMC46588) N Start LBA Length Start C/H/S End C/H/S boot Partition type 1 P 000000063 020980827 0000/001/01 1023/254/63 0C Fat32X 2 X 020980890 057143205 1023/000/01 1023/254/63 0F extended

Test Case DA-02-HIDDEN ILook IXimager Version 2.0, Feb 01 2006

```
 3 S 000000063 000032067 1023/001/01 1023/254/63    01 Fat12
 4 x 000032130 002104515 1023/000/01 1023/254/63    05 extended
 5 S 000000063 002104452 1023/001/01 1023/254/63    06 Fat16
 6 x 002136645 004192965 1023/000/01 1023/254/63    05 extended
 7 S 000000063 004192902 1023/001/01 1023/254/63    16 other
 8 x 006329610 008401995 1023/000/01 1023/254/63    05 extended
 9 S 000000063 008401932 1023/001/01 1023/254/63    0B Fat32
10 x 014731605 010490445 1023/000/01 1023/254/63    05 extended
11 S 000000063 010490382 1023/001/01 1023/254/63    83 Linux
12 x 025222050 004209030 1023/000/01 1023/254/63    05 extended
13 S 000000063 004208967 1023/001/01 1023/254/63    82 Linux swap
14 x 029431080 027712125 1023/000/01 1023/254/63    05 extended
15 S 000000063 027712062 1023/001/01 1023/254/63    07 NTFS
16 S 000000000 000000000 0000/000/00 0000/000/00    00 empty entry
17 P 000000000 000000000 0000/000/00 0000/000/00    00 empty entry
18 P 000000000 000000000 0000/000/00 0000/000/00    00 empty entry
 1 020980827 sectors 10742183424 bytes
 3 000032067 sectors 16418304 bytes
 5 002104452 sectors 1077479424 bytes
 7 004192902 sectors 2146765824 bytes
 9 008401932 sectors 4301789184 bytes
11 010490382 sectors 5371075584 bytes
13 004208967 sectors 2154991104 bytes
15 027712062 sectors 14188575744 bytes
```

Log Highlights:	
	IXImager Log file

```
SCSI device sdb: 17783249 512-byte hdwr sectors (9105 MB)
SCSI device sdc: 78125000 512-byte hdwr sectors (40000 MB)
SCSI device sdb: 17783249 512-byte hdwr sectors (9105 MB)
Initializing...
Opened input device '/dev/sdc7'
Opened output device '/dev/sdb'
Beginning Clone operation for 2146765824 bytes
Beginning Clone operation
Beginning Clone operation
Clone Complete
Clone was completed successfully.

Read            : 2.147 GB (2146765824 bytes)
Written         : 2.147 GB (2146765824 bytes)
Total Processed : 2.147 GB (2146765824 bytes)
Clone Speed     : 13.50 MB/sec
Elapsed Time    : 0h  2m 39s
Bad Sectors     : 0
Clearing computer memory...

Hashes of src and dst partitions
Src SHA1 Hash: 9D0C959EE797F223DA273F7CC18239C1A6769C47  -
Dst SHA1 Hash: 9D0C959EE797F223DA273F7CC18239C1A6769C47  -

Source SHA1 Hash: 888E2E7F7AD237DC7A732281DD93F325065E5871
```

Results:

Assertion & Expected Result	Actual Result
AM-01 Source acquired using interface AI.	as expected
AM-02 Source is type DS.	as expected
AM-03 Execution environment is XE.	as expected
AM-04 A clone is created.	as expected
AM-06 All visible sectors acquired.	as expected
AM-08 All sectors accurately acquired.	as expected
AO-11 A clone is created during acquisition.	as expected
AO-13 Clone created using interface AI.	as expected
AO-14 An unaligned clone is created.	as expected
AO-17 Excess sectors are unchanged.	as expected
AO-22 Tool calculates hashes by block.	option not available
AO-23 Logged information is correct.	as expected
AO-24 Source is unchanged by acquisition.	as expected

Analysis: Expected results achieved

5.2.14 DA-02-LX

Test Case DA-02-LX ILook IXimager Version 2.0, Feb 01 2006	
Description:	DA-02 Acquire a digital source of type DS to an unaligned clone.
Assertions:	AM-01 The tool uses access interface SRC-AI to access the digital source. AM-02 The tool acquires digital source DS. AM-03 The tool executes in execution environment XE. AM-04 If clone creation is specified, the tool creates a clone of the digital source. AM-06 All visible sectors are acquired from the digital source. AM-08 All sectors acquired from the digital source are acquired accurately. AO-11 If requested, a clone is created during an acquisition of a digital source. AO-13 A clone is created using access interface DST-AI to write to the clone device. AO-14 If an unaligned clone is created, each sector written to the clone is accurately written to the same disk address on the clone that the sector occupied on the digital source. AO-17 If requested, any excess sectors on a clone destination device are not modified. AO-22 If requested, the tool calculates block hashes for a specified block size during an acquisition for each block acquired from the digital source. AO-23 If the tool logs any log significant information, the information is accurately recorded in the log file. AO-24 If the tool executes in a forensically safe execution environment, the digital source is unchanged by the acquisition process.
Tester Name:	brl
Test Host:	Max
Test Date:	Thu Apr 20 14:11:48 2006
Drives:	src(44) dst (2C) other (none)
Source Setup:	src hash: < E196D36E7B322C0EF83923112AD1800581742B6E > 78165360 total sectors (40020664320 bytes) 65534/015/63 (max cyl/hd values) 65535/016/63 (number of cyl/hd) IDE disk: Model (WDC WD400JB-00FMA0) serial # (WD-WMAJC1011319) N Start LBA Length Start C/H/S End C/H/S boot Partition type 1 P 000000063 020980827 0000/001/01 1023/254/63 0C Fat32X 2 X 020980890 057175335 1023/000/01 1023/254/63 0F extended 3 S 000000063 000032067 1023/001/01 1023/254/63 01 Fat12 4 x 000032130 002104515 1023/000/01 1023/254/63 05 extended 5 S 000000063 002104452 1023/001/01 1023/254/63 06 Fat16 6 x 002136645 004192965 1023/000/01 1023/254/63 05 extended 7 S 000000063 004192902 1023/001/01 1023/254/63 16 other 8 x 006329610 008401995 1023/000/01 1023/254/63 05 extended 9 S 000000063 008401932 1023/001/01 1023/254/63 0B Fat32 10 x 014731605 010490445 1023/000/01 1023/254/63 05 extended 11 S 000000063 010490382 1023/001/01 1023/254/63 83 Linux 12 x 025222050 004209030 1023/000/01 1023/254/63 05 extended 13 S 000000063 004208967 1023/001/01 1023/254/63 82 Linux swap 14 x 029431080 027744255 1023/000/01 1023/254/63 05 extended 15 S 000000063 027744192 1023/001/01 1023/254/63 07 NTFS 16 S 000000000 000000000 0000/000/00 0000/000/00 00 empty entry 17 P 000000000 000000000 0000/000/00 0000/000/00 00 empty entry 18 P 000000000 000000000 0000/000/00 0000/000/00 00 empty entry 1 020980827 sectors 10742183424 bytes 3 000032067 sectors 16418304 bytes 5 002104452 sectors 1077479424 bytes 7 004192902 sectors 2146765824 bytes 9 008401932 sectors 4301789184 bytes 11 010490382 sectors 5371075584 bytes 13 004208967 sectors 2154991104 bytes 15 027744192 sectors 14205026304 bytes
Log Highlights:	IXImager Log file SCSI device sdb: 17783249 512-byte hdwr sectors (9105 MB) SCSI device sdc: 78165360 512-byte hdwr sectors (40021 MB) SCSI device sdb: 17783249 512-byte hdwr sectors (9105 MB) Initializing... Opened input device '/dev/sdc9' Opened output device '/dev/sdb'

```
Test Case DA-02-LX ILook IXimager Version 2.0, Feb 01 2006
```

	Beginning Clone operation for 5371075584 bytes Beginning Clone operation Beginning Clone operation Clone Complete Clone was completed successfully. Read : 5.371 GB (5371075584 bytes) Written : 5.371 GB (5371075584 bytes) Total Processed: 5.371 GB (5371075584 bytes) Clone Speed : 12.82 MB/sec Elapsed Time : 0h 6m 59s Bad Sectors : 0 Clearing computer memory... Hashes of src and dst partitions Src SHA1 Hash: DB95CCA2D36D79BD0CEEF189296CFF4F6F4D49C3 - Dst SHA1 Hash: DB95CCA2D36D79BD0CEEF189296CFF4F6F4D49C3 - Source SHA1 Hash: E196D36E7B322C0EF83923112AD1800581742B6E
Results:	

Assertion & Expected Result	Actual Result
AM-01 Source acquired using interface AI.	as expected
AM-02 Source is type DS.	as expected
AM-03 Execution environment is XE.	as expected
AM-04 A clone is created.	as expected
AM-06 All visible sectors acquired.	as expected
AM-08 All sectors accurately acquired.	as expected
AO-11 A clone is created during acquisition.	as expected
AO-13 Clone created using interface AI.	as expected
AO-14 An unaligned clone is created.	as expected
AO-17 Excess sectors are unchanged.	as expected
AO-22 Tool calculates hashes by block.	option not available
AO-23 Logged information is correct.	as expected
AO-24 Source is unchanged by acquisition.	as expected

Analysis:	Expected results achieved

5.2.15 DA-02-NT

Test Case DA-02-NT ILook IXimager Version 2.0, Feb 01 2006	
Description:	DA-02 Acquire a digital source of type DS to an unaligned clone.
Assertions:	AM-01 The tool uses access interface SRC-AI to access the digital source. AM-02 The tool acquires digital source DS. AM-03 The tool executes in execution environment XE. AM-04 If clone creation is specified, the tool creates a clone of the digital source. AM-06 All visible sectors are acquired from the digital source. AM-08 All sectors acquired from the digital source are acquired accurately. AO-11 If requested, a clone is created during an acquisition of a digital source. AO-13 A clone is created using access interface DST-AI to write to the clone device. AO-14 If an unaligned clone is created, each sector written to the clone is accurately written to the same disk address on the clone that the sector occupied on the digital source. AO-17 If requested, any excess sectors on a clone destination device are not modified. AO-22 If requested, the tool calculates block hashes for a specified block size during an acquisition for each block acquired from the digital source. AO-23 If the tool logs any log significant information, the information is accurately recorded in the log file. AO-24 If the tool executes in a forensically safe execution environment, the digital source is unchanged by the acquisition process.
Tester Name:	brl
Test Host:	Max
Test Date:	Fri Apr 21 08:14:26 2006
Drives:	src(44) dst (E6) other (none)

```
Test Case DA-02-NT ILook IXimager Version 2.0, Feb 01 2006
```

Source Setup:	```
	src hash: < E196D36E7B322C0EF83923112AD1800581742B6E >
	78165360 total sectors (40020664320 bytes)
	65534/015/63 (max cyl/hd values)
	65535/016/63 (number of cyl/hd)
	IDE disk: Model (WDC WD400JB-00FMA0) serial # (WD-WMAJC1011319)
	N Start LBA Length Start C/H/S End C/H/S boot Partition type
	1 P 000000063 020980827 0000/001/01 1023/254/63 0C Fat32X
	2 X 020980890 057175335 1023/000/01 1023/254/63 0F extended
	3 S 000000063 000032067 1023/001/01 1023/254/63 01 Fat12
	4 x 000032130 002104515 1023/000/01 1023/254/63 05 extended
	5 S 000000063 002104452 1023/001/01 1023/254/63 06 Fat16
	6 x 002136645 004192965 1023/000/01 1023/254/63 05 extended
	7 S 000000063 004192902 1023/001/01 1023/254/63 16 other
	8 x 006329610 008401995 1023/000/01 1023/254/63 05 extended
	9 S 000000063 008401932 1023/001/01 1023/254/63 0B Fat32
	10 x 014731605 010490445 1023/000/01 1023/254/63 05 extended
	11 S 000000063 010490382 1023/001/01 1023/254/63 83 Linux
	12 x 025222050 004209030 1023/000/01 1023/254/63 05 extended
	13 S 000000063 004208967 1023/001/01 1023/254/63 82 Linux swap
	14 x 029431080 027744255 1023/000/01 1023/254/63 05 extended
	15 S 000000063 027744192 1023/001/01 1023/254/63 07 NTFS
	16 S 000000000 000000000 0000/000/00 0000/000/00 00 empty entry
	17 P 000000000 000000000 0000/000/00 0000/000/00 00 empty entry
	18 P 000000000 000000000 0000/000/00 0000/000/00 00 empty entry
	1 020980827 sectors 10742183424 bytes
	3 000032067 sectors 16418304 bytes
	5 002104452 sectors 1077479424 bytes
	7 004192902 sectors 2146765824 bytes
	9 008401932 sectors 4301789184 bytes
	11 010490382 sectors 5371075584 bytes
	13 004208967 sectors 2154991104 bytes
	15 027744192 sectors 14205026304 bytes
Log Highlights:	IXImager Log file
	SCSI device sdb: 35843670 512-byte hdwr sectors (18352 MB)
	SCSI device sdc: 78165360 512-byte hdwr sectors (40021 MB)
	SCSI device sdb: 35843670 512-byte hdwr sectors (18352 MB)
	Initializing...
	Opened input device '/dev/sdc11'
	Opened output device '/dev/sdb'
	Beginning Clone operation for 14205026304 bytes
	Beginning Clone operation
	Beginning Clone operation
	Clone Complete
	Clone was completed successfully.
	Read : 14.21 GB (14205026304 bytes)
	Written : 14.21 GB (14205026304 bytes)
	Total Processed: 14.21 GB (14205026304 bytes)
	Clone Speed : 20.09 MB/sec
	Elapsed Time : 0h 11m 47s
	Bad Sectors : 0
	Clearing computer memory...
	Hashes of src and dst partitions
	Src SHA1 Hash: BD600A5EC643643D285C6C1C8A7D7A332B052D23 -
	Dst SHA1 Hash: BD600A5EC643643D285C6C1C8A7D7A332B052D23 -
	Source SHA1 Hash: E196D36E7B322C0EF83923112AD1800581742B6E

Results:

Assertion & Expected Result	Actual Result
AM-01 Source acquired using interface AI.	as expected
AM-02 Source is type DS.	as expected
AM-03 Execution environment is XE.	as expected
AM-04 A clone is created.	as expected
AM-06 All visible sectors acquired.	as expected
AM-08 All sectors accurately acquired.	as expected
AO-11 A clone is created during acquisition.	as expected
AO-13 Clone created using interface AI.	as expected
AO-14 An unaligned clone is created.	as expected

Test Case DA-02-NT ILook IXimager Version 2.0, Feb 01 2006		
	AO-17 Excess sectors are unchanged.	as expected
	AO-22 Tool calculates hashes by block.	option not available
	AO-23 Logged information is correct.	as expected
	AO-24 Source is unchanged by acquisition.	as expected
Analysis:	Expected results achieved	

5.2.16 DA-02-SWAP

Test Case DA-02-SWAP ILook IXimager Version 2.0, Feb 01 2006	
Description:	DA-02 Acquire a digital source of type DS to an unaligned clone.
Assertions:	AM-01 The tool uses access interface SRC-AI to access the digital source. AM-02 The tool acquires digital source DS. AM-03 The tool executes in execution environment XE. AM-04 If clone creation is specified, the tool creates a clone of the digital source. AM-06 All visible sectors are acquired from the digital source. AM-08 All sectors acquired from the digital source are acquired accurately. AO-11 If requested, a clone is created during an acquisition of a digital source. AO-13 A clone is created using access interface DST-AI to write to the clone device. AO-14 If an unaligned clone is created, each sector written to the clone is accurately written to the same disk address on the clone that the sector occupied on the digital source. AO-17 If requested, any excess sectors on a clone destination device are not modified. AO-22 If requested, the tool calculates block hashes for a specified block size during an acquisition for each block acquired from the digital source. AO-23 If the tool logs any log significant information, the information is accurately recorded in the log file. AO-24 If the tool executes in a forensically safe execution environment, the digital source is unchanged by the acquisition process.
Tester Name:	brl
Test Host:	Joe
Test Date:	Thu Apr 20 16:26:03 2006
Drives:	src(43) dst (2F) other (none)

Source Setup:	src hash: < 888E2E7F7AD237DC7A732281DD93F325065E5871 >
	78125000 total sectors (40000000000 bytes)
	Model (0BB-75JHC0) serial # (WD-WMAMC46588)
	  N Start LBA Length Start C/H/S End C/H/S boot Partition type
	  1 P 000000063 020980827 0000/001/01 1023/254/63 0C Fat32X
	  2 X 020980890 057143205 1023/001/01 1023/254/63 0F extended
	  3 S 000000063 000032067 1023/001/01 1023/254/63 01 Fat12
	  4 x 000032130 002104515 1023/000/01 1023/254/63 05 extended
	  5 S 000000063 002104452 1023/001/01 1023/254/63 06 Fat16
	  6 x 002136645 004192965 1023/000/01 1023/254/63 05 extended
	  7 S 000000063 004192902 1023/001/01 1023/254/63 16 other
	  8 x 006329610 008401995 1023/000/01 1023/254/63 05 extended
	  9 S 000000063 008401932 1023/001/01 1023/254/63 0B Fat32
	 10 x 014731605 010490445 1023/000/01 1023/254/63 05 extended
	 11 S 000000063 010490382 1023/001/01 1023/254/63 83 Linux
	 12 x 025222050 004209030 1023/000/01 1023/254/63 05 extended
	 13 S 000000063 004208967 1023/001/01 1023/254/63 82 Linux swap
	 14 x 029431080 027712125 1023/000/01 1023/254/63 05 extended
	 15 S 000000063 027712062 1023/001/01 1023/254/63 07 NTFS
	 16 S 000000000 000000000 0000/000/00 0000/000/00 00 empty entry
	 17 P 000000000 000000000 0000/000/00 0000/000/00 00 empty entry
	 18 P 000000000 000000000 0000/000/00 0000/000/00 00 empty entry
	  1 020980827 sectors 10742183424 bytes
	  3 000032067 sectors 16418304 bytes
	  5 002104452 sectors 1077479424 bytes
	  7 004192902 sectors 2146765824 bytes
	  9 008401932 sectors 4301789184 bytes
	 11 010490382 sectors 5371075584 bytes
	 13 004208967 sectors 2154991104 bytes
	 15 027712062 sectors 14188575744 bytes

Test Case DA-02-SWAP ILook IXimager Version 2.0, Feb 01 2006	
Log Highlights:	IXImager Log file SCSI device sdb: 17783249 512-byte hdwr sectors (9105 MB) SCSI device sdc: 78125000 512-byte hdwr sectors (40000 MB) SCSI device sdb: 17783249 512-byte hdwr sectors (9105 MB) Initializing... Opened input device '/dev/sdc10' Opened output device '/dev/sdb' Beginning Clone operation for 2154991104 bytes Beginning Clone operation Beginning Clone operation Clone Complete Clone was completed successfully. Read : 2.155 GB (2154991104 bytes) Written : 2.155 GB (2154991104 bytes) Total Processed: 2.155 GB (2154991104 bytes) Clone Speed : 13.39 MB/sec Elapsed Time : 0h 2m 41s Bad Sectors : 0 Clearing computer memory... Hashes of src and dst partitions Src SHA1 Hash: F5B062CC31DA088DF7FAF8F7A47E500BF4244BCF - Dst SHA1 Hash: F5B062CC31DA088DF7FAF8F7A47E500BF4244BCF - Source SHA1 Hash: 888E2E7F7AD237DC7A732281DD93F325065E5871
Results:	

Assertion & Expected Result	Actual Result
AM-01 Source acquired using interface AI.	as expected
AM-02 Source is type DS.	as expected
AM-03 Execution environment is XE.	as expected
AM-04 A clone is created.	as expected
AM-06 All visible sectors acquired.	as expected
AM-08 All sectors accurately acquired.	as expected
AO-11 A clone is created during acquisition.	as expected
AO-13 Clone created using interface AI.	as expected
AO-14 An unaligned clone is created.	as expected
AO-17 Excess sectors are unchanged.	as expected
AO-22 Tool calculates hashes by block.	option not available
AO-23 Logged information is correct.	as expected
AO-24 Source is unchanged by acquisition.	as expected

Analysis:	Expected results achieved

5.2.17   DA-02-THUMB

Test Case DA-02-THUMB ILook IXimager Version 2.0, Feb 01 2006	
Description:	DA-02 Acquire a digital source of type DS to an unaligned clone.
Assertions:	AM-01 The tool uses access interface SRC-AI to access the digital source. AM-02 The tool acquires digital source DS. AM-03 The tool executes in execution environment XE. AM-04 If clone creation is specified, the tool creates a clone of the digital source. AM-06 All visible sectors are acquired from the digital source. AM-08 All sectors acquired from the digital source are acquired accurately. AO-11 If requested, a clone is created during an acquisition of a digital source. AO-13 A clone is created using access interface DST-AI to write to the clone device. AO-14 If an unaligned clone is created, each sector written to the clone is accurately written to the same disk address on the clone that the sector occupied on the digital source. AO-17 If requested, any excess sectors on a clone destination device are not modified. AO-22 If requested, the tool calculates block hashes for a specified block size during an acquisition for each block acquired from the digital source. AO-23 If the tool logs any log significant information, the information is

```
Test Case DA-02-THUMB ILook IXimager Version 2.0, Feb 01 2006
```

	accurately recorded in the log file. AO-24 If the tool executes in a forensically safe execution environment, the digital source is unchanged by the acquisition process.
Tester Name:	brl
Test Host:	JohnSteed
Test Date:	Tue May 9 16:48:45 2006
Drives:	src(D2-THUMB) dst (D3-THUMB) other (none)
Source Setup:	src hash: < 712C9F59F598745977E4E19F235F83CE8F4EC7BA > 253400 total sectors (129740800 bytes) Model (TS128MJFLASHA) serial # () Removable media, no partition table.

Log Highlights:	Comparision of original to clone
	    Sectors compared: 253400
	    Sectors match: 253400
	    Sectors differ: 0
	    Bytes differ: 0
	    Diffs range
	0 source read errors, 0 destination read errors
	
	IXImager Log file
	hda: 156301488 sectors (80026 MB) w/8192KiB Cache, CHS=9729/255/63, UDMA(100)
	SCSI device sda: 253400 512-byte hdwr sectors (130 MB)
	SCSI device sdb: 253400 512-byte hdwr sectors (130 MB)
	SCSI device sdb: 253400 512-byte hdwr sectors (130 MB)
	Initializing...
	Opened input device '/dev/sda'
	Opened output device '/dev/sdb'
	Beginning Clone operation for 129740800 bytes
	Beginning Clone operation
	Beginning Clone operation
	Clone Complete
	Clone was completed successfully.
	
	Read : 129.7 MB (129740800 bytes)
	Written : 129.7 MB (129740800 bytes)
	Total Processed: 129.7 MB (129740800 bytes)
	Clone Speed : 655.3 kB/sec
	Elapsed Time : 0h 3m 18s
	Bad Sectors : 0
	Clearing computer memory...
	
	Source SHA1 Hash: 712C9F59F598745977E4E19F235F83CE8F4EC7BA

Results:	

Assertion & Expected Result	Actual Result
AM-01 Source acquired using interface AI.	as expected
AM-02 Source is type DS.	as expected
AM-03 Execution environment is XE.	as expected
AM-04 A clone is created.	as expected
AM-06 All visible sectors acquired.	as expected
AM-08 All sectors accurately acquired.	as expected
AO-11 A clone is created during acquisition.	as expected
AO-13 Clone created using interface AI.	as expected
AO-14 An unaligned clone is created.	as expected
AO-17 Excess sectors are unchanged.	as expected
AO-22 Tool calculates hashes by block.	option not available
AO-23 Logged information is correct.	as expected
AO-24 Source is unchanged by acquisition.	as expected

Analysis:	Expected results achieved

5.2.18 DA-02-ZIP

Test Case DA-02-ZIP ILook IXimager Version 2.0, Feb 01 2006	
Description:	DA-02 Acquire a digital source of type DS to an unaligned clone.
Assertions:	AM-01 The tool uses access interface SRC-AI to access the digital source. AM-02 The tool acquires digital source DS. AM-03 The tool executes in execution environment XE. AM-04 If clone creation is specified, the tool creates a clone of the digital source. AM-06 All visible sectors are acquired from the digital source. AM-08 All sectors acquired from the digital source are acquired accurately. AO-11 If requested, a clone is created during an acquisition of a digital source. AO-13 A clone is created using access interface DST-AI to write to the clone device. AO-14 If an unaligned clone is created, each sector written to the clone is accurately written to the same disk address on the clone that the sector occupied on the digital source. AO-17 If requested, any excess sectors on a clone destination device are not modified. AO-22 If requested, the tool calculates block hashes for a specified block size during an acquisition for each block acquired from the digital source. AO-23 If the tool logs any log significant information, the information is accurately recorded in the log file. AO-24 If the tool executes in a forensically safe execution environment, the digital source is unchanged by the acquisition process.
Tester Name:	brl
Test Host:	Nick
Test Date:	Thu May 11 10:18:03 2006
Drives:	src(E2-ZIP) dst (E1-ZIP) other (none)
Source Setup:	src hash: < AFEA6483060C6FAD1026B7094810674E91AEA5D7 > 196608 total sectors (100663296 bytes) Model (ZIP 250) serial # () Removable media, no partition table.
Log Highlights:	Comparision of original to clone Sectors compared: 196608 Sectors match: 196608 Sectors differ: 0 Bytes differ: 0 Diffs range Source (196608) has 292864 fewer sectors than destination (489472) Zero fill: 0 Src Byte fill (E2): 0 Dst Byte fill (E1): 292864 Other fill: 0 Other no fill: 0 Zero fill range: Src fill range: Dst fill range: 196608-489471 Other fill range: Other not filled range: 0 source read errors, 0 destination read errors IXImager Log file hda: 156250000 sectors (80000 MB) w/1821KiB Cache, CHS=9726/255/63, UDMA(100) SCSI device sda: 196608 512-byte hdwr sectors (101 MB) Initializing... Opened input device '/dev/sda' Opened output device '/dev/hdb' Beginning Clone operation for 100663296 bytes Beginning Clone operation Beginning Clone operation Clone Complete Clone was completed successfully. Read : 100.7 MB (100663296 bytes) Written : 100.7 MB (100663296 bytes)

Test Case DA-02-ZIP ILook IXimager Version 2.0, Feb 01 2006		
	Total Processed: 100.7 MB (100663296 bytes) Clone Speed : 756.9 kB/sec Elapsed Time : 0h 2m 13s Bad Sectors : 0 Clearing computer memory... Source SHA1 Hash: AFEA6483060C6FAD1026B7094810674E91AEA5D7	
Results:	Assertion & Expected Result	Actual Result
	AM-01 Source acquired using interface AI.	as expected
	AM-02 Source is type DS.	as expected
	AM-03 Execution environment is XE.	as expected
	AM-04 A clone is created.	as expected
	AM-06 All visible sectors acquired.	as expected
	AM-08 All sectors accurately acquired.	as expected
	AO-11 A clone is created during acquisition.	as expected
	AO-13 Clone created using interface AI.	as expected
	AO-14 An unaligned clone is created.	as expected
	AO-17 Excess sectors are unchanged.	as expected
	AO-22 Tool calculates hashes by block.	option not available
	AO-23 Logged information is correct.	as expected
	AO-24 Source is unchanged by acquisition.	as expected
Analysis:	Expected results achieved	

5.2.19   DA-04

Test Case DA-04 ILook IXimager Version 2.0, Feb 01 2006	
Description:	DA-04 Acquire a physical device to a truncated clone.
Assertions:	AM-01 The tool uses access interface SRC-AI to access the digital source. AM-02 The tool acquires digital source DS. AM-03 The tool executes in execution environment XE. AM-04 If clone creation is specified, the tool creates a clone of the digital source. AM-06 All visible sectors are acquired from the digital source. AM-08 All sectors acquired from the digital source are acquired accurately. AO-11 If requested, a clone is created during an acquisition of a digital source. AO-13 A clone is created using access interface DST-AI to write to the clone device. AO-14 If an unaligned clone is created, each sector written to the clone is accurately written to the same disk address on the clone that the sector occupied on the digital source. AO-19 If there is insufficient space to create a complete clone, a truncated clone is created using all available sectors of the clone device. AO-20 If a truncated clone is created, the tool notifies the user. AO-22 If requested, the tool calculates block hashes for a specified block size during an acquisition for each block acquired from the digital source. AO-23 If the tool logs any log significant information, the information is accurately recorded in the log file. AO-24 If the tool executes in a forensically safe execution environment, the digital source is unchanged by the acquisition process.
Tester Name:	brl
Test Host:	Max
Test Date:	Wed May 3 14:43:49 2006
Drives:	src(41) dst (5A) other (none)
Source Setup:	src hash: < 15CAA1A307271160D8372668BF8A03FC45A51CC9 > 78125000 total sectors (40000000000 bytes) 65534/015/63 (max cyl/hd values) 65535/016/63 (number of cyl/hd) IDE disk: Model (WDC WD400BB-75JHC0) serial # (WD-WMAMC4658355) N Start LBA Length Start C/H/S End C/H/S boot Partition type 1 P 000000063 078107967 0000/001/01 1023/254/63 Boot 07 NTFS 2 P 000000000 000000000 0000/000/00 0000/000/00 00 empty entry 3 P 000000000 000000000 0000/000/00 0000/000/00 00 empty entry 4 P 000000000 000000000 0000/000/00 0000/000/00 00 empty entry 1 078107967 sectors 39991279104 bytes

Test Case DA-04 ILook IXimager Version 2.0, Feb 01 2006	
Log Highlights:	Comparision of original to clone Sectors compared: 12692736 Sectors match: 12692736 Sectors differ: 0 Bytes differ: 0 Diffs range Source (78125000) has 65432264 more sectors than destination (12692736) 0 source read errors, 0 destination read errors IXImager Log file hda: 12692736 sectors (6498 MB) w/468KiB Cache, CHS=13431/15/63, UDMA(33) hdb: 78125000 sectors (40000 MB) w/2048KiB Cache, CHS=65535/16/63, UDMA(100) Initializing... Opened input device '/dev/hdb' Opened output device '/dev/hda' Beginning Clone operation for 40000000000 bytes Beginning Clone operation Beginning Clone operation Your target device has run out of free space! Clone Aborted Clone was aborted. Read : 6.507 GB (6506938368 bytes) Written : 6.499 GB (6498549760 bytes) Total Processed: 6.507 GB (6506938368 bytes) Expected Size : 40.00 GB (40000000000 bytes) Clone Speed : 53.30 kB/sec Elapsed Time : 33h 54m 35s Bad Sectors : 0 Clearing computer memory... Source SHA1 Hash: 15CAA1A307271160D8372668BF8A03FC45A51CC9
Results:	

Assertion & Expected Result	Actual Result
AM-01 Source acquired using interface AI.	as expected
AM-02 Source is type DS.	as expected
AM-03 Execution environment is XE.	as expected
AM-04 A clone is created.	as expected
AM-06 All visible sectors acquired.	as expected
AM-08 All sectors accurately acquired.	as expected
AO-11 A clone is created during acquisition.	as expected
AO-13 Clone created using interface AI.	as expected
AO-14 An unaligned clone is created.	as expected
AO-19 Truncated clone is created.	as expected
AO-20 User notified that clone is truncated.	as expected
AO-22 Tool calculates hashes by block.	option not available
AO-23 Logged information is correct.	as expected
AO-24 Source is unchanged by acquisition.	as expected

Analysis:	Expected results achieved

5.2.20 DA-06-ATA28

Test Case DA-06-ATA28 ILook IXimager Version 2.0, Feb 01 2006	
Description:	DA-06 Acquire a physical device using access interface AI to an image file.
Assertions:	AM-01 The tool uses access interface SRC-AI to access the digital source. AM-02 The tool acquires digital source DS. AM-03 The tool executes in execution environment XE. AM-05 If image file creation is specified, the tool creates an image file on file system type FS. AM-06 All visible sectors are acquired from the digital source. AM-08 All sectors acquired from the digital source are acquired accurately. AO-01 If the tool creates an image file, the data represented by the image file is the same as the data acquired by the tool. AO-05 If the tool creates a multi-file image of a requested size then all

	Test Case DA-06-ATA28 ILook IXimager Version 2.0, Feb 01 2006
	the individual files shall be no larger than the requested size. AO-22 If requested, the tool calculates block hashes for a specified block size during an acquisition for each block acquired from the digital source. AO-23 If the tool logs any log significant information, the information is accurately recorded in the log file. AO-24 If the tool executes in a forensically safe execution environment, the digital source is unchanged by the acquisition process.
Tester Name:	brl
Test Host:	Paladin
Test Date:	Wed Mar 29 11:47:49 2006
Drives:	src(41) dst (4D-FU2) other (none)
Source Setup:	src hash: < 15CAA1A307271160D8372668BF8A03FC45A51CC9 > 78125000 total sectors (40000000000 bytes) 65534/015/63 (max cyl/hd values) 65535/016/63 (number of cyl/hd) IDE disk: Model (WDC WD400BB-75JHC0) serial # (WD-WMAMC4658355) N Start LBA Length Start C/H/S End C/H/S boot Partition type 1 P 000000063 078107967 0000/001/01 1023/254/63 Boot 07 NTFS 2 P 000000000 000000000 0000/000/00 0000/000/00 00 empty entry 3 P 000000000 000000000 0000/000/00 0000/000/00 00 empty entry 4 P 000000000 000000000 0000/000/00 0000/000/00 00 empty entry 1 078107967 sectors 39991279104 bytes
Log Highlights:	IXImager Log file hda: 78125000 sectors (40000 MB) w/2048KiB Cache, CHS=4863/255/63, UDMA(100) SCSI device sda: 781443888 512-byte hdwr sectors (400099 MB) User selected ILook Default Image Format Initializing... Opened output file '/ILookImager/ILook.003/DA06ATA28001.asb' Beginning Image operation for 40000000000 bytes Beginning Image operation Beginning Image operation Opened output file '/ILookImager/ILook.003/DA06ATA28002.asb' continuing at byte 20948254720 Image is being stored to /ILook.003/DA06ATA28002.asb Opened output file '/ILookImager/ILook.003/DA06ATA28003.asb' continuing at byte 39119159296 Image is being stored to /ILook.003/DA06ATA28003.asb Image Complete Image was completed successfully. Read : 40.00 GB (40000000000 bytes) Written : 1.316 GB (1316466855 bytes) Total Processed: 40.00 GB (40000000000 bytes) Image Speed : 16.00 MB/sec Elapsed Time : 0h 41m 40s Compression : 96.71% Bad Sectors : 0 SHA-1 Value : 15caa1a307271160d8372668bf8a03fc45a51cc9 : for 40000000000 bytes Clearing computer memory... Source SHA1 Hash: 15CAA1A307271160D8372668BF8A03FC45A51CC9
Results:	

Assertion & Expected Result	Actual Result
AM-01 Source acquired using interface AI.	as expected
AM-02 Source is type DS.	as expected
AM-03 Execution environment is XE.	as expected
AM-05 An image is created on file system type FS.	as expected
AM-06 All visible sectors acquired.	as expected
AM-08 All sectors accurately acquired.	as expected
AO-01 Image file is complete and accurate.	as expected
AO-05 Multifile image created.	as expected
AO-22 Tool calculates hashes by block.	option not available
AO-23 Logged information is correct.	as expected
AO-24 Source is unchanged by acquisition.	as expected

Test Case DA-06-ATA28 ILook IXimager Version 2.0, Feb 01 2006	
Analysis:	Expected results achieved

5.2.21 DA-06-ATA48

Test Case DA-06-ATA48 ILook IXimager Version 2.0, Feb 01 2006	
Description:	DA-06 Acquire a physical device using access interface AI to an image file.
Assertions:	AM-01 The tool uses access interface SRC-AI to access the digital source. AM-02 The tool acquires digital source DS. AM-03 The tool executes in execution environment XE. AM-05 If image file creation is specified, the tool creates an image file on file system type FS. AM-06 All visible sectors are acquired from the digital source. AM-08 All sectors acquired from the digital source are acquired accurately. AO-01 If the tool creates an image file, the data represented by the image file is the same as the data acquired by the tool. AO-05 If the tool creates a multi-file image of a requested size then all the individual files shall be no larger than the requested size. AO-22 If requested, the tool calculates block hashes for a specified block size during an acquisition for each block acquired from the digital source. AO-23 If the tool logs any log significant information, the information is accurately recorded in the log file. AO-24 If the tool executes in a forensically safe execution environment, the digital source is unchanged by the acquisition process.
Tester Name:	brl
Test Host:	Max
Test Date:	Wed Apr 5 12:20:40 2006
Drives:	src(4C) dst (4D-FU2) other (none)
Source Setup:	src hash: < 8FF620D2BEDCCAFE8412EDAAD56C8554F872EFBF > 390721968 total sectors (200049647616 bytes) 24320/254/63 (max cyl/hd values) 24321/255/63 (number of cyl/hd) IDE disk: Model (WDC WD2000JB-00KFA0) serial # (WD-WMAMR1031111) N Start LBA Length Start C/H/S End C/H/S boot Partition type 1 P 000000063 390700737 0000/001/01 1023/254/63 Boot 07 NTFS 2 P 000000000 000000000 0000/000/00 0000/000/00 00 empty entry 3 P 000000000 000000000 0000/000/00 0000/000/00 00 empty entry 4 P 000000000 000000000 0000/000/00 0000/000/00 00 empty entry 1 390700737 sectors 200038777344 bytes
Log Highlights:	IXImager Log file hda: 390721968 sectors (200049 MB) w/8192KiB Cache, CHS=24321/255/63, UDMA(100) SCSI device sdb: 781443888 512-byte hdwr sectors (400099 MB) User selected ILook Default Image Format Initializing... Opened output file '/ILookImager/ILook.015/ATAB3001.asb' Beginning Image operation for 200049647616 bytes Beginning Image operation Beginning Image operation Opened output file '/ILookImager/ILook.015/ATAB3002.asb' continuing at byte 1274740736 Image is being stored to /ILook.015/ATAB3002.asb Opened output file '/ILookImager/ILook.015/ATAB3003.asb' continuing at byte 22620078080 Image is being stored to /ILook.015/ATAB3003.asb Opened output file '/ILookImager/ILook.015/ATAB3004.asb' continuing at byte 50723815424 Image is being stored to /ILook.015/ATAB3004.asb Opened output file '/ILookImager/ILook.015/ATAB3005.asb' continuing at byte 78889615360 Image is being stored to /ILook.015/ATAB3005.asb Opened output file '/ILookImager/ILook.015/ATAB3006.asb' continuing at byte 107052662784 Image is being stored to /ILook.015/ATAB3006.asb Opened output file '/ILookImager/ILook.015/ATAB3007.asb' continuing at byte 135218331648 Image is being stored to /ILook.015/ATAB3007.asb Opened output file '/ILookImager/ILook.015/ATAB3008.asb' continuing at byte 163384066048

```
Test Case DA-06-ATA48 ILook IXimager Version 2.0, Feb 01 2006
```

	Image is being stored to /ILook.015/ATAB3008.asb Opened output file '/ILookImager/ILook.015/ATAB3009.asb' continuing at byte 191549800448 Image is being stored to /ILook.015/ATAB3009.asb Image Complete Image was completed successfully. Read : 200.0 GB (200049647616 bytes) Written : 5.380 GB (5379855567 bytes) Total Processed : 200.0 GB (200049647616 bytes) Image Speed : 26.17 MB/sec Elapsed Time : 2h 7m 23s Compression : 97.31% Bad Sectors : 0 SHA-1 Value : 8ff620d2bedccafe8412edaad56c8554f872efbf : for 200049647616 bytes Clearing computer memory... Source SHA1 Hash: 8FF620D2BEDCCAFE8412EDAAD56C8554F872EFBF
Results:	

Assertion & Expected Result	Actual Result
AM-01 Source acquired using interface AI.	as expected
AM-02 Source is type DS.	as expected
AM-03 Execution environment is XE.	as expected
AM-05 An image is created on file system type FS.	as expected
AM-06 All visible sectors acquired.	as expected
AM-08 All sectors accurately acquired.	as expected
AO-01 Image file is complete and accurate.	as expected
AO-05 Multifile image created.	as expected
AO-22 Tool calculates hashes by block.	option not available
AO-23 Logged information is correct.	as expected
AO-24 Source is unchanged by acquisition.	as expected

Analysis:	Expected results achieved

5.2.22 DA-06-FIREWIRE

```
Test Case DA-06-FIREWIRE ILook IXimager Version 2.0, Feb 01 2006
```

Description:	DA-06 Acquire a physical device using access interface AI to an image file.
Assertions:	AM-01 The tool uses access interface SRC-AI to access the digital source. AM-02 The tool acquires digital source DS. AM-03 The tool executes in execution environment XE. AM-05 If image file creation is specified, the tool creates an image file on file system type FS. AM-06 All visible sectors are acquired from the digital source. AM-08 All sectors acquired from the digital source are acquired accurately. AO-01 If the tool creates an image file, the data represented by the image file is the same as the data acquired by the tool. AO-05 If the tool creates a multi-file image of a requested size then all the individual files shall be no larger than the requested size. AO-22 If requested, the tool calculates block hashes for a specified block size during an acquisition for each block acquired from the digital source. AO-23 If the tool logs any log significant information, the information is accurately recorded in the log file. AO-24 If the tool executes in a forensically safe execution environment, the digital source is unchanged by the acquisition process.
Tester Name:	brl
Test Host:	JohnSteed
Test Date:	Tue Apr 4 09:26:17 2006
Drives:	src(83-FU2) dst (4D-FU2) other (none)
Source Setup:	src hash: < 9B0D0FEA3023476FA5D24436C0CEFCB585EB8695 > 160836480 total sectors (82348277760 bytes) 10010/254/63 (max cyl/hd values) 10011/255/63 (number of cyl/hd) Model (HDS722580VLAT20) serial # ()

Log Highlights:	IXImager Log file hda: 156301488 sectors (80026 MB) w/8192KiB Cache, CHS=9729/255/63, UDMA(100) SCSI device sda: 781443888 512-byte hdwr sectors (400099 MB) SCSI device sdb: 160836480 512-byte hdwr sectors (82348 MB) User selected ILook Default Image Format Initializing... Opened output file '/ILookImager/ILook.009/DA06FIREWIRE001.asb' Beginning Image operation for 82348277760 bytes Beginning Image operation Beginning Image operation Opened output file '/ILookImager/ILook.009/DA06FIREWIRE002.asb' continuing at byte 28174450688 Image is being stored to /ILook.009/DA06FIREWIRE002.asb Opened output file '/ILookImager/ILook.009/DA06FIREWIRE003.asb' continuing at byte 56342872064 Image is being stored to /ILook.009/DA06FIREWIRE003.asb Image Complete Image was completed successfully. Read : 82.35 GB (82348277760 bytes) Written : 1.894 GB (1894487827 bytes) Total Processed: 82.35 GB (82348277760 bytes) Image Speed : 7.943 MB/sec Elapsed Time : 2h 52m 48s Compression : 97.70% Bad Sectors : 0 SHA-1 Value : 9b0d0fea3023476fa5d24436c0cefcb585eb8695 : for 82348277760 bytes Clearing computer memory... Source SHA1 Hash: 9B0D0FEA3023476FA5D24436C0CEFCB585EB8695
Results:	

Assertion & Expected Result	Actual Result
AM-01 Source acquired using interface AI.	as expected
AM-02 Source is type DS.	as expected
AM-03 Execution environment is XE.	as expected
AM-05 An image is created on file system type FS.	as expected
AM-06 All visible sectors acquired.	as expected
AM-08 All sectors accurately acquired.	as expected
AO-01 Image file is complete and accurate.	as expected
AO-05 Multifile image created.	as expected
AO-22 Tool calculates hashes by block.	option not available
AO-23 Logged information is correct.	as expected
AO-24 Source is unchanged by acquisition.	as expected

Analysis:	Expected results achieved

5.2.23 DA-06-SATA28

Test Case DA-06-SATA28 ILook IXimager Version 2.0, Feb 01 2006	
Description:	DA-06 Acquire a physical device using access interface AI to an image file.
Assertions:	AM-01 The tool uses access interface SRC-AI to access the digital source. AM-02 The tool acquires digital source DS. AM-03 The tool executes in execution environment XE. AM-05 If image file creation is specified, the tool creates an image file on file system type FS. AM-06 All visible sectors are acquired from the digital source. AM-08 All sectors acquired from the digital source are acquired accurately. AO-01 If the tool creates an image file, the data represented by the image file is the same as the data acquired by the tool. AO-05 If the tool creates a multi-file image of a requested size then all the individual files shall be no larger than the requested size. AO-22 If requested, the tool calculates block hashes for a specified block size during an acquisition for each block acquired from the digital source. AO-23 If the tool logs any log significant information, the information is accurately recorded in the log file.

\multicolumn{2}{|l|}{Test Case DA-06-SATA28 ILook IXimager Version 2.0, Feb 01 2006}
	AO-24 If the tool executes in a forensically safe execution environment, the digital source is unchanged by the acquisition process.
Tester Name:	brl
Test Host:	Joe
Test Date:	Thu Mar 30 14:04:53 2006
Drives:	src(07) dst (4D-FU2) other (none)

Source Setup:	src hash: < 655E9BDDB36A3F9C5C4CC8BF32B8C5B41AF9F52E >
	 156301488 total sectors (80026361856 bytes)
	 Model (WDC WD800JD-32HK) serial # (WD-WMAJ91510044)
	  N Start LBA Length Start C/H/S End C/H/S boot Partition type
	  1 P 000000063 156280257 0000/001/01 1023/254/63 Boot 07 NTFS
	  2 P 000000000 000000000 0000/000/00 0000/000/00 00 empty entry
	  3 P 000000000 000000000 0000/000/00 0000/000/00 00 empty entry
	  4 P 000000000 000000000 0000/000/00 0000/000/00 00 empty entry
	 1 156280257 sectors 80015491584 bytes

Log Highlights:	IXImager Log file ata1: dev 0 ATA-6, max UDMA/133, 156301488 sectors: LBA SCSI device sdb: 156301488 512-byte hdwr sectors (80026 MB) SCSI device sdc: 781443888 512-byte hdwr sectors (400099 MB) User selected ILook Default Image Format Initializing... Opened output file '/ILookImager/ILook.007/DA06SATA48001.asb' Beginning Image operation for 80026361856 bytes Beginning Image operation Beginning Image operation Opened output file '/ILookImager/ILook.007/DA06SATA48002.asb' continuing at byte 1286864896 Image is being stored to /ILook.007/DA06SATA48002.asb Opened output file '/ILookImager/ILook.007/DA06SATA48003.asb' continuing at byte 22481928192 Image is being stored to /ILook.007/DA06SATA48003.asb Opened output file '/ILookImager/ILook.007/DA06SATA48004.asb' continuing at byte 50646089728 Image is being stored to /ILook.007/DA06SATA48004.asb Opened output file '/ILookImager/ILook.007/DA06SATA48005.asb' continuing at byte 78812282880 Image is being stored to /ILook.007/DA06SATA48005.asb Image Complete Image was completed successfully. Read : 80.03 GB (80026361856 bytes) Written : 2.620 GB (2620183743 bytes) Total Processed: 80.03 GB (80026361856 bytes) Image Speed : 25.81 MB/sec Elapsed Time : 0h 51m 40s Compression : 96.73% Bad Sectors : 0 SHA-1 Value : 655e9bddb36a3f9c5c4cc8bf32b8c5b41af9f52e : for 80026361856 bytes Clearing computer memory... Source SHA1 Hash: 655E9BDDB36A3F9C5C4CC8BF32B8C5B41AF9F52E
Results:	

Assertion & Expected Result	Actual Result
AM-01 Source acquired using interface AI.	as expected
AM-02 Source is type DS.	as expected
AM-03 Execution environment is XE.	as expected
AM-05 An image is created on file system type FS.	as expected
AM-06 All visible sectors acquired.	as expected
AM-08 All sectors accurately acquired.	as expected
AO-01 Image file is complete and accurate.	as expected
AO-05 Multifile image created.	as expected
AO-22 Tool calculates hashes by block.	option not available
AO-23 Logged information is correct.	as expected
AO-24 Source is unchanged by acquisition.	as expected

Analysis:	Expected results achieved

5.2.24 DA-06-SATA48

Test Case DA-06-SATA48 ILook IXimager Version 2.0, Feb 01 2006	
Description:	DA-06 Acquire a physical device using access interface AI to an image file.
Assertions:	AM-01 The tool uses access interface SRC-AI to access the digital source. AM-02 The tool acquires digital source DS. AM-03 The tool executes in execution environment XE. AM-05 If image file creation is specified, the tool creates an image file on file system type FS. AM-06 All visible sectors are acquired from the digital source. AM-08 All sectors acquired from the digital source are acquired accurately. AO-01 If the tool creates an image file, the data represented by the image file is the same as the data acquired by the tool. AO-05 If the tool creates a multi-file image of a requested size then all the individual files shall be no larger than the requested size. AO-22 If requested, the tool calculates block hashes for a specified block size during an acquisition for each block acquired from the digital source. AO-23 If the tool logs any log significant information, the information is accurately recorded in the log file. AO-24 If the tool executes in a forensically safe execution environment, the digital source is unchanged by the acquisition process.
Tester Name:	brl
Test Host:	Joe
Test Date:	Wed Apr 5 09:51:02 2006
Drives:	src(16) dst (4D-FU2) other (none)
Source Setup:	src hash: < F82982A9C63133988C1D2B4DA7C9C25CCA2D77A5 > 312581808 total sectors (160041885696 bytes) 19456/254/63 (max cyl/hd values) 19457/255/63 (number of cyl/hd) Model (WDC WD1600JD-00G) serial # (WD-WMAES2058252) N Start LBA Length Start C/H/S End C/H/S boot Partition type 1 P 000000063 312560577 0000/001/01 1023/254/63 Boot 07 NTFS 2 P 000000000 000000000 0000/000/00 0000/000/00 00 empty entry 3 P 000000000 000000000 0000/000/00 0000/000/00 00 empty entry 4 P 000000000 000000000 0000/000/00 0000/000/00 00 empty entry 1 312560577 sectors 160031015424 bytes
Log Highlights:	IXImager Log file ata2: dev 0 ATA-6, max UDMA/100, 312581808 sectors: LBA48 SCSI device sdb: 312581808 512-byte hdwr sectors (160042 MB) SCSI device sdc: 781443888 512-byte hdwr sectors (400099 MB) User selected ILook Default Image Format Initializing... Opened output file '/ILookImager/ILook.010/DA06SATA48001.asb' Beginning Image operation for 160041885696 bytes Beginning Image operation Beginning Image operation Opened output file '/ILookImager/ILook.010/DA06SATA48002.asb' continuing at byte 1267662848 Image is being stored to /ILook.010/DA06SATA48002.asb Opened output file '/ILookImager/ILook.010/DA06SATA48003.asb' continuing at byte 22621192192 Image is being stored to /ILook.010/DA06SATA48003.asb Opened output file '/ILookImager/ILook.010/DA06SATA48004.asb' continuing at byte 50723553280 Image is being stored to /ILook.010/DA06SATA48004.asb Opened output file '/ILookImager/ILook.010/DA06SATA48005.asb' continuing at byte 78889680896 Image is being stored to /ILook.010/DA06SATA48005.asb Opened output file '/ILookImager/ILook.010/DA06SATA48006.asb' continuing at byte 107052138496 Image is being stored to /ILook.010/DA06SATA48006.asb Opened output file '/ILookImager/ILook.010/DA06SATA48007.asb' continuing at byte 135218266112 Image is being stored to /ILook.010/DA06SATA48007.asb Image Complete Image was completed successfully. Read : 160.0 GB (160041885696 bytes) Written : 4.459 GB (4459320703 bytes)

Test Case DA-06-SATA48 ILook IXimager Version 2.0, Feb 01 2006	
	Total Processed: 160.0 GB (160041885696 bytes) Image Speed : 22.83 MB/sec Elapsed Time : 1h 56m 50s Compression : 97.21% Bad Sectors : 0 SHA-1 Value : f82982a9c63133988c1d2b4da7c9c25cca2d77a5 : for 160041885696 bytes Clearing computer memory... Source SHA1 Hash: F82982A9C63133988C1D2B4DA7C9C25CCA2D77A5
Results:	

Assertion & Expected Result	Actual Result
AM-01 Source acquired using interface AI.	as expected
AM-02 Source is type DS.	as expected
AM-03 Execution environment is XE.	as expected
AM-05 An image is created on file system type FS.	as expected
AM-06 All visible sectors acquired.	as expected
AM-08 All sectors accurately acquired.	as expected
AO-01 Image file is complete and accurate.	as expected
AO-05 Multifile image created.	as expected
AO-22 Tool calculates hashes by block.	option not available
AO-23 Logged information is correct.	as expected
AO-24 Source is unchanged by acquisition.	as expected

Analysis:	Expected results achieved

5.2.25 DA-06-SCSI

Test Case DA-06-SCSI ILook IXimager Version 2.0, Feb 01 2006	
Description:	DA-06 Acquire a physical device using access interface AI to an image file.
Assertions:	AM-01 The tool uses access interface SRC-AI to access the digital source. AM-02 The tool acquires digital source DS. AM-03 The tool executes in execution environment XE. AM-05 If image file creation is specified, the tool creates an image file on file system type FS. AM-06 All visible sectors are acquired from the digital source. AM-08 All sectors acquired from the digital source are acquired accurately. AO-01 If the tool creates an image file, the data represented by the image file is the same as the data acquired by the tool. AO-05 If the tool creates a multi-file image of a requested size then all the individual files shall be no larger than the requested size. AO-22 If requested, the tool calculates block hashes for a specified block size during an acquisition for each block acquired from the digital source. AO-23 If the tool logs any log significant information, the information is accurately recorded in the log file. AO-24 If the tool executes in a forensically safe execution environment, the digital source is unchanged by the acquisition process.
Tester Name:	brl
Test Host:	Paladin
Test Date:	Wed Mar 29 09:39:34 2006
Drives:	src(2A) dst (4D-FU2) other (none)
Source Setup:	src hash: < F5F9F2903DCAB895F36E270FB22A722E27918125 > 17783249 total sectors (9105023488 bytes) Model (QM39100TD-SCA) serial # (PCB=20-116711-06 HDAQM39100TD-SCA) N Start LBA Length Start C/H/S End C/H/S boot Partition type 1 P 000000063 017751762 0000/001/01 1023/254/63 Boot 07 NTFS 2 P 000000000 000000000 0000/000/00 0000/000/00 00 empty entry 3 P 000000000 000000000 0000/000/00 0000/000/00 00 empty entry 4 P 000000000 000000000 0000/000/00 0000/000/00 00 empty entry 1 017751762 sectors 9088902144 bytes
Log Highlights:	IXImager Log file SCSI device sda: 17783249 512-byte hdwr sectors (9105 MB) SCSI device sdb: 781443888 512-byte hdwr sectors (400099 MB) User selected ILook Default Image Format Initializing...

	Test Case DA-06-SCSI ILook IXimager Version 2.0, Feb 01 2006
	Opened output file '/ILookImager/ILook.002/DA06SCSI001.asb' Beginning Image operation for 9105023488 bytes Beginning Image operation Beginning Image operation Image Complete Image was completed successfully. Read : 9.105 GB (9105023488 bytes) Written : 606.9 MB (606900616 bytes) Total Processed: 9.105 GB (9105023488 bytes) Image Speed : 11.66 MB/sec Elapsed Time : 0h 13m 1s Compression : 93.33% Bad Sectors : 0 SHA-1 Value : f5f9f2903dcab895f36e270fb22a722e27918125 : for 9105023488 bytes Clearing computer memory... Source SHA1 Hash: F5F9F2903DCAB895F36E270FB22A722E27918125
Results:	

Assertion & Expected Result	Actual Result
AM-01 Source acquired using interface AI.	as expected
AM-02 Source is type DS.	as expected
AM-03 Execution environment is XE.	as expected
AM-05 An image is created on file system type FS.	as expected
AM-06 All visible sectors acquired.	as expected
AM-08 All sectors accurately acquired.	as expected
AO-01 Image file is complete and accurate.	as expected
AO-05 Multifile image created.	as expected
AO-22 Tool calculates hashes by block.	option not available
AO-23 Logged information is correct.	as expected
AO-24 Source is unchanged by acquisition.	as expected

Analysis:	Expected results achieved

5.2.26 DA-06-USB

	Test Case DA-06-USB ILook IXimager Version 2.0, Feb 01 2006
Description:	DA-06 Acquire a physical device using access interface AI to an image file.
Assertions:	AM-01 The tool uses access interface SRC-AI to access the digital source. AM-02 The tool acquires digital source DS. AM-03 The tool executes in execution environment XE. AM-05 If image file creation is specified, the tool creates an image file on file system type FS. AM-06 All visible sectors are acquired from the digital source. AM-08 All sectors acquired from the digital source are acquired accurately. AO-01 If the tool creates an image file, the data represented by the image file is the same as the data acquired by the tool. AO-05 If the tool creates a multi-file image of a requested size then all the individual files shall be no larger than the requested size. AO-22 If requested, the tool calculates block hashes for a specified block size during an acquisition for each block acquired from the digital source. AO-23 If the tool logs any log significant information, the information is accurately recorded in the log file. AO-24 If the tool executes in a forensically safe execution environment, the digital source is unchanged by the acquisition process.
Tester Name:	brl
Test Host:	JohnSteed
Test Date:	Wed Mar 29 16:33:12 2006
Drives:	src(63-FU2) dst (4D-FU2) other (none)
Source Setup:	src hash: < F7069EDCBEAC863C88DECED82159F22DA96BE99B > 117304992 total sectors (60060155904 bytes) Model (SP0612N) serial # () N Start LBA Length Start C/H/S End C/H/S boot Partition type 1 P 000000063 004192902 0000/001/01 0260/254/63 Boot 06 Fat16 2 X 004192965 113097600 0261/000/01 1023/254/63 0F extended 3 S 000000063 113097537 0261/001/01 1023/254/63 0B Fat32

Test Case DA-06-USB ILook IXimager Version 2.0, Feb 01 2006	
| | ```
                  4 S 000000000 000000000 0000/000/00 0000/000/00      00 empty entry
                  5 P 000000000 000000000 0000/000/00 0000/000/00      00 empty entry
                  6 P 000000000 000000000 0000/000/00 0000/000/00      00 empty entry
              1 004192902 sectors 2146765824 bytes
              3 113097537 sectors 57905938944 bytes
``` |
| Log Highlights: | IXImager Log file
hda: 156301488 sectors (80026 MB) w/8192KiB Cache, CHS=9729/255/63, UDMA(100)
SCSI device sda: 117304992 512-byte hdwr sectors (60060 MB)
SCSI device sda: 117304992 512-byte hdwr sectors (60060 MB)
SCSI device sdb: 781443888 512-byte hdwr sectors (400099 MB)
User selected ILook Default Image Format
Initializing...
Opened output file '/ILookImager/ILook.004/DA06USB001.asb'
Beginning Image operation for 60060155904 bytes
Beginning Image operation
Beginning Image operation
Opened output file '/ILookImager/ILook.004/DA06USB002.asb'
continuing at byte 28180283392
Image is being stored to /ILook.004/DA06USB002.asb
Opened output file '/ILookImager/ILook.004/DA06USB003.asb'
continuing at byte 56343855104
Image is being stored to /ILook.004/DA06USB003.asb
Image Complete
Image was completed successfully.

Read   : 60.06 GB (60060155904 bytes)
Written   : 1.382 GB (1381727236 bytes)
Total Processed : 60.06 GB (60060155904 bytes)
Image Speed   : 14.97 MB/sec
Elapsed Time   : 1h 6m 53s
Compression   : 97.70%
Bad Sectors   : 0
SHA-1 Value   : f7069edcbeac863c88deced82159f22da96be99b
                : for 60060155904 bytes
Clearing computer memory...

Source SHA1 Hash: F7069EDCBEAC863C88DECED82159F22DA96BE99B |
| Results: | |

Assertion & Expected Result	Actual Result
AM-01 Source acquired using interface AI.	as expected
AM-02 Source is type DS.	as expected
AM-03 Execution environment is XE.	as expected
AM-05 An image is created on file system type FS.	as expected
AM-06 All visible sectors acquired.	as expected
AM-08 All sectors accurately acquired.	as expected
AO-01 Image file is complete and accurate.	as expected
AO-05 Multifile image created.	as expected
AO-22 Tool calculates hashes by block.	option not available
AO-23 Logged information is correct.	as expected
AO-24 Source is unchanged by acquisition.	as expected

Analysis:	Expected results achieved

5.2.27 DA-07-CF

Test Case DA-07-CF ILook IXimager Version 2.0, Feb 01 2006	
Description:	DA-07 Acquire a digital source of type DS to an image file.
Assertions:	AM-01 The tool uses access interface SRC-AI to access the digital source. AM-02 The tool acquires digital source DS. AM-03 The tool executes in execution environment XE. AM-05 If image file creation is specified, the tool creates an image file on file system type FS. AM-06 All visible sectors are acquired from the digital source. AM-08 All sectors acquired from the digital source are acquired accurately. AO-01 If the tool creates an image file, the data represented by the image
```

	Test Case DA-07-CF ILook IXimager Version 2.0, Feb 01 2006
	file is the same as the data acquired by the tool. AO-05 If the tool creates a multi-file image of a requested size then all the individual files shall be no larger than the requested size. AO-22 If requested, the tool calculates block hashes for a specified block size during an acquisition for each block acquired from the digital source. AO-23 If the tool logs any log significant information, the information is accurately recorded in the log file. AO-24 If the tool executes in a forensically safe execution environment, the digital source is unchanged by the acquisition process.
Tester Name:	brl
Test Host:	JohnSteed
Test Date:	Wed May 10 16:19:56 2006
Drives:	src(C1-CF) dst (4D-FU2) other (none)
Source Setup:	src hash: < 5B8235178DF99FA307430C088F81746606638A0B > 503808 total sectors (257949696 bytes) Removable media, no partition table.
Log Highlights:	IXImager Log file hda: 156301488 sectors (80026 MB) w/8192KiB Cache, CHS=9729/255/63, UDMA(100) SCSI device sda: 503808 512-byte hdwr sectors (258 MB) SCSI device sdb: 781443888 512-byte hdwr sectors (400099 MB) User selected ILook Default Image Format Initializing... Opened output file '/ILookImager/ILook.026/DA07CF001.asb' Beginning Image operation for 257949696 bytes Beginning Image operation Beginning Image operation Image Complete Image was completed successfully. Read : 257.9 MB (257949696 bytes) Written : 6.038 MB (6037753 bytes) Total Processed: 257.9 MB (257949696 bytes) Image Speed : 4.961 MB/sec Elapsed Time : 0h 0m 52s Compression : 97.66% Bad Sectors : 0 SHA-1 Value : 5b8235178df99fa307430c088f81746606638a0b : for 257949696 bytes Clearing computer memory... Source SHA1 Hash: 5B8235178DF99FA307430C088F81746606638A0B
Results:	

Assertion & Expected Result	Actual Result
AM-01 Source acquired using interface AI.	as expected
AM-02 Source is type DS.	as expected
AM-03 Execution environment is XE.	as expected
AM-05 An image is created on file system type FS.	as expected
AM-06 All visible sectors acquired.	as expected
AM-08 All sectors accurately acquired.	as expected
AO-01 Image file is complete and accurate.	as expected
AO-05 Multifile image created.	as expected
AO-22 Tool calculates hashes by block.	option not available
AO-23 Logged information is correct.	as expected
AO-24 Source is unchanged by acquisition.	as expected

Analysis:	Expected results achieved

5.2.28 DA-07-F12

	Test Case DA-07-F12 ILook IXimager Version 2.0, Feb 01 2006
Description:	DA-07 Acquire a digital source of type DS to an image file.
Assertions:	AM-01 The tool uses access interface SRC-AI to access the digital source. AM-02 The tool acquires digital source DS. AM-03 The tool executes in execution environment XE.

Test Case DA-07-F12 ILook IXimager Version 2.0, Feb 01 2006

	AM-05 If image file creation is specified, the tool creates an image file on file system type FS. AM-06 All visible sectors are acquired from the digital source. AM-08 All sectors acquired from the digital source are acquired accurately. AO-01 If the tool creates an image file, the data represented by the image file is the same as the data acquired by the tool. AO-05 If the tool creates a multi-file image of a requested size then all the individual files shall be no larger than the requested size. AO-22 If requested, the tool calculates block hashes for a specified block size during an acquisition for each block acquired from the digital source. AO-23 If the tool logs any log significant information, the information is accurately recorded in the log file. AO-24 If the tool executes in a forensically safe execution environment, the digital source is unchanged by the acquisition process.
Tester Name:	brl
Test Host:	Joe
Test Date:	Fri Apr 21 13:53:43 2006
Drives:	src(43) dst (4D-FU2) other (none)
Source Setup:	src hash: < 888E2E7F7AD237DC7A732281DD93F325065E5871 > 78125000 total sectors (40000000000 bytes) Model (0BB-75JHC0) serial # (WD-WMAMC46588) N Start LBA Length Start C/H/S End C/H/S boot Partition type 1 P 000000063 020980827 0000/001/01 1023/254/63 0C Fat32X 2 X 020980890 057143205 1023/000/01 1023/254/63 0F extended 3 S 000000063 000032067 1023/001/01 1023/254/63 01 Fat12 4 x 000032130 002104515 1023/000/01 1023/254/63 05 extended 5 S 000000063 002104452 1023/001/01 1023/254/63 06 Fat16 6 x 002136645 004192965 1023/000/01 1023/254/63 05 extended 7 S 000000063 004192902 1023/001/01 1023/254/63 16 other 8 x 006329610 008401995 1023/000/01 1023/254/63 05 extended 9 S 000000063 008401932 1023/001/01 1023/254/63 0B Fat32 10 x 014731605 010490445 1023/000/01 1023/254/63 05 extended 11 S 000000063 010490382 1023/001/01 1023/254/63 83 Linux 12 x 025222050 004209030 1023/000/01 1023/254/63 05 extended 13 S 000000063 004208967 1023/001/01 1023/254/63 82 Linux swap 14 x 029431080 027712125 1023/000/01 1023/254/63 05 extended 15 S 000000063 027712062 1023/001/01 1023/254/63 07 NTFS 16 S 000000000 000000000 0000/000/00 0000/000/00 00 empty entry 17 P 000000000 000000000 0000/000/00 0000/000/00 00 empty entry 18 P 000000000 000000000 0000/000/00 0000/000/00 00 empty entry 1 020980827 sectors 10742183424 bytes 3 000032067 sectors 16418304 bytes 5 002104452 sectors 1077479424 bytes 7 004192902 sectors 2146765824 bytes 9 008401932 sectors 4301789184 bytes 11 010490382 sectors 5371075584 bytes 13 004208967 sectors 2154991104 bytes 15 027712062 sectors 14188575744 bytes
Log Highlights:	IXImager Log file SCSI device sdb: 78125000 512-byte hdwr sectors (40000 MB) SCSI device sdc: 781443888 512-byte hdwr sectors (400099 MB) User selected ILook Default Image Format Initializing... Opened output file '/ILookImager/ILook.012/DA07F12001.asb' Beginning Image operation for 16418304 bytes Beginning Image operation Beginning Image operation Image Complete Image was completed successfully. Read : 16.42 MB (16418304 bytes) Written : 593.0 kB (593021 bytes) Total Processed: 16.42 MB (16418304 bytes) Image Speed : 8.209 MB/sec Elapsed Time : 0h 0m 2s Compression : 96.39% Bad Sectors : 0 SHA-1 Value : 6853b517f50bf3ccaded3db5feae08c18c62fca0 : for 16418304 bytes Clearing computer memory...

Test Case DA-07-F12 ILook IXimager Version 2.0, Feb 01 2006		
	Source SHA1 Hash: 888E2E7F7AD237DC7A732281DD93F325065E5871	
Results:	Assertion & Expected Result	Actual Result
	AM-01 Source acquired using interface AI.	as expected
	AM-02 Source is type DS.	as expected
	AM-03 Execution environment is XE.	as expected
	AM-05 An image is created on file system type FS.	as expected
	AM-06 All visible sectors acquired.	as expected
	AM-08 All sectors accurately acquired.	as expected
	AO-01 Image file is complete and accurate.	as expected
	AO-05 Multifile image created.	as expected
	AO-22 Tool calculates hashes by block.	option not available
	AO-23 Logged information is correct.	as expected
	AO-24 Source is unchanged by acquisition.	as expected
Analysis:	Expected results achieved	

5.2.29 DA-07-F16

Test Case DA-07-F16 ILook IXimager Version 2.0, Feb 01 2006	
Description:	DA-07 Acquire a digital source of type DS to an image file.
Assertions:	AM-01 The tool uses access interface SRC-AI to access the digital source. AM-02 The tool acquires digital source DS. AM-03 The tool executes in execution environment XE. AM-05 If image file creation is specified, the tool creates an image file on file system type FS. AM-06 All visible sectors are acquired from the digital source. AM-08 All sectors acquired from the digital source are acquired accurately. AO-01 If the tool creates an image file, the data represented by the image file is the same as the data acquired by the tool. AO-05 If the tool creates a multi-file image of a requested size then all the individual files shall be no larger than the requested size. AO-22 If requested, the tool calculates block hashes for a specified block size during an acquisition for each block acquired from the digital source. AO-23 If the tool logs any log significant information, the information is accurately recorded in the log file. AO-24 If the tool executes in a forensically safe execution environment, the digital source is unchanged by the acquisition process.
Tester Name:	brl
Test Host:	Max
Test Date:	Fri Apr 21 14:01:44 2006
Drives:	src(44) dst (4D-FU2) other (none)
Source Setup:	src hash: < E196D36E7B322C0EF83923112AD1800581742B6E > 78165360 total sectors (40020664320 bytes) 65534/015/63 (max cyl/hd values) 65535/016/63 (number of cyl/hd) IDE disk: Model (WDC WD400JB-00FMA0) serial # (WD-WMAJC1011319) N Start LBA Length Start C/H/S End C/H/S boot Partition type 1 P 000000063 020980827 0000/001/01 1023/254/63 0C Fat32X 2 X 020980890 057175335 1023/000/01 1023/254/63 0F extended 3 S 000000063 000032067 1023/001/01 1023/254/63 01 Fat12 4 x 000032130 002104515 1023/000/01 1023/254/63 05 extended 5 S 000000063 002104452 1023/001/01 1023/254/63 06 Fat16 6 x 002136645 004192965 1023/000/01 1023/254/63 05 extended 7 S 000000063 004192902 1023/001/01 1023/254/63 16 other 8 x 006329610 008401995 1023/000/01 1023/254/63 05 extended 9 S 000000063 008401932 1023/001/01 1023/254/63 0B Fat32 10 x 014731605 010490445 1023/000/01 1023/254/63 05 extended 11 S 000000063 010490382 1023/001/01 1023/254/63 83 Linux 12 x 025222050 004209030 1023/000/01 1023/254/63 05 extended 13 S 000000063 004208967 1023/001/01 1023/254/63 82 Linux swap 14 x 029431080 027744255 1023/000/01 1023/254/63 05 extended 15 S 000000063 027744192 1023/001/01 1023/254/63 07 NTFS 16 S 000000000 000000000 0000/000/00 0000/000/00 00 empty entry 17 P 000000000 000000000 0000/000/00 0000/000/00 00 empty entry 18 P 000000000 000000000 0000/000/00 0000/000/00 00 empty entry

```
Test Case DA-07-F16 ILook IXimager Version 2.0, Feb 01 2006
                    1 020980827 sectors 10742183424 bytes
                    3 000032067 sectors    16418304 bytes
                    5 002104452 sectors  1077479424 bytes
                    7 004192902 sectors  2146765824 bytes
                    9 008401932 sectors  4301789184 bytes
                   11 010490382 sectors  5371075584 bytes
                   13 004208967 sectors  2154991104 bytes
                   15 027744192 sectors 14205026304 bytes
```

Log Highlights:	IXImager Log file SCSI device sdb: 78165360 512-byte hdwr sectors (40021 MB) SCSI device sdc: 781443888 512-byte hdwr sectors (400099 MB) User selected ILook Default Image Format Initializing... Opened output file '/ILookImager/ILook.013/DA07F16001.asb' Beginning Image operation for 1077479424 bytes Beginning Image operation Beginning Image operation Image Complete Image was completed successfully. Read : 1.077 GB (1077479424 bytes) Written : 24.93 MB (24932422 bytes) Total Processed: 1.077 GB (1077479424 bytes) Image Speed : 7.865 MB/sec Elapsed Time : 0h 2m 17s Compression : 97.69% Bad Sectors : 0 SHA-1 Value : f26795072562849a38bb46c94aa54b7d1ca65660 : for 1077479424 bytes Clearing computer memory... Source SHA1 Hash: E196D36E7B322C0EF83923112AD1800581742B6E
Results:	

Assertion & Expected Result	Actual Result
AM-01 Source acquired using interface AI.	as expected
AM-02 Source is type DS.	as expected
AM-03 Execution environment is XE.	as expected
AM-05 An image is created on file system type FS.	as expected
AM-06 All visible sectors acquired.	as expected
AM-08 All sectors accurately acquired.	as expected
AO-01 Image file is complete and accurate.	as expected
AO-05 Multifile image created.	as expected
AO-22 Tool calculates hashes by block.	option not available
AO-23 Logged information is correct.	as expected
AO-24 Source is unchanged by acquisition.	as expected

Analysis:	Expected results achieved

5.2.30 DA-07-F32

Test Case DA-07-F32 ILook IXimager Version 2.0, Feb 01 2006	
Description:	DA-07 Acquire a digital source of type DS to an image file.
Assertions:	AM-01 The tool uses access interface SRC-AI to access the digital source. AM-02 The tool acquires digital source DS. AM-03 The tool executes in execution environment XE. AM-05 If image file creation is specified, the tool creates an image file on file system type FS. AM-06 All visible sectors are acquired from the digital source. AM-08 All sectors acquired from the digital source are acquired accurately. AO-01 If the tool creates an image file, the data represented by the image file is the same as the data acquired by the tool. AO-05 If the tool creates a multi-file image of a requested size then all the individual files shall be no larger than the requested size. AO-22 If requested, the tool calculates block hashes for a specified block size during an acquisition for each block acquired from the digital source. AO-23 If the tool logs any log significant information, the information is

	Test Case DA-07-F32 ILook IXimager Version 2.0, Feb 01 2006
	accurately recorded in the log file. AO-24 If the tool executes in a forensically safe execution environment, the digital source is unchanged by the acquisition process.
Tester Name:	brl
Test Host:	Joe
Test Date:	Fri Apr 21 15:48:08 2006
Drives:	src(43) dst (4D-FU2) other (none)

Source Setup:	src hash: < 888E2E7F7AD237DC7A732281DD93F325065E5871 >
	78125000 total sectors (40000000000 bytes)
	Model (0BB-75JHC0) serial # (WD-WMAMC46588)
	  N Start LBA Length Start C/H/S End C/H/S boot Partition type
	  1 P 000000063 020980827 0000/001/01 1023/254/63 0C Fat32X
	  2 X 020980890 057143205 1023/000/01 1023/254/63 0F extended
	  3 S 000000063 000032067 1023/001/01 1023/254/63 01 Fat12
	  4 x 000032130 002104515 1023/000/01 1023/254/63 05 extended
	  5 S 000000063 002104452 1023/001/01 1023/254/63 06 Fat16
	  6 x 002136645 004192965 1023/000/01 1023/254/63 05 extended
	  7 S 000000063 004192902 1023/001/01 1023/254/63 16 other
	  8 x 006329610 008401995 1023/000/01 1023/254/63 05 extended
	  9 S 000000063 008401932 1023/001/01 1023/254/63 0B Fat32
	 10 x 014731605 010490445 1023/000/01 1023/254/63 05 extended
	 11 S 000000063 010490382 1023/001/01 1023/254/63 83 Linux
	 12 x 025222050 004209030 1023/000/01 1023/254/63 05 extended
	 13 S 000000063 004208967 1023/001/01 1023/254/63 82 Linux swap
	 14 x 029431080 027712125 1023/000/01 1023/254/63 05 extended
	 15 S 000000063 027712062 1023/001/01 1023/254/63 07 NTFS
	 16 S 000000000 000000000 0000/000/00 0000/000/00 00 empty entry
	 17 P 000000000 000000000 0000/000/00 0000/000/00 00 empty entry
	 18 P 000000000 000000000 0000/000/00 0000/000/00 00 empty entry
	  1 020980827 sectors 10742183424 bytes
	  3 000032067 sectors 16418304 bytes
	  5 002104452 sectors 1077479424 bytes
	  7 004192902 sectors 2146765824 bytes
	  9 008401932 sectors 4301789184 bytes
	 11 010490382 sectors 5371075584 bytes
	 13 004208967 sectors 2154991104 bytes
	 15 027712062 sectors 14188575744 bytes

Log Highlights:	IXImager Log file SCSI device sdb: 78125000 512-byte hdwr sectors (40000 MB) SCSI device sdc: 781443888 512-byte hdwr sectors (400099 MB) User selected ILook Default Image Format Initializing... Opened output file '/ILookImager/ILook.014/DA07F32001.asb' Beginning Image operation for 4301789184 bytes Beginning Image operation Beginning Image operation Image Complete Image was completed successfully. Read : 4.302 GB (4301789184 bytes) Written : 98.98 MB (98984710 bytes) Total Processed: 4.302 GB (4301789184 bytes) Image Speed : 7.922 MB/sec Elapsed Time : 0h 9m 3s Compression : 97.70% Bad Sectors : 0 SHA-1 Value : 72462489bcf79a98b59b6a8cd938feb46fa2a781 : for 4301789184 bytes Clearing computer memory... Source SHA1 Hash: 888E2E7F7AD237DC7A732281DD93F325065E5871
Results:	

Assertion & Expected Result	Actual Result
AM-01 Source acquired using interface AI.	as expected
AM-02 Source is type DS.	as expected
AM-03 Execution environment is XE.	as expected
AM-05 An image is created on file system type FS.	as expected
AM-06 All visible sectors acquired.	as expected

	Test Case DA-07-F32 ILook IXimager Version 2.0, Feb 01 2006	
	AM-08 All sectors accurately acquired.	as expected
	AO-01 Image file is complete and accurate.	as expected
	AO-05 Multifile image created.	as expected
	AO-22 Tool calculates hashes by block.	option not available
	AO-23 Logged information is correct.	as expected
	AO-24 Source is unchanged by acquisition.	as expected
Analysis:	Expected results achieved	

5.2.31   DA-07-F32X

Test Case DA-07-F32X ILook IXimager Version 2.0, Feb 01 2006	
Description:	DA-07 Acquire a digital source of type DS to an image file.
Assertions:	AM-01 The tool uses access interface SRC-AI to access the digital source. AM-02 The tool acquires digital source DS. AM-03 The tool executes in execution environment XE. AM-05 If image file creation is specified, the tool creates an image file on file system type FS. AM-06 All visible sectors are acquired from the digital source. AM-08 All sectors acquired from the digital source are acquired accurately. AO-01 If the tool creates an image file, the data represented by the image file is the same as the data acquired by the tool. AO-05 If the tool creates a multi-file image of a requested size then all the individual files shall be no larger than the requested size. AO-22 If requested, the tool calculates block hashes for a specified block size during an acquisition for each block acquired from the digital source. AO-23 If the tool logs any log significant information, the information is accurately recorded in the log file. AO-24 If the tool executes in a forensically safe execution environment, the digital source is unchanged by the acquisition process.
Tester Name:	brl
Test Host:	Max
Test Date:	Fri Apr 21 15:51:32 2006
Drives:	src(44) dst (4D-FU2) other (none)

Source Setup:	src hash: < E196D36E7B322C0EF83923112AD1800581742B6E >
	78165360 total sectors (40020664320 bytes)
	65534/015/63 (max cyl/hd values)
	65535/016/63 (number of cyl/hd)
	IDE disk: Model (WDC WD400JB-00FMA0) serial # (WD-WMAJC1011319)
	  N Start LBA Length Start C/H/S End C/H/S boot Partition type
	  1 P 000000063 020980827 0000/001/01 1023/254/63 0C Fat32X
	  2 X 020980890 057175335 1023/000/01 1023/254/63 0F extended
	  3 S 000000063 000032067 1023/001/01 1023/254/63 01 Fat12
	  4 x 000032130 002104515 1023/000/01 1023/254/63 05 extended
	  5 S 000000063 002104452 1023/001/01 1023/254/63 06 Fat16
	  6 x 002136645 004192965 1023/000/01 1023/254/63 05 extended
	  7 S 000000063 004192902 1023/001/01 1023/254/63 16 other
	  8 x 006329610 008401995 1023/000/01 1023/254/63 05 extended
	  9 S 000000063 008401932 1023/001/01 1023/254/63 0B Fat32
	10 x 014731605 010490445 1023/000/01 1023/254/63 05 extended
	11 S 000000063 010490382 1023/001/01 1023/254/63 83 Linux
	12 x 025222050 004209030 1023/000/01 1023/254/63 05 extended
	13 S 000000063 004208967 1023/001/01 1023/254/63 82 Linux swap
	14 x 029431080 027744255 1023/000/01 1023/254/63 05 extended
	15 S 000000063 027744192 1023/001/01 1023/254/63 07 NTFS
	16 S 000000000 000000000 0000/000/00 0000/000/00 00 empty entry
	17 P 000000000 000000000 0000/000/00 0000/000/00 00 empty entry
	18 P 000000000 000000000 0000/000/00 0000/000/00 00 empty entry
	 1 020980827 sectors 10742183424 bytes
	 3 000032067 sectors 16418304 bytes
	 5 002104452 sectors 1077479424 bytes
	 7 004192902 sectors 2146765824 bytes
	 9 008401932 sectors 4301789184 bytes
	11 010490382 sectors 5371075584 bytes
	13 004208967 sectors 2154991104 bytes
	15 027744192 sectors 14205026304 bytes

Log Highlights:	IXImager Log file SCSI device sdb: 78165360 512-byte hdwr sectors (40021 MB) SCSI device sdc: 781443888 512-byte hdwr sectors (400099 MB) User selected ILook Default Image Format Initializing... Opened output file '/ILookImager/ILook.015/DA07F32X001.asb' Beginning Image operation for 10742183424 bytes Beginning Image operation Beginning Image operation Image Complete Image was completed successfully. Read : 10.74 GB (10742183424 bytes) Written : 247.0 MB (247043065 bytes) Total Processed: 10.74 GB (10742183424 bytes) Image Speed : 7.934 MB/sec Elapsed Time : 0h 22m 34s Compression : 97.70% Bad Sectors : 0 SHA-1 Value : d190a47b60a17fe6912ca26be237e923ad592fae : for 10742183424 bytes Clearing computer memory... Source SHA1 Hash: E196D36E7B322C0EF83923112AD1800581742B6E
Results:	

Assertion & Expected Result	Actual Result
AM-01 Source acquired using interface AI.	as expected
AM-02 Source is type DS.	as expected
AM-03 Execution environment is XE.	as expected
AM-05 An image is created on file system type FS.	as expected
AM-06 All visible sectors acquired.	as expected
AM-08 All sectors accurately acquired.	as expected
AO-01 Image file is complete and accurate.	as expected
AO-05 Multifile image created.	as expected
AO-22 Tool calculates hashes by block.	option not available
AO-23 Logged information is correct.	as expected
AO-24 Source is unchanged by acquisition.	as expected

Analysis:	Expected results achieved

5.2.32 DA-07-FLOPPY

Test Case DA-07-FLOPPY ILook IXimager Version 2.0, Feb 01 2006	
Description:	DA-07 Acquire a digital source of type DS to an image file.
Assertions:	AM-01 The tool uses access interface SRC-AI to access the digital source. AM-02 The tool acquires digital source DS. AM-03 The tool executes in execution environment XE. AM-05 If image file creation is specified, the tool creates an image file on file system type FS. AM-06 All visible sectors are acquired from the digital source. AM-08 All sectors acquired from the digital source are acquired accurately. AO-01 If the tool creates an image file, the data represented by the image file is the same as the data acquired by the tool. AO-05 If the tool creates a multi-file image of a requested size then all the individual files shall be no larger than the requested size. AO-22 If requested, the tool calculates block hashes for a specified block size during an acquisition for each block acquired from the digital source. AO-23 If the tool logs any log significant information, the information is accurately recorded in the log file. AO-24 If the tool executes in a forensically safe execution environment, the digital source is unchanged by the acquisition process.
Tester Name:	brl
Test Host:	JohnSteed
Test Date:	Wed May 3 09:40:50 2006
Drives:	src(floppy) dst (4D-FU2) other (none)
Source	src hash: < E2863334AC7EAABC7C8A0D62EB0D3B3AF29F2C40 >

```
Test Case DA-07-FLOPPY ILook IXimager Version 2.0, Feb 01 2006
```

Setup:	Floppy disk
Log Highlights:	IXImager Log file hda: 156301488 sectors (80026 MB) w/8192KiB Cache, CHS=9729/255/63, UDMA(100) SCSI device sda: 781443888 512-byte hdwr sectors (400099 MB) User selected ILook Default Image Format Initializing... Opened output file '/ILookImager/ILook.021/DA07FLOPPY001.asb' Beginning Image operation for 1474560 bytes Beginning Image operation Beginning Image operation Image Complete Image was completed successfully. Read : 1.475 MB (1474560 bytes) Written : 141.8 kB (141815 bytes) Total Processed: 1.475 MB (1474560 bytes) Image Speed : 27.82 kB/sec Elapsed Time : 0h 0m 53s Compression : 90.38% Bad Sectors : 0 SHA-1 Value : e2863334ac7eaabc7c8a0d62eb0d3b3af29f2c40 : for 1474560 bytes Clearing computer memory... Source SHA1 Hash: E2863334AC7EAABC7C8A0D62EB0D3B3AF29F2C40
Results:	

Assertion & Expected Result	Actual Result
AM-01 Source acquired using interface AI.	as expected
AM-02 Source is type DS.	as expected
AM-03 Execution environment is XE.	as expected
AM-05 An image is created on file system type FS.	as expected
AM-06 All visible sectors acquired.	as expected
AM-08 All sectors accurately acquired.	as expected
AO-01 Image file is complete and accurate.	as expected
AO-05 Multifile image created.	as expected
AO-22 Tool calculates hashes by block.	option not available
AO-23 Logged information is correct.	as expected
AO-24 Source is unchanged by acquisition.	as expected

Analysis:	Expected results achieved

5.2.33 DA-07-HIDDEN

```
Test Case DA-07-HIDDEN ILook IXimager Version 2.0, Feb 01 2006
```

Description:	DA-07 Acquire a digital source of type DS to an image file.
Assertions:	AM-01 The tool uses access interface SRC-AI to access the digital source. AM-02 The tool acquires digital source DS. AM-03 The tool executes in execution environment XE. AM-05 If image file creation is specified, the tool creates an image file on file system type FS. AM-06 All visible sectors are acquired from the digital source. AM-08 All sectors acquired from the digital source are acquired accurately. AO-01 If the tool creates an image file, the data represented by the image file is the same as the data acquired by the tool. AO-05 If the tool creates a multi-file image of a requested size then all the individual files shall be no larger than the requested size. AO-22 If requested, the tool calculates block hashes for a specified block size during an acquisition for each block acquired from the digital source. AO-23 If the tool logs any log significant information, the information is accurately recorded in the log file. AO-24 If the tool executes in a forensically safe execution environment, the digital source is unchanged by the acquisition process.
Tester Name:	brl
Test Host:	Max
Test Date:	Mon Apr 24 10:52:28 2006

Test Case DA-07-HIDDEN ILook IXimager Version 2.0, Feb 01 2006	
Drives:	src(44) dst (4D-FU2) other (none)
Source Setup:	src hash: < E196D36E7B322C0EF83923112AD1800581742B6E > 78165360 total sectors (40020664320 bytes) 65534/015/63 (max cyl/hd values) 65535/016/63 (number of cyl/hd) IDE disk: Model (WDC WD400JB-00FMA0) serial # (WD-WMAJC1011319) N Start LBA Length Start C/H/S End C/H/S boot Partition type 1 P 000000063 020980827 0000/001/01 1023/254/63 0C Fat32X 2 X 020980890 057175335 1023/000/01 1023/254/63 0F extended 3 S 000000063 000032067 1023/001/01 1023/254/63 01 Fat12 4 x 000032130 002104515 1023/000/01 1023/254/63 05 extended 5 S 000000063 002104452 1023/001/01 1023/254/63 06 Fat16 6 x 002136645 004192965 1023/000/01 1023/254/63 05 extended 7 S 000000063 004192902 1023/001/01 1023/254/63 16 other 8 x 006329610 008401995 1023/000/01 1023/254/63 05 extended 9 S 000000063 008401932 1023/001/01 1023/254/63 0B Fat32 10 x 014731605 010490445 1023/000/01 1023/254/63 05 extended 11 S 000000063 010490382 1023/001/01 1023/254/63 83 Linux 12 x 025222050 004209030 1023/000/01 1023/254/63 05 extended 13 S 000000063 004208967 1023/001/01 1023/254/63 82 Linux swap 14 x 029431080 027744255 1023/000/01 1023/254/63 05 extended 15 S 000000063 027744192 1023/001/01 1023/254/63 07 NTFS 16 S 000000000 000000000 0000/000/00 0000/000/00 00 empty entry 17 P 000000000 000000000 0000/000/00 0000/000/00 00 empty entry 18 P 000000000 000000000 0000/000/00 0000/000/00 00 empty entry 1 020980827 sectors 10742183424 bytes 3 000032067 sectors 16418304 bytes 5 002104452 sectors 1077479424 bytes 7 004192902 sectors 2146765824 bytes 9 008401932 sectors 4301789184 bytes 11 010490382 sectors 5371075584 bytes 13 004208967 sectors 2154991104 bytes 15 027744192 sectors 14205026304 bytes
Log Highlights:	IXImager Log file SCSI device sdb: 78165360 512-byte hdwr sectors (40021 MB) SCSI device sdc: 781443888 512-byte hdwr sectors (400099 MB) User selected ILook Default Image Format Initializing... Opened output file '/ILookImager/ILook.020/DA07HIDDEN001.asb' Beginning Image operation for 2146765824 bytes Beginning Image operation Beginning Image operation Image Complete Image was completed successfully. Read : 2.147 GB (2146765824 bytes) Written : 49.54 MB (49537184 bytes) Total Processed: 2.147 GB (2146765824 bytes) Image Speed : 7.922 MB/sec Elapsed Time : 0h 4m 31s Compression : 97.69% Bad Sectors : 0 SHA-1 Value : 0893c80edc0e9074fd139b67fb6de3ce9390c550 : for 2146765824 bytes Clearing computer memory... Source SHA1 Hash: E196D36E7B322C0EF83923112AD1800581742B6E

Results:		
	Assertion & Expected Result	Actual Result
	AM-01 Source acquired using interface AI.	as expected
	AM-02 Source is type DS.	as expected
	AM-03 Execution environment is XE.	as expected
	AM-05 An image is created on file system type FS.	as expected
	AM-06 All visible sectors acquired.	as expected
	AM-08 All sectors accurately acquired.	as expected
	AO-01 Image file is complete and accurate.	as expected
	AO-05 Multifile image created.	as expected
	AO-22 Tool calculates hashes by block.	option not available
	AO-23 Logged information is correct.	as expected

Test Case DA-07-HIDDEN ILook IXimager Version 2.0, Feb 01 2006		
	AO-24 Source is unchanged by acquisition.	as expected
Analysis:	Expected results achieved	

5.2.34 DA-07-NT

Test Case DA-07-NT ILook IXimager Version 2.0, Feb 01 2006	
Description:	DA-07 Acquire a digital source of type DS to an image file.
Assertions:	AM-01 The tool uses access interface SRC-AI to access the digital source. AM-02 The tool acquires digital source DS. AM-03 The tool executes in execution environment XE. AM-05 If image file creation is specified, the tool creates an image file on file system type FS. AM-06 All visible sectors are acquired from the digital source. AM-08 All sectors acquired from the digital source are acquired accurately. AO-01 If the tool creates an image file, the data represented by the image file is the same as the data acquired by the tool. AO-05 If the tool creates a multi-file image of a requested size then all the individual files shall be no larger than the requested size. AO-22 If requested, the tool calculates block hashes for a specified block size during an acquisition for each block acquired from the digital source. AO-23 If the tool logs any log significant information, the information is accurately recorded in the log file. AO-24 If the tool executes in a forensically safe execution environment, the digital source is unchanged by the acquisition process.
Tester Name:	brl
Test Host:	Joe
Test Date:	Mon Apr 24 10:38:49 2006
Drives:	src(43) dst (4D-FU2) other (none)

Source Setup:	src hash: < 888E2E7F7AD237DC7A732281DD93F325065E5871 >
	78125000 total sectors (40000000000 bytes)
	Model (0BB-75JHC0) serial # (WD-WMAMC46588)
	  N Start LBA Length Start C/H/S End C/H/S boot Partition type
	  1 P 000000063 020980827 0000/001/01 1023/254/63 0C Fat32X
	  2 X 020980890 057143205 1023/000/01 1023/254/63 0F extended
	  3 S 000000063 000032067 1023/001/01 1023/254/63 01 Fat12
	  4 x 000032130 002104515 1023/000/01 1023/254/63 05 extended
	  5 S 000000063 002104452 1023/001/01 1023/254/63 06 Fat16
	  6 x 002136645 004192965 1023/000/01 1023/254/63 05 extended
	  7 S 000000063 004192902 1023/001/01 1023/254/63 16 other
	  8 x 006329610 008401995 1023/000/01 1023/254/63 05 extended
	  9 S 000000063 008401932 1023/001/01 1023/254/63 0B Fat32
	 10 x 014731605 010490445 1023/000/01 1023/254/63 05 extended
	 11 S 000000063 010490382 1023/001/01 1023/254/63 83 Linux
	 12 x 025222050 004209030 1023/000/01 1023/254/63 05 extended
	 13 S 000000063 004208967 1023/001/01 1023/254/63 82 Linux swap
	 14 x 029431080 027712125 1023/000/01 1023/254/63 05 extended
	 15 S 000000063 027712062 1023/001/01 1023/254/63 07 NTFS
	 16 S 000000000 000000000 0000/000/00 0000/000/00 00 empty entry
	 17 P 000000000 000000000 0000/000/00 0000/000/00 00 empty entry
	 18 P 000000000 000000000 0000/000/00 0000/000/00 00 empty entry
	 1 020980827 sectors 10742183424 bytes
	 3 000032067 sectors 16418304 bytes
	 5 002104452 sectors 1077479424 bytes
	 7 004192902 sectors 2146765824 bytes
	 9 008401932 sectors 4301789184 bytes
	11 010490382 sectors 5371075584 bytes
	13 004208967 sectors 2154991104 bytes
	15 027712062 sectors 14188575744 bytes

Log Highlights:	IXImager Log file SCSI device sdb: 78125000 512-byte hdwr sectors (40000 MB) SCSI device sdc: 781443888 512-byte hdwr sectors (400099 MB) User selected ILook Default Image Format Initializing... Opened output file '/ILookImager/ILook.019/DA07NT001.asb' Beginning Image operation for 14188575744 bytes

```
Test Case DA-07-NT ILook IXimager Version 2.0, Feb 01 2006
```
	Beginning Image operation Beginning Image operation Image Complete Image was completed successfully. Read : 14.19 GB (14188575744 bytes) Written : 324.5 MB (324528081 bytes) Total Processed: 14.19 GB (14188575744 bytes) Image Speed : 8.293 MB/sec Elapsed Time : 0h 28m 31s Compression : 97.71% Bad Sectors : 0 SHA-1 Value : 73eb2d27564b060db796efb78694a10e6b43d23f : for 14188575744 bytes Clearing computer memory... Source SHA1 Hash: 888E2E7F7AD237DC7A732281DD93F325065E5871
Results:	

Assertion & Expected Result	Actual Result
AM-01 Source acquired using interface AI.	as expected
AM-02 Source is type DS.	as expected
AM-03 Execution environment is XE.	as expected
AM-05 An image is created on file system type FS.	as expected
AM-06 All visible sectors acquired.	as expected
AM-08 All sectors accurately acquired.	as expected
AO-01 Image file is complete and accurate.	as expected
AO-05 Multifile image created.	as expected
AO-22 Tool calculates hashes by block.	option not available
AO-23 Logged information is correct.	as expected
AO-24 Source is unchanged by acquisition.	as expected

Analysis:	Expected results achieved

5.2.35   DA-07-R1

```
Test Case DA-07-R1 ILook IXimager Version 2.0, Feb 01 2006
```
Description:	DA-07 Acquire a digital source of type DS to an image file.
Assertions:	AM-01 The tool uses access interface SRC-AI to access the digital source. AM-02 The tool acquires digital source DS. AM-03 The tool executes in execution environment XE. AM-05 If image file creation is specified, the tool creates an image file on file system type FS. AM-06 All visible sectors are acquired from the digital source. AM-08 All sectors acquired from the digital source are acquired accurately. AO-01 If the tool creates an image file, the data represented by the image file is the same as the data acquired by the tool. AO-05 If the tool creates a multi-file image of a requested size then all the individual files shall be no larger than the requested size. AO-22 If requested, the tool calculates block hashes for a specified block size during an acquisition for each block acquired from the digital source. AO-23 If the tool logs any log significant information, the information is accurately recorded in the log file. AO-24 If the tool executes in a forensically safe execution environment, the digital source is unchanged by the acquisition process.
Tester Name:	Brl
Test Host:	SamSpade
Test Date:	Tue Jun 27 13:33:33 2006
Drives:	src(A1) dst (2A-FU2) other (none)

Source Setup:	src hash: < 229F00E5E9232A47E69E30ED4DCD57F0DFFEA1F7 >
	4192256 total sectors (2146435072 bytes)
	18446744073709551615/063/32 (max cyl/hd values)
	Model (Logical Disk 2) serial # ()
	  N Start LBA Length Start C/H/S End C/H/S boot Partition type
	  1 P 000000063 004160772 0000/001/01 0258/254/63 Boot 07 NTFS
	  2 P 000000000 000000000 0000/000/00 0000/000/00 00 empty entry
	  3 P 000000000 000000000 0000/000/00 0000/000/00 00 empty entry
	  4 P 000000000 000000000 0000/000/00 0000/000/00 00 empty entry

Test Case DA-07-R1 ILook IXimager Version 2.0, Feb 01 2006	
	1 004160772 sectors 2130315264 bytes A1 is a raid 1 consisting of drives 48 and 49.
Log Highlights:	IXImager Log file SCSI device sda: 488397168 512-byte hdwr sectors (250059 MB) SCSI device sdb: 4192256 512-byte hdwr sectors (2146 MB) User selected ILook Default Image Format Initializing... Opened output file '/ILookImager/ILook.004/DA07R1001.asb' Beginning Image operation for 2146435072 bytes Beginning Image operation Beginning Image operation Opened output file '/ILookImager/ILook.004/DA07R1002.asb' continuing at byte 1488781312 Image is being stored to /ILook.004/DA07R1002.asb Image Complete Image was completed successfully. Read : 2.146 GB (2146435072 bytes) Written : 749.6 MB (749551753 bytes) Total Processed: 2.146 GB (2146435072 bytes) Image Speed : 13.76 MB/sec Elapsed Time : 0h 2m 36s Compression : 65.08% Bad Sectors : 0 SHA-1 Value : 229f00e5e9232a47e69e30ed4dcd57f0dffea1f7 : for 2146435072 bytes Clearing computer memory... Source SHA1 Hash: 229F00E5E9232A47E69E30ED4DCD57F0DFFEA1F7
Results:	

Assertion & Expected Result	Actual Result
AM-01 Source acquired using interface AI.	as expected
AM-02 Source is type DS.	as expected
AM-03 Execution environment is XE.	as expected
AM-05 An image is created on file system type FS.	as expected
AM-06 All visible sectors acquired.	as expected
AM-08 All sectors accurately acquired.	as expected
AO-01 Image file is complete and accurate.	as expected
AO-05 Multifile image created.	as expected
AO-22 Tool calculates hashes by block.	option not available
AO-23 Logged information is correct.	as expected
AO-24 Source is unchanged by acquisition.	as expected

Analysis:	Expected results achieved

5.2.36   DA-07-R5

Test Case DA-07-R5 ILook IXimager Version 2.0, Feb 01 2006	
Description:	DA-07 Acquire a digital source of type DS to an image file.
Assertions:	AM-01 The tool uses access interface SRC-AI to access the digital source. AM-02 The tool acquires digital source DS. AM-03 The tool executes in execution environment XE. AM-05 If image file creation is specified, the tool creates an image file on file system type FS. AM-06 All visible sectors are acquired from the digital source. AM-08 All sectors acquired from the digital source are acquired accurately. AO-01 If the tool creates an image file, the data represented by the image file is the same as the data acquired by the tool. AO-05 If the tool creates a multi-file image of a requested size then all the individual files shall be no larger than the requested size. AO-22 If requested, the tool calculates block hashes for a specified block size during an acquisition for each block acquired from the digital source. AO-23 If the tool logs any log significant information, the information is accurately recorded in the log file. AO-24 If the tool executes in a forensically safe execution environment,

	Test Case DA-07-R5 ILook IXimager Version 2.0, Feb 01 2006
	the digital source is unchanged by the acquisition process.
Tester Name:	Brl
Test Host:	SamSpade
Test Date:	Tue Jun 27 09:46:00 2006
Drives:	src(A5) dst (2A-FU2) other (none)

Source Setup:	src hash: < EEF618B63B5A55893CFB685E20344D9030BBA94B >
	 12576768 total sectors (6439305216 bytes)
	 18446744073709551615/063/32 (max cyl/hd values)
	 Model (Logical Disk 0) serial # ()
	  N Start LBA Length Start C/H/S End C/H/S boot Partition type
	  1 P 000000063 012546702 0000/001/01 0780/254/63 Boot 07 NTFS
	  2 P 000000000 000000000 0000/000/00 0000/000/00 00 empty entry
	  3 P 000000000 000000000 0000/000/00 0000/000/00 00 empty entry
	  4 P 000000000 000000000 0000/000/00 0000/000/00 00 empty entry
	 1 012546702 sectors 6423911424 bytes
	
	 A5 is a Raid 5 consisting of drives 40, 45, 46 and 47

Log Highlights:	IXImager Log file SCSI device sda: 488397168 512-byte hdwr sectors (250059 MB) SCSI device sdb: 12576768 512-byte hdwr sectors (6439 MB) User selected ILook Default Image Format Initializing... Opened output file '/ILookImager/ILook.002/DA07R5001.asb' Beginning Image operation for 6439305216 bytes Beginning Image operation Beginning Image operation Opened output file '/ILookImager/ILook.002/DA07R5002.asb' continuing at byte 2048327680 Image is being stored to /ILook.002/DA07R5002.asb Image Complete Image was completed successfully. Read : 6.439 GB (6439305216 bytes) Written : 1.019 GB (1019166787 bytes) Total Processed : 6.439 GB (6439305216 bytes) Image Speed : 13.85 MB/sec Elapsed Time : 0h 7m 45s Compression : 84.17% Bad Sectors : 0 SHA-1 Value : eef618b63b5a55893cfb685e20344d9030bba94b : for 6439305216 bytes Clearing computer memory... Source SHA1 Hash: EEF618B63B5A55893CFB685E20344D9030BBA94B
Results:	

Assertion & Expected Result	Actual Result
AM-01 Source acquired using interface AI.	as expected
AM-02 Source is type DS.	as expected
AM-03 Execution environment is XE.	as expected
AM-05 An image is created on file system type FS.	as expected
AM-06 All visible sectors acquired.	as expected
AM-08 All sectors accurately acquired.	as expected
AO-01 Image file is complete and accurate.	as expected
AO-05 Multifile image created.	as expected
AO-22 Tool calculates hashes by block.	option not available
AO-23 Logged information is correct.	as expected
AO-24 Source is unchanged by acquisition.	as expected

Analysis:	Expected results achieved

5.2.37 DA-07-SWAP

Test Case DA-07-SWAP ILook IXimager Version 2.0, Feb 01 2006	
Description:	DA-07 Acquire a digital source of type DS to an image file.
Assertions:	AM-01 The tool uses access interface SRC-AI to access the digital source.

Test Case DA-07-SWAP ILook IXimager Version 2.0, Feb 01 2006

	AM-02 The tool acquires digital source DS. AM-03 The tool executes in execution environment XE. AM-05 If image file creation is specified, the tool creates an image file on file system type FS. AM-06 All visible sectors are acquired from the digital source. AM-08 All sectors acquired from the digital source are acquired accurately. AO-01 If the tool creates an image file, the data represented by the image file is the same as the data acquired by the tool. AO-05 If the tool creates a multi-file image of a requested size then all the individual files shall be no larger than the requested size. AO-22 If requested, the tool calculates block hashes for a specified block size during an acquisition for each block acquired from the digital source. AO-23 If the tool logs any log significant information, the information is accurately recorded in the log file. AO-24 If the tool executes in a forensically safe execution environment, the digital source is unchanged by the acquisition process.
Tester Name:	brl
Test Host:	Max
Test Date:	Mon Apr 24 10:16:22 2006
Drives:	src(44) dst (4D-FU2) other (none)
Source Setup:	src hash: < E196D36E7B322C0EF83923112AD1800581742B6E > 78165360 total sectors (40020664320 bytes) 65534/015/63 (max cyl/hd values) 65535/016/63 (number of cyl/hd) IDE disk: Model (WDC WD400JB-00FMA0) serial # (WD-WMAJC1011319) N Start LBA Length Start C/H/S End C/H/S boot Partition type 1 P 000000063 020980827 0000/001/01 1023/254/63 0C Fat32X 2 X 020980890 057175335 1023/000/01 1023/254/63 0F extended 3 S 000000063 000032067 1023/001/01 1023/254/63 01 Fat12 4 x 000032130 002104515 1023/000/01 1023/254/63 05 extended 5 S 000000063 002104452 1023/001/01 1023/254/63 06 Fat16 6 x 002136645 004192965 1023/000/01 1023/254/63 05 extended 7 S 000000063 004192902 1023/001/01 1023/254/63 16 other 8 x 006329610 008401995 1023/000/01 1023/254/63 05 extended 9 S 000000063 008401932 1023/001/01 1023/254/63 0B Fat32 10 x 014731605 010490445 1023/000/01 1023/254/63 05 extended 11 S 000000063 010490382 1023/001/01 1023/254/63 83 Linux 12 x 025222050 004209030 1023/000/01 1023/254/63 05 extended 13 S 000000063 004208967 1023/001/01 1023/254/63 82 Linux swap 14 x 029431080 027744255 1023/000/01 1023/254/63 05 extended 15 S 000000063 027744192 1023/001/01 1023/254/63 07 NTFS 16 S 000000000 000000000 0000/000/00 0000/000/00 00 empty entry 17 P 000000000 000000000 0000/000/00 0000/000/00 00 empty entry 18 P 000000000 000000000 0000/000/00 0000/000/00 00 empty entry 1 020980827 sectors 10742183424 bytes 3 000032067 sectors 16418304 bytes 5 002104452 sectors 1077479424 bytes 7 004192902 sectors 2146765824 bytes 9 008401932 sectors 4301789184 bytes 11 010490382 sectors 5371075584 bytes 13 004208967 sectors 2154991104 bytes 15 027744192 sectors 14205026304 bytes
Log Highlights:	IXImager Log file SCSI device sdb: 78165360 512-byte hdwr sectors (40021 MB) SCSI device sdc: 781443888 512-byte hdwr sectors (400099 MB) User selected ILook Default Image Format Initializing... Opened output file '/ILookImager/ILook.017/DA07SWAP001.asb' Beginning Image operation for 2154991104 bytes Beginning Image operation Beginning Image operation Image Complete Image was completed successfully. Read : 2.155 GB (2154991104 bytes) Written : 49.74 MB (49737188 bytes) Total Processed: 2.155 GB (2154991104 bytes) Image Speed : 7.923 MB/sec Elapsed Time : 0h 4m 32s Compression : 97.69%

Test Case DA-07-SWAP ILook IXimager Version 2.0, Feb 01 2006		
	Bad Sectors : 0 SHA-1 Value : 7bdd19b23e43ab62042fbf47fad69bb878f1ec6a : for 2154991104 bytes Clearing computer memory... Source SHA1 Hash: E196D36E7B322C0EF83923112AD1800581742B6E	
Results:	Assertion & Expected Result	Actual Result
	AM-01 Source acquired using interface AI.	as expected
	AM-02 Source is type DS.	as expected
	AM-03 Execution environment is XE.	as expected
	AM-05 An image is created on file system type FS.	as expected
	AM-06 All visible sectors acquired.	as expected
	AM-08 All sectors accurately acquired.	as expected
	AO-01 Image file is complete and accurate.	as expected
	AO-05 Multifile image created.	as expected
	AO-22 Tool calculates hashes by block.	option not available
	AO-23 Logged information is correct.	as expected
	AO-24 Source is unchanged by acquisition.	as expected
Analysis:	Expected results achieved	

5.2.38 DA-07-X2

Test Case DA-07-X2 ILook IXimager Version 2.0, Feb 01 2006	
Description:	DA-07 Acquire a digital source of type DS to an image file.
Assertions:	AM-01 The tool uses access interface SRC-AI to access the digital source. AM-02 The tool acquires digital source DS. AM-03 The tool executes in execution environment XE. AM-05 If image file creation is specified, the tool creates an image file on file system type FS. AM-06 All visible sectors are acquired from the digital source. AM-08 All sectors acquired from the digital source are acquired accurately. AO-01 If the tool creates an image file, the data represented by the image file is the same as the data acquired by the tool. AO-05 If the tool creates a multi-file image of a requested size then all the individual files shall be no larger than the requested size. AO-22 If requested, the tool calculates block hashes for a specified block size during an acquisition for each block acquired from the digital source. AO-23 If the tool logs any log significant information, the information is accurately recorded in the log file. AO-24 If the tool executes in a forensically safe execution environment, the digital source is unchanged by the acquisition process.
Tester Name:	brl
Test Host:	Joe
Test Date:	Fri Apr 21 16:53:30 2006
Drives:	src(43) dst (4D-FU2) other (none)
Source Setup:	src hash: < 888E2E7F7AD237DC7A732281DD93F325065E5871 > 78125000 total sectors (40000000000 bytes) Model (0BB-75JHC0) serial # (WD-WMAMC46588) N Start LBA Length Start C/H/S End C/H/S boot Partition type 1 P 000000063 020980827 0000/001/01 1023/254/63 0C Fat32X 2 X 020980890 057143205 1023/000/01 1023/254/63 0F extended 3 S 000000063 000032067 1023/001/01 1023/254/63 01 Fat12 4 x 000032130 002104515 1023/000/01 1023/254/63 05 extended 5 S 000000063 002104452 1023/001/01 1023/254/63 06 Fat16 6 x 002136645 004192965 1023/000/01 1023/254/63 05 extended 7 S 000000063 004192902 1023/001/01 1023/254/63 16 other 8 x 006329610 008401995 1023/000/01 1023/254/63 05 extended 9 S 000000063 008401932 1023/001/01 1023/254/63 0B Fat32 10 x 014731605 010490445 1023/000/01 1023/254/63 05 extended 11 S 000000063 010490382 1023/001/01 1023/254/63 83 Linux 12 x 025222050 004209030 1023/000/01 1023/254/63 05 extended 13 S 000000063 004208967 1023/001/01 1023/254/63 82 Linux swap 14 x 029431080 027712125 1023/000/01 1023/254/63 05 extended 15 S 000000063 027712062 1023/001/01 1023/254/63 07 NTFS 16 S 000000000 000000000 0000/000/00 0000/000/00 00 empty entry

Test Case DA-07-X2 ILook IXimager Version 2.0, Feb 01 2006	
	17 P 000000000 000000000 0000/000/00 0000/000/00 00 empty entry 18 P 000000000 000000000 0000/000/00 0000/000/00 00 empty entry 1 020980827 sectors 10742183424 bytes 3 000032067 sectors 16418304 bytes 5 002104452 sectors 1077479424 bytes 7 004192902 sectors 2146765824 bytes 9 008401932 sectors 4301789184 bytes 11 010490382 sectors 5371075584 bytes 13 004208967 sectors 2154991104 bytes 15 027712062 sectors 14188575744 bytes
Log Highlights:	IXImager Log file SCSI device sdb: 78125000 512-byte hdwr sectors (40000 MB) SCSI device sdc: 781443888 512-byte hdwr sectors (400099 MB) User selected ILook Default Image Format Initializing... Opened output file '/ILookImager/ILook.016/DA07X2001.asb' Beginning Image operation for 5371075584 bytes Beginning Image operation Beginning Image operation Image Complete Image was completed successfully. Read : 5.371 GB (5371075584 bytes) Written : 125.1 MB (125099895 bytes) Total Processed: 5.371 GB (5371075584 bytes) Image Speed : 7.934 MB/sec Elapsed Time : 0h 11m 17s Compression : 97.67% Bad Sectors : 0 SHA-1 Value : 283bcc32de892c12c37698af7e38703619e57f57 : for 5371075584 bytes Clearing computer memory... Source SHA1 Hash: 888E2E7F7AD237DC7A732281DD93F325065E5871
Results:	

Assertion & Expected Result	Actual Result
AM-01 Source acquired using interface AI.	as expected
AM-02 Source is type DS.	as expected
AM-03 Execution environment is XE.	as expected
AM-05 An image is created on file system type FS.	as expected
AM-06 All visible sectors acquired.	as expected
AM-08 All sectors accurately acquired.	as expected
AO-01 Image file is complete and accurate.	as expected
AO-05 Multifile image created.	as expected
AO-22 Tool calculates hashes by block.	option not available
AO-23 Logged information is correct.	as expected
AO-24 Source is unchanged by acquisition.	as expected

Analysis:	Expected results achieved

5.2.39   DA-08-ATA28

Test Case DA-08-ATA28 ILook IXimager Version 2.0, Feb 01 2006	
Description:	DA-08 Acquire a physical drive with hidden sectors to an image file.
Assertions:	AM-01 The tool uses access interface SRC-AI to access the digital source. AM-02 The tool acquires digital source DS. AM-03 The tool executes in execution environment XE. AM-05 If image file creation is specified, the tool creates an image file on file system type FS. AM-06 All visible sectors are acquired from the digital source. AM-07 All hidden sectors are acquired from the digital source. AM-08 All sectors acquired from the digital source are acquired accurately. AO-01 If the tool creates an image file, the data represented by the image file is the same as the data acquired by the tool. AO-05 If the tool creates a multi-file image of a requested size then all the individual files shall be no larger than the requested size.

	Test Case DA-08-ATA28 ILook IXimager Version 2.0, Feb 01 2006
	AO-22 If requested, the tool calculates block hashes for a specified block size during an acquisition for each block acquired from the digital source. AO-23 If the tool logs any log significant information, the information is accurately recorded in the log file. AO-24 If the tool executes in a forensically safe execution environment, the digital source is unchanged by the acquisition process.
Tester Name:	Brl
Test Host:	Joe
Test Date:	Thu May 25 15:03:06 2006
Drives:	src(42) dst (4D-FU2) other (none)
Source Setup:	src hash: < 5A75399023056E0EB905082B35F8FAA1DB049229 > 78165360 total sectors (40020664320 bytes) 65534/015/63 (max cyl/hd values) 65535/016/63 (number of cyl/hd) IDE disk: Model (WDC WD400JB-00JJC0) serial # (WD-WCAMA3958512) N Start LBA Length Start C/H/S End C/H/S boot Partition type 1 P 000000063 070348572 0000/001/01 1023/254/63 Boot 07 NTFS 2 P 000000000 000000000 0000/000/00 0000/000/00 00 empty entry 3 P 000000000 000000000 0000/000/00 0000/000/00 00 empty entry 4 P 000000000 000000000 0000/000/00 0000/000/00 00 empty entry 1 070348572 sectors 36018468864 bytes HPA created BIOS, XBIOS and Direct disk geometry Reporter (BXDR) BXDR 128 /S70000000 /P /fbxdrlog.txt Setting Maximum Addressable Sector to 70000000 MAS now set to 70000000
Log Highlights:	IXImager Log file hda: 70000001 sectors (35840 MB) w/8192KiB Cache, CHS=65535/16/63, UDMA(100) SCSI device sdb: 781443888 512-byte hdwr sectors (400099 MB) Maximum HPA address: /dev/hda: 78165360 (40.02 GB) An HPA area hiding 4.181 GB has been detected on Hard Drive device '/dev/hda'. Unless this HPA is disabled, the imaged the HPA. Would you like to disable the HPA so the IXimager can obtain the additional data hidden within the HPA area? User selected ILook Default Image Format Initializing... Opened output file '/ILookImager/ILook.035/DA08ATA28001.asb' Beginning Image operation for 40020664320 bytes Beginning Image operation Beginning Image operation Opened output file '/ILookImager/ILook.035/DA08ATA28002.asb' continuing at byte 1281622016 Image is being stored to /ILook.035/DA08ATA28002.asb Opened output file '/ILookImager/ILook.035/DA08ATA28003.asb' continuing at byte 22366126080 Image is being stored to /ILook.035/DA08ATA28003.asb Image Complete Image was completed successfully. Read : 40.02 GB (40020664320 bytes) Written : 1.702 GB (1702413859 bytes) Total Processed: 40.02 GB (40020664320 bytes) Image Speed : 25.22 MB/sec Elapsed Time : 0h 26m 27s Compression : 95.75% Bad Sectors : 0 SHA-1 Value : 5a75399023056e0eb905082b35f8faa1db049229 : for 40020664320 bytes Clearing computer memory... Source SHA1 Hash: 5A75399023056E0EB905082B35F8FAA1DB049229
Results:	

Assertion & Expected Result	Actual Result
AM-01 Source acquired using interface AI.	as expected
AM-02 Source is type DS.	as expected
AM-03 Execution environment is XE.	as expected

Test Case DA-08-ATA28 ILook IXimager Version 2.0, Feb 01 2006		
	AM-05 An image is created on file system type FS.	as expected
	AM-06 All visible sectors acquired.	as expected
	AM-07 All hidden sectors acquired.	as expected
	AM-08 All sectors accurately acquired.	as expected
	AO-01 Image file is complete and accurate.	as expected
	AO-05 Multifile image created.	as expected
	AO-22 Tool calculates hashes by block.	option not available
	AO-23 Logged information is correct.	as expected
	AO-24 Source is unchanged by acquisition.	as expected
Analysis:	Expected results achieved	

5.2.40 DA-08-ATA48

Test Case DA-08-ATA48 ILook IXimager Version 2.0, Feb 01 2006	
Description:	DA-08 Acquire a physical drive with hidden sectors to an image file.
Assertions:	AM-01 The tool uses access interface SRC-AI to access the digital source. AM-02 The tool acquires digital source DS. AM-03 The tool executes in execution environment XE. AM-05 If image file creation is specified, the tool creates an image file on file system type FS. AM-06 All visible sectors are acquired from the digital source. AM-07 All hidden sectors are acquired from the digital source. AM-08 All sectors acquired from the digital source are acquired accurately. AO-01 If the tool creates an image file, the data represented by the image file is the same as the data acquired by the tool. AO-05 If the tool creates a multi-file image of a requested size then all the individual files shall be no larger than the requested size. AO-22 If requested, the tool calculates block hashes for a specified block size during an acquisition for each block acquired from the digital source. AO-23 If the tool logs any log significant information, the information is accurately recorded in the log file. AO-24 If the tool executes in a forensically safe execution environment, the digital source is unchanged by the acquisition process.
Tester Name:	brl
Test Host:	Max
Test Date:	Thu May 25 15:17:34 2006
Drives:	src(4B) dst (4D-FU2) other (none)
Source Setup:	src hash: < F409920836FED76DBB60DEEEF467A6DDED5BF48E > 390721968 total sectors (200049647616 bytes) 24320/254/63 (max cyl/hd values) 24321/255/63 (number of cyl/hd) IDE disk: Model (WDC WD2000JB-00GVC0) serial # (WD-WCAL78252964) N Start LBA Length Start C/H/S End C/H/S boot Partition type 1 P 000000063 351646722 0000/001/01 1023/254/63 Boot 07 NTFS 2 P 000000000 000000000 0000/000/00 0000/000/00 00 empty entry 3 P 000000000 000000000 0000/000/00 0000/000/00 00 empty entry 4 P 000000000 000000000 0000/000/00 0000/000/00 00 empty entry 1 351646722 sectors 180043121664 bytes HPA created BIOS, XBIOS and Direct disk geometry Reporter (BXDR) BXDR 128 /S351000000 /P /fHPA.TXT Setting Maximum Addressable Sector to 351000000 MAS now set to 351000000
Log Highlights:	IXImager Log file hda: 351000001 sectors (179712 MB) w/8192KiB Cache, CHS=21848/255/63, UDMA(100) SCSI device sdb: 781443888 512-byte hdwr sectors (400099 MB) Maximum HPA address: /dev/hda: 390721968 (200.0 GB) An HPA area hiding 20.34 GB has been detected on Hard Drive device '/dev/hda'. Unless this HPA is disabled, the imaged the HPA. Would you like to disable the HPA so the IXimager can obtain the additional data hidden within the HPA area? User selected ILook Default Image Format Initializing...

Test Case DA-08-ATA48 ILook IXimager Version 2.0, Feb 01 2006	
	Opened output file '/ILookImager/ILook.036/da08ata48001.asb' Beginning Image operation for 200049647616 bytes Beginning Image operation Beginning Image operation Opened output file '/ILookImager/ILook.036/da08ata48002.asb' continuing at byte 1263861760 Image is being stored to /ILook.036/da08ata48002.asb Opened output file '/ILookImager/ILook.036/da08ata48003.asb' continuing at byte 22317760512 Image is being stored to /ILook.036/da08ata48003.asb Opened output file '/ILookImager/ILook.036/da08ata48004.asb' continuing at byte 50487296000 Image is being stored to /ILook.036/da08ata48004.asb Opened output file '/ILookImager/ILook.036/da08ata48005.asb' continuing at byte 78653292544 Image is being stored to /ILook.036/da08ata48005.asb Opened output file '/ILookImager/ILook.036/da08ata48006.asb' continuing at byte 106816536576 Image is being stored to /ILook.036/da08ata48006.asb Opened output file '/ILookImager/ILook.036/da08ata48007.asb' continuing at byte 134982467584 Image is being stored to /ILook.036/da08ata48007.asb Opened output file '/ILookImager/ILook.036/da08ata48008.asb' continuing at byte 163148464128 Image is being stored to /ILook.036/da08ata48008.asb Opened output file '/ILookImager/ILook.036/da08ata48009.asb' continuing at byte 191314460672 Image is being stored to /ILook.036/da08ata48009.asb Image Complete Image was completed successfully. Read : 200.0 GB (200049647616 bytes) Written : 5.385 GB (5385219933 bytes) Total Processed: 200.0 GB (200049647616 bytes) Image Speed : 26.23 MB/sec Elapsed Time : 2h 7m 6s Compression : 97.31% Bad Sectors : 0 SHA-1 Value : f409920836fed76dbb60deeef467a6dded5bf48e : for 200049647616 bytes Clearing computer memory... Source SHA1 Hash: F409920836FED76DBB60DEEEF467A6DDED5BF48E
Results:	

Assertion & Expected Result	Actual Result
AM-01 Source acquired using interface AI.	as expected
AM-02 Source is type DS.	as expected
AM-03 Execution environment is XE.	as expected
AM-05 An image is created on file system type FS.	as expected
AM-06 All visible sectors acquired.	as expected
AM-07 All hidden sectors acquired.	as expected
AM-08 All sectors accurately acquired.	as expected
AO-01 Image file is complete and accurate.	as expected
AO-05 Multifile image created.	as expected
AO-22 Tool calculates hashes by block.	option not available
AO-23 Logged information is correct.	as expected
AO-24 Source is unchanged by acquisition.	as expected

Analysis:	Expected results achieved

5.2.41 DA-08-DCO

Test Case DA-08-DCO ILook IXimager Version 2.0, Feb 01 2006	
Case Summary:	DA-08 Acquire a physical drive with hidden sectors to an image file.
Assertions:	AM-01 The tool uses access interface SRC-AI to access the digital source. AM-02 The tool acquires digital source DS. AM-03 The tool executes in execution environment XE.

Test Case DA-08-DCO ILook IXimager Version 2.0, Feb 01 2006	
	AM-05 If image file creation is specified, the tool creates an image file on file system type FS. AM-06 All visible sectors are acquired from the digital source. AM-07 All hidden sectors are acquired from the digital source. AM-08 All sectors acquired from the digital source are acquired accurately. AO-01 If the tool creates an image file, the data represented by the image file is the same as the data acquired by the tool. AO-05 If the tool creates a multi-file image of a requested size then all the individual files shall be no larger than the requested size. AO-22 If requested, the tool calculates block hashes for a specified block size during an acquisition for each block acquired from the digital source. AO-23 If the tool logs any log significant information, the information is accurately recorded in the log file. AO-24 If the tool executes in a forensically safe execution environment, the digital source is unchanged by the acquisition process.
Tester Name:	brl
Test Host:	McCloud
Test Date:	Thu Oct 12 14:22:38 2006
Drives:	src(92) dst (50-IDE) other (none)
Source Setup:	src hash: < 63E6F7BD3040A8ADA2CF8FBF66A805B76DF10481 > 58633344 total sectors (30020272128 bytes) 58167/015/63 (max cyl/hd values) 58168/016/63 (number of cyl/hd) IDE disk: Model (WDC WD300BB-00CAA0) serial # (WD-WMA8H2140350) N Start LBA Length Start C/H/S End C/H/S boot Partition type 1 P 000000063 058605057 0000/001/01 1023/254/63 Boot 07 NTFS 2 P 000000000 000000000 0000/000/00 0000/000/00 00 empty entry 3 P 000000000 000000000 0000/000/00 0000/000/00 00 empty entry 4 P 000000000 000000000 0000/000/00 0000/000/00 00 empty entry 1 058605057 sectors 30005789184 bytes After DCO Created: 52770010 Sectors, 27018245120 src with DCO hash: 55A3CFE756B7B0034DCCE71F7D7A477D8681B781
Log Highlights:	IXImager Log file hda: 52770010 sectors (27018 MB) w/2048KiB Cache, CHS=3284/255/63, UDMA(100) hdb: 156301488 sectors (80026 MB) w/8192KiB Cache, CHS=9729/255/63, UDMA(100) User selected ILook Default Image Format Initializing... Opened output file '/ILookImager/ILook.038/da08dco001.asb' Beginning Image operation for 30020272128 bytes Beginning Image operation Beginning Image operation Opened output file '/ILookImager/ILook.038/da08dco002.asb' continuing at byte 1256980480 Image is being stored to /ILook.038/da08dco002.asb Opened output file '/ILookImager/ILook.038/da08dco003.asb' continuing at byte 24723062784 Image is being stored to /ILook.038/da08dco003.asb Image Complete Image was completed successfully. Read : 30.02 GB (30020272128 bytes) Written : 1.418 GB (1418092899 bytes) Total Processed: 30.02 GB (30020272128 bytes) Image Speed : 14.57 MB/sec Elapsed Time : 0h 34m 21s Compression : 95.28% Bad Sectors : 0 SHA-1 Value : 63e6f7bd3040a8ada2cf8fbf66a805b76df10481 : for 30020272128 bytes Clearing computer memory... Source SHA1 Hash: 55A3CFE756B7B0034DCCE71F7D7A477D8681B781
Results:	
	Assertion & Expected Result Actual Result

Test Case DA-08-DCO ILook IXimager Version 2.0, Feb 01 2006		
	am-01 Source acquired using interface AI.	as expected
	am-02 Source is type DS.	as expected
	am-03 Execution environment is XE.	as expected
	am-05 An image is created on file system type FS.	as expected
	am-06 All visible sectors acquired.	as expected
	am-07 All hidden sectors acquired.	as expected
	am-08 All sectors accurately acquired.	as expected
	ao-01 Image file is complete and accurate.	as expected
	ao-05 Multifile image created.	as expected
	ao-22 Tool calculates hashes by block.	option not available
	ao-23 Logged information is correct.	as expected
	ao-24 Source is unchanged by acquisition.	as expected
Analysis:	Expected results achieved	

5.2.42 DA-09

Test Case DA-09 ILook IXimager Version 2.0, Feb 01 2006	
Description:	DA-09 Acquire a digital source that has at least one faulty data sector.
Assertions:	AM-01 The tool uses access interface SRC-AI to access the digital source. AM-02 The tool acquires digital source DS. AM-03 The tool executes in execution environment XE. AM-05 If image file creation is specified, the tool creates an image file on file system type FS. AM-06 All visible sectors are acquired from the digital source. AM-08 All sectors acquired from the digital source are acquired accurately. AM-09 If unresolved errors occur while reading from the selected digital source, the tool notifies the user of the error type and location within the digital source. AM-10 If unresolved errors occur while reading from the selected digital source, the tool uses a benign fill in the destination object in place of the inaccessible data. AO-01 If the tool creates an image file, the data represented by the image file is the same as the data acquired by the tool. AO-05 If the tool creates a multi-file image of a requested size then all the individual files shall be no larger than the requested size. AO-22 If requested, the tool calculates block hashes for a specified block size during an acquisition for each block acquired from the digital source. AO-23 If the tool logs any log significant information, the information is accurately recorded in the log file. AO-24 If the tool executes in a forensically safe execution environment, the digital source is unchanged by the acquisition process.
Tester Name:	Brl
Test Host:	Frank
Test Date:	Tue Jun 27 15:37:17 2006
Drives:	src(BE) dst (0B) other (BF)

Source Setup:	No before hash for be total sectors (bytes)
	  Drive with known bad sectors
	  Vendor: WDC WD20 Model: 00JB-00GVC0 Rev: 08.0
	  390721968 512-byte hdwr sectors (200050 MB)
	
	Bad sectors present on drive: 0, 512, 1024-1025, 2048-2050, 4096-4099, 195360979-195360983, 195360985-195360989, 390721967

Log Highlights:	Comparision of original to clone Sectors compared: 390721968 Sectors match: 390721946 Sectors differ: 22 Bytes differ: 10941 Diffs range 0, 512, 1024-1025, 2048-2050, 4096-4099, 195360979-195360983, 195360985-195360989, 390721967 Source (390721968) has 97675200 fewer sectors than destination (488397168) Zero fill: 0 Src Byte fill (BF): 0

```
Test Case DA-09 ILook IXimager Version 2.0, Feb 01 2006
                    Dst Byte fill (0B): 97675200
                    Other fill:                 0
                    Other no fill:              0
                    Zero fill range:
                    Src fill range:
                    Dst fill range:    390721968-488397167
                    Other fill range:
                    Other not filled range:
                    0 source read errors, 0 destination read errors

                    IXImager Log file
                    hda: 390721968 sectors (200049 MB) w/8192KiB Cache, CHS=24321/255/63,
                    UDMA(100)
                     hda:hda (dev 03:00): I/O error reading 8 sectors, sector 0
                    ata1: dev 0 ATA-6, max UDMA/100, 488397168 sectors: LBA48
                    SCSI device sdb: 488397168 512-byte hdwr sectors (250059 MB)
                    SCSI device sdb: 488397168 512-byte hdwr sectors (250059 MB)
                    hda: 390721968 sectors (200049 MB) w/8192KiB Cache, CHS=24321/255/63,
                    UDMA(100)
                     hda:hda (dev 03:00): I/O error reading 8 sectors, sector 0
                     sda:/dev/sda: I/O error reading 8 sectors, sector 0
                    /dev/sda: I/O error reading 8 sectors, sector 0
                     sda:/dev/sda: I/O error reading 8 sectors, sector 0
                    /dev/sda: I/O error reading 8 sectors, sector 0
                     sda:/dev/sda: I/O error reading 8 sectors, sector 0
                    /dev/sda: I/O error reading 8 sectors, sector 0
                    Initializing...
                    Opened input device '/dev/hda'
                    Opened output device '/dev/sdb'
                    Beginning Clone operation for 200049647616 bytes
                    Beginning Clone operation
                    Beginning Clone operation
                    Bad sector: position 0 (sector 0)
                    Bad sector: position 262144 (sector 512)
                    Bad sector: position 524288 (sector 1024)
                    Bad sector: position 524800 (sector 1025)
                    Bad sector: position 1048576 (sector 2048)
                    Bad sector: position 1049088 (sector 2049)
                    Bad sector: position 1049600 (sector 2050)
                    Bad sector: position 2097152 (sector 4096)
                    Bad sector: position 2097664 (sector 4097)
                    Bad sector: position 2098176 (sector 4098)
                    Bad sector: position 2098688 (sector 4099)
                    Bad sector: position 100024821248 (sector 195360979)
                    Bad sector: position 100024821760 (sector 195360980)
                    Bad sector: position 100024822272 (sector 195360981)
                    Bad sector: position 100024822784 (sector 195360982)
                    Bad sector: position 100024823296 (sector 195360983)
                    Bad sector: position 100024824320 (sector 195360985)
                    Bad sector: position 100024824832 (sector 195360986)
                    Bad sector: position 100024825344 (sector 195360987)
                    Bad sector: position 100024825856 (sector 195360988)
                    Bad sector: position 100024826368 (sector 195360989)
                    Bad sector: position 200049647104 (sector 390721967)
                    Clone Complete
                    Clone was completed successfully.

                    Read           :  200.0 GB (200049647616 bytes)
                    Written        :  200.0 GB (200049647616 bytes)
                    Total Processed:  200.0 GB (200049647616 bytes)
                    Clone Speed    :  49.15 MB/sec
                    Elapsed Time   :  1h  7m 50s
                    Bad Sectors    :  22
                    Clearing computer memory...
                    Initializing...

                    Opened input device '/dev/hda', continuing at byte 0
                    Beginning Verify operation for 200049647616 bytes
                    Bad sector: position 0 (sector 0)
                    Bad sector: position 262144 (sector 512)
                    Bad sector: position 524288 (sector 1024)
                    Bad sector: position 524800 (sector 1025)
                    Bad sector: position 1048576 (sector 2048)
```

Test Case DA-09 ILook IXimager Version 2.0, Feb 01 2006	
	Bad sector: position 1049088 (sector 2049) Bad sector: position 1049600 (sector 2050) Bad sector: position 2097152 (sector 4096) Bad sector: position 2097664 (sector 4097) Bad sector: position 2098176 (sector 4098) Bad sector: position 2098688 (sector 4099) Bad sector: position 100024821248 (sector 195360979) Bad sector: position 100024821760 (sector 195360980) Bad sector: position 100024822272 (sector 195360981) Bad sector: position 100024822784 (sector 195360982) Bad sector: position 100024823296 (sector 195360983) Bad sector: position 100024824320 (sector 195360985) Bad sector: position 100024824832 (sector 195360986) Bad sector: position 100024825344 (sector 195360987) Bad sector: position 100024825856 (sector 195360988) Bad sector: position 100024826368 (sector 195360989) Bad sector: position 200049647104 (sector 390721967) Verify Complete Verify was completed successfully. Read : 200.0 GB (200049647616 bytes) Written : 0.000 MB (0 bytes) Total Processed: 200.0 GB (200049647616 bytes) Verify Speed : 45.85 MB/sec Elapsed Time : 1h 12m 43s Bad Sectors : 22 SHA-1 Value : 55f30dbab3fbd80459235a26335ddf5af5899496 : for 200049647616 bytes Clearing computer memory...
Results:	
	Assertion & Expected Result **Actual Result**
	AM-01 Source acquired using interface AI. — as expected
	AM-02 Source is type DS. — as expected
	AM-03 Execution environment is XE. — as expected
	AM-05 An image is created on file system type FS. — as expected
	AM-06 All visible sectors acquired. — as expected
	AM-08 All sectors accurately acquired. — as expected
	AM-09 Error logged. — as expected
	AM-10 Benign fill replaces inaccessible sectors. — as expected
	AO-01 Image file is complete and accurate. — as expected
	AO-05 Multifile image created. — as expected
	AO-22 Tool calculates hashes by block. — option not available
	AO-23 Logged information is correct. — as expected
	AO-24 Source is unchanged by acquisition. — as expected
Analysis:	Expected results achieved

5.2.43 DA-10-ENCRYPTED

Test Case DA-10-ENCRYPTED ILook IXimager Version 2.0, Feb 01 2006	
Description:	DA-10 Acquire a digital source to an image file in an alternate format.
Assertions:	AM-01 The tool uses access interface SRC-AI to access the digital source. AM-02 The tool acquires digital source DS. AM-03 The tool executes in execution environment XE. AM-05 If image file creation is specified, the tool creates an image file on file system type FS. AM-06 All visible sectors are acquired from the digital source. AM-08 All sectors acquired from the digital source are acquired accurately. AO-01 If the tool creates an image file, the data represented by the image file is the same as the data acquired by the tool. AO-02 If an image file format is specified, the tool creates an image file in the specified format. AO-05 If the tool creates a multi-file image of a requested size then all the individual files shall be no larger than the requested size. AO-22 If requested, the tool calculates block hashes for a specified block size during an acquisition for each block acquired from the digital source. AO-23 If the tool logs any log significant information, the information is accurately recorded in the log file.

Test Case DA-10-ENCRYPTED ILook IXimager Version 2.0, Feb 01 2006	
	AO-24 If the tool executes in a forensically safe execution environment, the digital source is unchanged by the acquisition process.
Tester Name:	brl
Test Host:	Joe
Test Date:	Thu May 4 09:09:57 2006
Drives:	src(2A) dst (4D-FU2) other (none)
Source Setup:	src hash: < F5F9F2903DCAB895F36E270FB22A722E27918125 > 17783249 total sectors (9105023488 bytes) Model (QM39100TD-SCA) serial # (PCB=20-116711-06 HDAQM39100TD-SCA) N Start LBA Length Start C/H/S End C/H/S boot Partition type 1 P 000000063 017751762 0000/001/01 1023/254/63 Boot 07 NTFS 2 P 000000000 000000000 0000/000/00 0000/000/00 00 empty entry 3 P 000000000 000000000 0000/000/00 0000/000/00 00 empty entry 4 P 000000000 000000000 0000/000/00 0000/000/00 00 empty entry 1 017751762 sectors 9088902144 bytes
Log Highlights:	IXImager Log file SCSI device sdb: 17783249 512-byte hdwr sectors (9105 MB) SCSI device sdc: 781443888 512-byte hdwr sectors (400099 MB) User selected ILook Encrypted Image Format Initializing... Opened output file '/ILookImager/ILook.023/DA10ENCRYPTED001.asb' Beginning Image operation for 9105023488 bytes Beginning Image operation Beginning Image operation Image Complete Image was completed successfully. Read : 9.105 GB (9105023488 bytes) Written : 609.1 MB (609137424 bytes) Total Processed: 9.105 GB (9105023488 bytes) Image Speed : 11.98 MB/sec Elapsed Time : 0h 12m 40s Compression : 93.31% Bad Sectors : 0 SHA-1 Value : f5f9f2903dcab895f36e270fb22a722e27918125 : for 9105023488 bytes Clearing computer memory... Source SHA1 Hash: F5F9F2903DCAB895F36E270FB22A722E27918125
Results:	

Assertion & Expected Result	Actual Result
AM-01 Source acquired using interface AI.	as expected
AM-02 Source is type DS.	as expected
AM-03 Execution environment is XE.	as expected
AM-05 An image is created on file system type FS.	as expected
AM-06 All visible sectors acquired.	as expected
AM-08 All sectors accurately acquired.	as expected
AO-01 Image file is complete and accurate.	as expected
AO-02 Image file in specified format.	as expected
AO-05 Multifile image created.	as expected
AO-22 Tool calculates hashes by block.	option not available
AO-23 Logged information is correct.	as expected
AO-24 Source is unchanged by acquisition.	as expected

Analysis:	Expected results achieved

5.2.44   DA-10-RAW

Test Case DA-10-RAW ILook IXimager Version 2.0, Feb 01 2006	
Description:	DA-10 Acquire a digital source to an image file in an alternate format.
Assertions:	AM-01 The tool uses access interface SRC-AI to access the digital source. AM-02 The tool acquires digital source DS. AM-03 The tool executes in execution environment XE. AM-05 If image file creation is specified, the tool creates an image file on file system type FS.

Test Case DA-10-RAW ILook IXimager Version 2.0, Feb 01 2006

	AM-06 All visible sectors are acquired from the digital source. AM-08 All sectors acquired from the digital source are acquired accurately. AO-01 If the tool creates an image file, the data represented by the image file is the same as the data acquired by the tool. AO-02 If an image file format is specified, the tool creates an image file in the specified format. AO-05 If the tool creates a multi-file image of a requested size then all the individual files shall be no larger than the requested size. AO-22 If requested, the tool calculates block hashes for a specified block size during an acquisition for each block acquired from the digital source. AO-23 If the tool logs any log significant information, the information is accurately recorded in the log file. AO-24 If the tool executes in a forensically safe execution environment, the digital source is unchanged by the acquisition process.
Tester Name:	brl
Test Host:	Joe
Test Date:	Fri Jun 2 14:09:15 2006
Drives:	src(2A) dst (4D-FU2) other (none)
Source Setup:	src hash: < F5F9F2903DCAB895F36E270FB22A722E27918125 > 17783249 total sectors (9105023488 bytes) Model (QM39100TD-SCA) serial # (PCB=20-116711-06 HDAQM39100TD-SCA) N Start LBA Length Start C/H/S End C/H/S boot Partition type 1 P 000000063 017751762 0000/001/01 1023/254/63 Boot 07 NTFS 2 P 000000000 000000000 0000/000/00 0000/000/00 00 empty entry 3 P 000000000 000000000 0000/000/00 0000/000/00 00 empty entry 4 P 000000000 000000000 0000/000/00 0000/000/00 00 empty entry 1 017751762 sectors 9088902144 bytes
Log Highlights:	IXImager Log file SCSI device sdb: 17783249 512-byte hdwr sectors (9105 MB) SCSI device sdc: 781443888 512-byte hdwr sectors (400099 MB) User selected ILook Raw Image Format Initializing... Opened output file '/ILookImager/ILook.022/DA10RAW001.asb' Beginning Image operation for 9105023488 bytes Beginning Image operation Beginning Image operation Opened output file '/ILookImager/ILook.022/DA10RAW002.asb' continuing at byte 648740864 Image is being stored to /ILook.022/DA10RAW002.asb Opened output file '/ILookImager/ILook.022/DA10RAW003.asb' continuing at byte 1295450112 Image is being stored to /ILook.022/DA10RAW003.asb Opened output file '/ILookImager/ILook.022/DA10RAW004.asb' continuing at byte 1942159360 Image is being stored to /ILook.022/DA10RAW004.asb Opened output file '/ILookImager/ILook.022/DA10RAW005.asb' continuing at byte 2588868608 Image is being stored to /ILook.022/DA10RAW005.asb Opened output file '/ILookImager/ILook.022/DA10RAW006.asb' continuing at byte 3235577856 Image is being stored to /ILook.022/DA10RAW006.asb Opened output file '/ILookImager/ILook.022/DA10RAW007.asb' continuing at byte 3882287104 Image is being stored to /ILook.022/DA10RAW007.asb Opened output file '/ILookImager/ILook.022/DA10RAW008.asb' continuing at byte 4528996352 Image is being stored to /ILook.022/DA10RAW008.asb Opened output file '/ILookImager/ILook.022/DA10RAW009.asb' continuing at byte 5175705600 Image is being stored to /ILook.022/DA10RAW009.asb Opened output file '/ILookImager/ILook.022/DA10RAW010.asb' continuing at byte 5822414848 Image is being stored to /ILook.022/DA10RAW010.asb Opened output file '/ILookImager/ILook.022/DA10RAW011.asb' continuing at byte 6469124096 Image is being stored to /ILook.022/DA10RAW011.asb Opened output file '/ILookImager/ILook.022/DA10RAW012.asb' continuing at byte 7115833344 Image is being stored to /ILook.022/DA10RAW012.asb Opened output file '/ILookImager/ILook.022/DA10RAW013.asb'

```
Test Case DA-10-RAW ILook IXimager Version 2.0, Feb 01 2006
```

	continuing at byte 7762542592 Image is being stored to /ILook.022/DA10RAW013.asb Opened output file '/ILookImager/ILook.022/DA10RAW014.asb' continuing at byte 8409251840 Image is being stored to /ILook.022/DA10RAW014.asb Opened output file '/ILookImager/ILook.022/DA10RAW015.asb' continuing at byte 9055961088 Image is being stored to /ILook.022/DA10RAW015.asb Image Complete Image was completed successfully. Read : 9.105 GB (9105023488 bytes) Written : 9.123 GB (9122743904 bytes) Total Processed : 9.105 GB (9105023488 bytes) Image Speed : 10.65 MB/sec Elapsed Time : 0h 14m 15s Bad Sectors : 0 SHA-1 Value : f5f9f2903dcab895f36e270fb22a722e27918125 : for 9105023488 bytes Clearing computer memory... Source SHA1 Hash: F5F9F2903DCAB895F36E270FB22A722E27918125
Results:	

Assertion & Expected Result	Actual Result
AM-01 Source acquired using interface AI.	as expected
AM-02 Source is type DS.	as expected
AM-03 Execution environment is XE.	as expected
AM-05 An image is created on file system type FS.	as expected
AM-06 All visible sectors acquired.	as expected
AM-08 All sectors accurately acquired.	as expected
AO-01 Image file is complete and accurate.	as expected
AO-02 Image file in specified format.	as expected
AO-05 Multifile image created.	as expected
AO-22 Tool calculates hashes by block.	option not available
AO-23 Logged information is correct.	as expected
AO-24 Source is unchanged by acquisition.	as expected

Analysis:	Expected results achieved

5.2.45 DA-12

Test Case DA-12 ILook IXimager Version 2.0, Feb 01 2006	
Description:	DA-12 Attempt to create an image file where there is insufficient space.
Assertions:	AM-01 The tool uses access interface SRC-AI to access the digital source. AM-02 The tool acquires digital source DS. AM-03 The tool executes in execution environment XE. AM-05 If image file creation is specified, the tool creates an image file on file system type FS. AO-04 If the tool is creating an image file and there is insufficient space on the image destination device to contain the image file, the tool shall notify the user. AO-23 If the tool logs any log significant information, the information is accurately recorded in the log file. AO-24 If the tool executes in a forensically safe execution environment, the digital source is unchanged by the acquisition process.
Tester Name:	brl
Test Host:	Max
Test Date:	Thu May 4 16:59:09 2006
Drives:	src(07) dst (8E-FU2) other (none)

Source Setup:	src hash: < 655E9BDDB36A3F9C5C4CC8BF32B8C5B41AF9F52E >
	156301488 total sectors (80026361856 bytes)
	Model (WDC WD800JD-32HK) serial # (WD-WMAJ91510044)
	  N Start LBA Length Start C/H/S End C/H/S boot Partition type
	  1 P 000000063 156280257 0000/001/01 1023/254/63 Boot 07 NTFS
	  2 P 000000000 000000000 0000/000/00 0000/000/00 00 empty entry
	  3 P 000000000 000000000 0000/000/00 0000/000/00 00 empty entry
	  4 P 000000000 000000000 0000/000/00 0000/000/00 00 empty entry

Test Case DA-12 ILook IXimager Version 2.0, Feb 01 2006	
	1 156280257 sectors 80015491584 bytes
Log Highlights:	IXImager Log file ata1: dev 0 ATA-6, max UDMA/133, 156301488 sectors: LBA SCSI device sdb: 156301488 512-byte hdwr sectors (80026 MB) SCSI device sdc: 78140160 512-byte hdwr sectors (40008 MB) User selected ILook Default Image Format Initializing... It appears your target device is significantly smaller then your source device. Even though you have compression enabled there is no guarantee that everything will compress to fit on your selected target device. If you choose to continue this operation, when your target device becomes full - you will need to change the output media to complete the operation. Would you like to continue this operation anyway? User selected: Yes Opened output file '/ILookImager/ILook.001/DA12001.asb' Beginning Image operation for 80026361856 bytes Beginning Image operation Beginning Image operation Opened output file '/ILookImager/ILook.001/DA12002.asb' continuing at byte 1287651328 Image is being stored to /ILook.001/DA12002.asb Opened output file '/ILookImager/ILook.001/DA12003.asb' continuing at byte 22496018432 Image is being stored to /ILook.001/DA12003.asb Scanning for devices. Please wait... User entered the Select Next Output Device Menu Do you really want to abort this operation? User selected: Yes Image Aborted Image was aborted. Read : 50.66 GB (50659196928 bytes) Written : 1.944 GB (1944057180 bytes) Total Processed: 50.66 GB (50659131392 bytes) Expected Size : 80.03 GB (80026361856 bytes) Image Speed : 13.59 MB/sec Elapsed Time : 1h 2m 9s Bad Sectors : 0 Clearing computer memory... Source SHA1 Hash: 655E9BDDB36A3F9C5C4CC8BF32B8C5B41AF9F52E
Results:	

Assertion & Expected Result	Actual Result
AM-01 Source acquired using interface AI.	as expected
AM-02 Source is type DS.	as expected
AM-03 Execution environment is XE.	as expected
AM-05 An image is created on file system type FS.	as expected
AO-04 User notified if space exhausted.	as expected
AO-23 Logged information is correct.	as expected
AO-24 Source is unchanged by acquisition.	as expected

Analysis:	Expected results achieved

5.2.46 DA-13

Test Case DA-13 ILook IXimager Version 2.0, Feb 01 2006	
Description:	DA-13 Create an image file where there is insufficient space on a single volume, and use destination device switching to continue on another volume.
Assertions:	AM-01 The tool uses access interface SRC-AI to access the digital source. AM-02 The tool acquires digital source DS. AM-03 The tool executes in execution environment XE. AM-05 If image file creation is specified, the tool creates an image file on file system type FS. AM-06 All visible sectors are acquired from the digital source. AM-08 All sectors acquired from the digital source are acquired accurately.

	Test Case DA-13 ILook IXimager Version 2.0, Feb 01 2006
	AO-01 If the tool creates an image file, the data represented by the image file is the same as the data acquired by the tool. AO-04 If the tool is creating an image file and there is insufficient space on the image destination device to contain the image file, the tool shall notify the user. AO-05 If the tool creates a multi-file image of a requested size then all the individual files shall be no larger than the requested size. AO-10 If there is insufficient space to contain all files of a multi-file image and if destination device switching is supported, the image is continued on another device. AO-22 If requested, the tool calculates block hashes for a specified block size during an acquisition for each block acquired from the digital source. AO-23 If the tool logs any log significant information, the information is accurately recorded in the log file. AO-24 If the tool executes in a forensically safe execution environment, the digital source is unchanged by the acquisition process.
Tester Name:	brl
Test Host:	Joe
Test Date:	Fri May 5 13:59:05 2006
Drives:	src(07) dst (8F-FU2) other (8D-FU2)

Source Setup:	src hash: < 655E9BDDB36A3F9C5C4CC8BF32B8C5B41AF9F52E >
	156301488 total sectors (80026361856 bytes)
	Model (WDC WD800JD-32HK) serial # (WD-WMAJ91510044)
	  N Start LBA Length Start C/H/S End C/H/S boot Partition type
	  1 P 000000063 156280257 0000/001/01 1023/254/63 Boot 07 NTFS
	  2 P 000000000 000000000 0000/000/00 0000/000/00 00 empty entry
	  3 P 000000000 000000000 0000/000/00 0000/000/00 00 empty entry
	  4 P 000000000 000000000 0000/000/00 0000/000/00 00 empty entry
	1 156280257 sectors 80015491584 bytes

Log Highlights:	IXImager Log file ata2: dev 0 ATA-6, max UDMA/133, 156301488 sectors: LBA SCSI device sdb: 156301488 512-byte hdwr sectors (80026 MB) SCSI device sdc: 78140160 512-byte hdwr sectors (40008 MB) SCSI device sdd: 781422768 512-byte hdwr sectors (400088 MB) User selected ILook Default Image Format Initializing... It appears your target device is significantly smaller then your source device. Even though you have compression enabled there is no guarantee that everything will compress to fit on your selected target device. If you choose to continue this operation, when your target device becomes full - you will need to change the output media to complete the operation. Would you like to continue this operation anyway? User selected: Yes Opened output file '/ILookImager/ILook.001/DA13001.asb' Beginning Image operation for 80026361856 bytes Beginning Image operation Beginning Image operation Opened output file '/ILookImager/ILook.001/DA13002.asb' continuing at byte 1287585792 Image is being stored to /ILook.001/DA13002.asb Opened output file '/ILookImager/ILook.001/DA13003.asb' continuing at byte 22494773248 Image is being stored to /ILook.001/DA13003.asb Scanning for devices. Please wait... User entered the Select Next Output Device Menu Scanning for devices. Please wait... Please wait while I check for media... Checking target device... User selected device '/dev/sdd' for output Making an image of /dev/sdb A 80.03 GB WDC WD800JD-32HK Hard Drive Image is being stored to /dev/sdd1 A 400.1 GB Win95 FAT32 (LBA) Partition on Firewire0,1 Opened output file '/ILookImager/ILook.003/DA13004.asb' continuing at byte 50657951744 Image is being stored to /ILook.003/DA13004.asb Opened output file '/ILookImager/ILook.003/DA13005.asb' continuing at byte 78822965248 Image is being stored to /ILook.003/DA13005.asb

Test Case DA-13 ILook IXimager Version 2.0, Feb 01 2006

```
                Image Complete
                Image was completed successfully.

                Read             :  80.03 GB (80026361856 bytes)
                Written          :  2.620 GB (2619912273 bytes)
                Total Processed  :  80.03 GB (80026361856 bytes)
                Image Speed      :  7.681 MB/sec
                Elapsed Time     :  2h 53m 39s
                Compression      :  96.73%
                Bad Sectors      :  0
                SHA-1 Value      :  655e9bddb36a3f9c5c4cc8bf32b8c5b41af9f52e
                                 :  for 80026361856 bytes
                Clearing computer memory...

                Source SHA1 Hash: 655E9BDDB36A3F9C5C4CC8BF32B8C5B41AF9F52E
```

Results:	Assertion & Expected Result	Actual Result
	AM-01 Source acquired using interface AI.	as expected
	AM-02 Source is type DS.	as expected
	AM-03 Execution environment is XE.	as expected
	AM-05 An image is created on file system type FS.	as expected
	AM-06 All visible sectors acquired.	as expected
	AM-08 All sectors accurately acquired.	as expected
	AO-01 Image file is complete and accurate.	as expected
	AO-04 User notified if space exhausted.	as expected
	AO-05 Multifile image created.	as expected
	AO-10 Image file continued on new device.	as expected
	AO-22 Tool calculates hashes by block.	option not available
	AO-23 Logged information is correct.	as expected
	AO-24 Source is unchanged by acquisition.	as expected

Analysis:	Expected results achieved

5.2.47 DA-14-ATA28

Test Case DA-14-ATA28 ILook IXimager Version 2.0, Feb 01 2006	
Description:	DA-14 Create an unaligned clone from an image file.
Assertions:	AM-03 The tool executes in execution environment XE. AO-12 If requested, a clone is created from an image file. AO-13 A clone is created using access interface DST-AI to write to the clone device. AO-14 If an unaligned clone is created, each sector written to the clone is accurately written to the same disk address on the clone that the sector occupied on the digital source. AO-17 If requested, any excess sectors on a clone destination device are not modified. AO-23 If the tool logs any log significant information, the information is accurately recorded in the log file.
Tester Name:	brl
Test Host:	Paladin
Test Date:	Fri Mar 31 11:05:56 2006
Drives:	src(41) dst (85) other (4D-FU2)
Source Setup:	src hash: < 15CAA1A307271160D8372668BF8A03FC45A51CC9 > 78125000 total sectors (40000000000 bytes) 65534/015/63 (max cyl/hd values) 65535/016/63 (number of cyl/hd) IDE disk: Model (WDC WD400BB-75JHC0) serial # (WD-WMAMC4658355) N Start LBA Length Start C/H/S End C/H/S boot Partition type 1 P 000000063 078107967 0000/001/01 1023/254/63 Boot 07 NTFS 2 P 000000000 000000000 0000/000/00 0000/000/00 00 empty entry 3 P 000000000 000000000 0000/000/00 0000/000/00 00 empty entry 4 P 000000000 000000000 0000/000/00 0000/000/00 00 empty entry 1 078107967 sectors 39991279104 bytes
Log Highlights:	Comparision of original to clone Sectors compared: 78125000

```
Test Case DA-14-ATA28 ILook IXimager Version 2.0, Feb 01 2006
                    Sectors match:     78125000
                    Sectors differ:           0
                    Bytes differ:             0
                    Diffs range
                    Source (78125000) has 78176488 fewer sectors than destination (156301488)
                    Zero fill:                0
                    Src Byte fill (41):       0
                    Dst Byte fill (85): 78176488
                    Other fill:               0
                    Other no fill:            0
                    Zero fill range:
                    Src fill range:
                    Dst fill range:   78125000-156301487
                    Other fill range:
                    Other not filled range:
                    0 source read errors, 0 destination read errors

                    IXImager Log file
                    hda: 156301488 sectors (80026 MB) w/2048KiB Cache, CHS=9729/255/63,
                    UDMA(100)
                    SCSI device sda: 781443888 512-byte hdwr sectors (400099 MB)
                    Initializing...
                    Opened output device '/dev/hda'
                    Beginning Restore operation for 40000000000 bytes
                    Beginning Restore operation
                    Beginning Restore operation
                    Opened input file '/ILookImager/ILook.003/DA06ATA28002.asb'
                    continuing at byte 20946223104
                    Restoring from /ILook.003/DA06ATA28002.asb
                    Opened input file '/ILookImager/ILook.003/DA06ATA28003.asb'
                    continuing at byte 39117127680
                    Restoring from /ILook.003/DA06ATA28003.asb
                    Restore Complete
                    Restore was completed successfully.

                    Read           : 1.316 GB (1316466855 bytes)
                    Written        : 40.00 GB (40000000000 bytes)
                    Total Processed: 40.00 GB (40000000000 bytes)
                    Restore Speed  : 38.31 MB/sec
                    Elapsed Time   : 0h 17m 24s
                    Bad Sectors    : 0
                    Clearing computer memory...
```

Results:	Assertion & Expected Result	Actual Result
	AM-03 Execution environment is XE.	as expected
	AO-12 A clone is created from an image file.	as expected
	AO-13 Clone created using interface AI.	as expected
	AO-14 An unaligned clone is created.	as expected
	AO-17 Excess sectors are unchanged.	as expected
	AO-23 Logged information is correct.	as expected

Analysis:	Expected results achieved

5.2.48 DA-14-ATA48

Test Case DA-14-ATA48 ILook IXimager Version 2.0, Feb 01 2006	
Description:	DA-14 Create an unaligned clone from an image file.
Assertions:	AM-03 The tool executes in execution environment XE. AO-12 If requested, a clone is created from an image file. AO-13 A clone is created using access interface DST-AI to write to the clone device. AO-14 If an unaligned clone is created, each sector written to the clone is accurately written to the same disk address on the clone that the sector occupied on the digital source. AO-17 If requested, any excess sectors on a clone destination device are not modified. AO-23 If the tool logs any log significant information, the information is accurately recorded in the log file.

Test Case DA-14-ATA48 ILook IXimager Version 2.0, Feb 01 2006	
Tester Name:	brl
Test Host:	Paladin
Test Date:	Thu Apr 6 09:29:09 2006
Drives:	src(4C) dst (4D) other (4D-FU2)
Source Setup:	src hash: < 8FF620D2BEDCCAFE8412EDAAD56C8554F872EFBF > 390721968 total sectors (200049647616 bytes) 24320/254/63 (max cyl/hd values) 24321/255/63 (number of cyl/hd) IDE disk: Model (WDC WD2000JB-00KFA0) serial # (WD-WMAMR1031111) N Start LBA Length Start C/H/S End C/H/S boot Partition type 1 P 000000063 390700737 0000/001/01 1023/254/63 Boot 07 NTFS 2 P 000000000 000000000 0000/000/00 0000/000/00 00 empty entry 3 P 000000000 000000000 0000/000/00 0000/000/00 00 empty entry 4 P 000000000 000000000 0000/000/00 0000/000/00 00 empty entry 1 390700737 sectors 200038777344 bytes
Log Highlights:	Comparision of original to clone Sectors compared: 390721968 Sectors match: 390721968 Sectors differ: 0 Bytes differ: 0 Diffs range Source (390721968) has 97675200 fewer sectors than destination (488397168) Zero fill: 0 Src Byte fill (4C): 0 Dst Byte fill (4D): 97675200 Other fill: 0 Other no fill: 0 Zero fill range: Src fill range: Dst fill range: 390721968-488397167 Other fill range: Other not filled range: 0 source read errors, 0 destination read errors IXImager Log file hda: 488397168 sectors (250059 MB) w/8192KiB Cache, CHS=30401/255/63, UDMA(100) SCSI device sda: 781443888 512-byte hdwr sectors (400099 MB) Initializing... Opened output device '/dev/hda' Beginning Restore operation for 200049647616 bytes Beginning Restore operation Beginning Restore operation Opened input file '/ILookImager/ILook.011/DA06ATA484C002.asb' continuing at byte 1272381440 Restoring from /ILook.011/DA06ATA484C002.asb Opened input file '/ILookImager/ILook.011/DA06ATA484C003.asb' continuing at byte 22615228416 Restoring from /ILook.011/DA06ATA484C003.asb Opened input file '/ILookImager/ILook.011/DA06ATA484C004.asb' continuing at byte 50719096832 Restoring from /ILook.011/DA06ATA484C004.asb Opened input file '/ILookImager/ILook.011/DA06ATA484C005.asb' continuing at byte 78885093376 Restoring from /ILook.011/DA06ATA484C005.asb Opened input file '/ILookImager/ILook.011/DA06ATA484C006.asb' continuing at byte 107048337408 Restoring from /ILook.011/DA06ATA484C006.asb Opened input file '/ILookImager/ILook.011/DA06ATA484C007.asb' continuing at byte 135214202880 Restoring from /ILook.011/DA06ATA484C007.asb Opened input file '/ILookImager/ILook.011/DA06ATA484C008.asb' continuing at byte 163380002816 Restoring from /ILook.011/DA06ATA484C008.asb Opened input file '/ILookImager/ILook.011/DA06ATA484C009.asb' continuing at byte 191545737216 Restoring from /ILook.011/DA06ATA484C009.asb Restore Complete Restore was completed successfully.

Test Case DA-14-ATA48 ILook IXimager Version 2.0, Feb 01 2006		
	Read : 5.380 GB (5379859104 bytes) Written : 200.0 GB (200049647616 bytes) Total Processed: 200.0 GB (200049647616 bytes) Restore Speed : 38.54 MB/sec Elapsed Time : 1h 26m 31s Bad Sectors : 0 Clearing computer memory...	
Results:	Assertion & Expected Result	Actual Result
	AM-03 Execution environment is XE.	as expected
	AO-12 A clone is created from an image file.	as expected
	AO-13 Clone created using interface AI.	as expected
	AO-14 An unaligned clone is created.	as expected
	AO-17 Excess sectors are unchanged.	as expected
	AO-23 Logged information is correct.	as expected
Analysis:	Expected results achieved	

5.2.49 DA-14-CF

Test Case DA-14-CF ILook IXimager Version 2.0, Feb 01 2006	
Description:	DA-14 Create an unaligned clone from an image file.
Assertions:	AM-03 The tool executes in execution environment XE. AO-12 If requested, a clone is created from an image file. AO-13 A clone is created using access interface DST-AI to write to the clone device. AO-14 If an unaligned clone is created, each sector written to the clone is accurately written to the same disk address on the clone that the sector occupied on the digital source. AO-17 If requested, any excess sectors on a clone destination device are not modified. AO-23 If the tool logs any log significant information, the information is accurately recorded in the log file.
Tester Name:	brl
Test Host:	JohnSteed
Test Date:	Wed May 10 16:34:22 2006
Drives:	src(C1-CF) dst (C2-CF) other (4D-FU2)
Source Setup:	src hash: < 5B8235178DF99FA307430C088F81746606638A0B > 503808 total sectors (257949696 bytes) Removable media, no partition table.
Log Highlights:	Comparision of original to clone Sectors compared: 503808 Sectors match: 503808 Sectors differ: 0 Bytes differ: 0 Diffs range 0 source read errors, 0 destination read errors IXImager Log file hda: 156301488 sectors (80026 MB) w/8192KiB Cache, CHS=9729/255/63, UDMA(100) SCSI device sda: 503808 512-byte hdwr sectors (258 MB) SCSI device sdb: 781443888 512-byte hdwr sectors (400099 MB) SCSI device sda: 503808 512-byte hdwr sectors (258 MB) Initializing... Opened output device '/dev/sda' Beginning Restore operation for 257949696 bytes Beginning Restore operation Beginning Restore operation Restore Complete Restore was completed successfully. Read : 6.038 MB (6037753 bytes) Written : 257.9 MB (257949696 bytes) Total Processed: 257.9 MB (257949696 bytes)

	Restore Speed : 5.862 MB/sec Elapsed Time : 0h 0m 44s Bad Sectors : 0 Clearing computer memory...
Results:	

Assertion & Expected Result	Actual Result
AM-03 Execution environment is XE.	as expected
AO-12 A clone is created from an image file.	as expected
AO-13 Clone created using interface AI.	as expected
AO-14 An unaligned clone is created.	as expected
AO-17 Excess sectors are unchanged.	as expected
AO-23 Logged information is correct.	as expected

Analysis:	Expected results achieved

5.2.50 DA-14-ENCRYPTED

Test Case DA-14-ENCRYPTED ILook IXimager Version 2.0, Feb 01 2006

Description:	DA-14 Create an unaligned clone from an image file.
Assertions:	AM-03 The tool executes in execution environment XE. AO-12 If requested, a clone is created from an image file. AO-13 A clone is created using access interface DST-AI to write to the clone device. AO-14 If an unaligned clone is created, each sector written to the clone is accurately written to the same disk address on the clone that the sector occupied on the digital source. AO-17 If requested, any excess sectors on a clone destination device are not modified. AO-23 If the tool logs any log significant information, the information is accurately recorded in the log file.
Tester Name:	brl
Test Host:	Joe
Test Date:	Thu May 4 14:55:47 2006
Drives:	src(2A) dst(E6) other(4D-FU2)
Source Setup:	src hash: < F5F9F2903DCAB895F36E270FB22A722E27918125 > 17783249 total sectors (9105023488 bytes) Model (QM39100TD-SCA) serial # (PCB=20-116711-06 HDAQM39100TD-SCA) N Start LBA Length Start C/H/S End C/H/S boot Partition type 1 P 000000063 017751762 0000/001/01 1023/254/63 Boot 07 NTFS 2 P 000000000 000000000 0000/000/00 0000/000/00 00 empty entry 3 P 000000000 000000000 0000/000/00 0000/000/00 00 empty entry 4 P 000000000 000000000 0000/000/00 0000/000/00 00 empty entry 1 017751762 sectors 9088902144 bytes
Log Highlights:	Comparision of original to clone Sectors compared: 17783249 Sectors match: 17783249 Sectors differ: 0 Bytes differ: 0 Diffs range Source (17783249) has 18060421 fewer sectors than destination (35843670) Zero fill: 0 Src Byte fill (2A): 0 Dst Byte fill (E6): 18060421 Other fill: 0 Other no fill: 0 Zero fill range: Src fill range: Dst fill range: 17783249-35843669 Other fill range: Other not filled range: 0 source read errors, 0 destination read errors IXImager Log file SCSI device sdb: 17783249 512-byte hdwr sectors (9105 MB) SCSI device sdc: 35843670 512-byte hdwr sectors (18352 MB)

	Test Case DA-14-ENCRYPTED ILook IXimager Version 2.0, Feb 01 2006
	SCSI device sdd: 781443888 512-byte hdwr sectors (400099 MB) SCSI device sdc: 35843670 512-byte hdwr sectors (18352 MB) Initializing... Opened output device '/dev/sdc' Beginning Restore operation for 9105023488 bytes Beginning Restore operation Beginning Restore operation Restore Complete Restore was completed successfully. Read : 609.1 MB (609137424 bytes) Written : 9.105 GB (9105023488 bytes) Total Processed: 9.105 GB (9105023488 bytes) Restore Speed : 30.97 MB/sec Elapsed Time : 0h 4m 54s Bad Sectors : 0 Clearing computer memory...
Results:	<table><tr><th>Assertion & Expected Result</th><th>Actual Result</th></tr><tr><td>AM-03 Execution environment is XE.</td><td>as expected</td></tr><tr><td>AO-12 A clone is created from an image file.</td><td>as expected</td></tr><tr><td>AO-13 Clone created using interface AI.</td><td>as expected</td></tr><tr><td>AO-14 An unaligned clone is created.</td><td>as expected</td></tr><tr><td>AO-17 Excess sectors are unchanged.</td><td>as expected</td></tr><tr><td>AO-23 Logged information is correct.</td><td>as expected</td></tr></table>
Analysis:	Expected results achieved

5.2.51 DA-14-F12

	Test Case DA-14-F12 ILook IXimager Version 2.0, Feb 01 2006
Description:	DA-14 Create an unaligned clone from an image file.
Assertions:	AM-03 The tool executes in execution environment XE. AO-12 If requested, a clone is created from an image file. AO-13 A clone is created using access interface DST-AI to write to the clone device. AO-14 If an unaligned clone is created, each sector written to the clone is accurately written to the same disk address on the clone that the sector occupied on the digital source. AO-17 If requested, any excess sectors on a clone destination device are not modified. AO-23 If the tool logs any log significant information, the information is accurately recorded in the log file.
Tester Name:	brl
Test Host:	Joe
Test Date:	Mon Apr 24 14:28:18 2006
Drives:	src(43) dst (2F) other (4D-FU2)
Source Setup:	src hash: < 888E2E7F7AD237DC7A732281DD93F325065E5871 > 78125000 total sectors (40000000000 bytes) Model (0BB-75JHC0) serial # (WD-WMAMC46588) N Start LBA Length Start C/H/S End C/H/S boot Partition type 1 P 000000063 020980827 0000/001/01 1023/254/63 0C Fat32X 2 X 020980890 057143205 1023/000/01 1023/254/63 0F extended 3 S 000000063 000032067 1023/001/01 1023/254/63 01 Fat12 4 x 000032130 002104515 1023/000/01 1023/254/63 05 extended 5 S 000000063 002104452 1023/001/01 1023/254/63 06 Fat16 6 x 002136645 004192965 1023/000/01 1023/254/63 05 extended 7 S 000000063 004192902 1023/001/01 1023/254/63 16 other 8 x 006329610 008401995 1023/000/01 1023/254/63 05 extended 9 S 000000063 008401932 1023/001/01 1023/254/63 0B Fat32 10 x 014731605 010490445 1023/000/01 1023/254/63 05 extended 11 S 000000063 010490382 1023/001/01 1023/254/63 83 Linux 12 x 025222050 004209030 1023/000/01 1023/254/63 05 extended 13 S 000000063 004208967 1023/001/01 1023/254/63 82 Linux swap 14 x 029431080 027712125 1023/000/01 1023/254/63 05 extended 15 S 000000063 027712062 1023/001/01 1023/254/63 07 NTFS 16 S 000000000 000000000 0000/000/00 0000/000/00 00 empty entry

Test Case DA-14-F12 ILook IXimager Version 2.0, Feb 01 2006	
	17 P 000000000 000000000 0000/000/00 0000/000/00 00 empty entry 18 P 000000000 000000000 0000/000/00 0000/000/00 00 empty entry 1 020980827 sectors 10742183424 bytes 3 000032067 sectors 16418304 bytes 5 002104452 sectors 1077479424 bytes 7 004192902 sectors 2146765824 bytes 9 008401932 sectors 4301789184 bytes 11 010490382 sectors 5371075584 bytes 13 004208967 sectors 2154991104 bytes 15 027712062 sectors 14188575744 bytes
Log Highlights:	IXImager Log file SCSI device sdb: 17783249 512-byte hdwr sectors (9105 MB) SCSI device sdc: 78125000 512-byte hdwr sectors (40000 MB) SCSI device sdd: 781443888 512-byte hdwr sectors (400099 MB) SCSI device sdb: 17783249 512-byte hdwr sectors (9105 MB) Initializing... Opened output device '/dev/sdb' Beginning Restore operation for 16418304 bytes Beginning Restore operation Beginning Restore operation Restore Complete Restore was completed successfully. Read : 593.0 kB (593021 bytes) Written : 16.42 MB (16418304 bytes) Total Processed : 16.42 MB (16418304 bytes) Restore Speed : 8.209 MB/sec Elapsed Time : 0h 0m 2s Bad Sectors : 0 Clearing computer memory... Hashes of src and dst partitions Src SHA1 Hash: 6853B517F50BF3CCADED3DB5FEAE08C18C62FCA0 - Dst SHA1 Hash: 6853B517F50BF3CCADED3DB5FEAE08C18C62FCA0 -
Results:	

Assertion & Expected Result	Actual Result
AM-03 Execution environment is XE.	as expected
AO-12 A clone is created from an image file.	as expected
AO-13 Clone created using interface AI.	as expected
AO-14 An unaligned clone is created.	as expected
AO-17 Excess sectors are unchanged.	as expected
AO-23 Logged information is correct.	as expected

Analysis:	Expected results achieved

5.2.52 DA-14-F16

Test Case DA-14-F16 ILook IXimager Version 2.0, Feb 01 2006	
Description:	DA-14 Create an unaligned clone from an image file.
Assertions:	AM-03 The tool executes in execution environment XE. AO-12 If requested, a clone is created from an image file. AO-13 A clone is created using access interface DST-AI to write to the clone device. AO-14 If an unaligned clone is created, each sector written to the clone is accurately written to the same disk address on the clone that the sector occupied on the digital source. AO-17 If requested, any excess sectors on a clone destination device are not modified. AO-23 If the tool logs any log significant information, the information is accurately recorded in the log file.
Tester Name:	brl
Test Host:	Max
Test Date:	Mon Apr 24 16:31:24 2006
Drives:	src(44) dst (2C) other (4D-FU2)
Source	src hash: < E196D36E7B322C0EF83923112AD1800581742B6E >

Test Case DA-14-F16 ILook IXimager Version 2.0, Feb 01 2006	
Setup:	78165360 total sectors (40020664320 bytes) 65534/015/63 (max cyl/hd values) 65535/016/63 (number of cyl/hd) IDE disk: Model (WDC WD400JB-00FMA0) serial # (WD-WMAJC1011319) N Start LBA Length Start C/H/S End C/H/S boot Partition type 1 P 000000063 020980827 0000/001/01 1023/254/63 0C Fat32X 2 X 020980890 057175335 1023/000/01 1023/254/63 0F extended 3 S 000000063 000032067 1023/001/01 1023/254/63 01 Fat12 4 x 000032130 002104515 1023/000/01 1023/254/63 05 extended 5 S 000000063 002104452 1023/001/01 1023/254/63 06 Fat16 6 x 002136645 004192965 1023/000/01 1023/254/63 05 extended 7 S 000000063 004192902 1023/001/01 1023/254/63 16 other 8 x 006329610 008401995 1023/000/01 1023/254/63 05 extended 9 S 000000063 008401932 1023/001/01 1023/254/63 0B Fat32 10 x 014731605 010490445 1023/000/01 1023/254/63 05 extended 11 S 000000063 010490382 1023/001/01 1023/254/63 83 Linux 12 x 025222050 004209030 1023/000/01 1023/254/63 05 extended 13 S 000000063 004208967 1023/001/01 1023/254/63 82 Linux swap 14 x 029431080 027744255 1023/000/01 1023/254/63 05 extended 15 S 000000063 027744192 1023/001/01 1023/254/63 07 NTFS 16 S 000000000 000000000 0000/000/00 0000/000/00 00 empty entry 17 P 000000000 000000000 0000/000/00 0000/000/00 00 empty entry 18 P 000000000 000000000 0000/000/00 0000/000/00 00 empty entry 1 020980827 sectors 10742183424 bytes 3 000032067 sectors 16418304 bytes 5 002104452 sectors 1077479424 bytes 7 004192902 sectors 2146765824 bytes 9 008401932 sectors 4301789184 bytes 11 010490382 sectors 5371075584 bytes 13 004208967 sectors 2154991104 bytes 15 027744192 sectors 14205026304 bytes
Log Highlights:	IXImager Log file SCSI device sdb: 17783249 512-byte hdwr sectors (9105 MB) SCSI device sdc: 78165360 512-byte hdwr sectors (40021 MB) SCSI device sdd: 781443888 512-byte hdwr sectors (400099 MB) SCSI device sdb: 17783249 512-byte hdwr sectors (9105 MB) Initializing... Opened output device '/dev/sdb' Beginning Restore operation for 1077479424 bytes Beginning Restore operation Beginning Restore operation Restore Complete Restore was completed successfully. Read : 24.93 MB (24932422 bytes) Written : 1.077 GB (1077479424 bytes) Total Processed: 1.077 GB (1077479424 bytes) Restore Speed : 13.30 MB/sec Elapsed Time : 0h 1m 21s Bad Sectors : 0 Clearing computer memory... Hashes of src and dst partitions Src SHA1 Hash: F26795072562849A38BB46C94AA54B7D1CA65660 - Dst SHA1 Hash: F26795072562849A38BB46C94AA54B7D1CA65660 -
Results:	

Assertion & Expected Result	Actual Result
AM-03 Execution environment is XE.	as expected
AO-12 A clone is created from an image file.	as expected
AO-13 Clone created using interface AI.	as expected
AO-14 An unaligned clone is created.	as expected
AO-17 Excess sectors are unchanged.	as expected
AO-23 Logged information is correct.	as expected

Analysis:	Expected results achieved

5.2.53 DA-14-F32

Test Case DA-14-F32 ILook IXimager Version 2.0, Feb 01 2006	
Description:	DA-14 Create an unaligned clone from an image file.
Assertions:	AM-03 The tool executes in execution environment XE. AO-12 If requested, a clone is created from an image file. AO-13 A clone is created using access interface DST-AI to write to the clone device. AO-14 If an unaligned clone is created, each sector written to the clone is accurately written to the same disk address on the clone that the sector occupied on the digital source. AO-17 If requested, any excess sectors on a clone destination device are not modified. AO-23 If the tool logs any log significant information, the information is accurately recorded in the log file.
Tester Name:	brl
Test Host:	Joe
Test Date:	Mon Apr 24 17:04:40 2006
Drives:	src(43) dst (2F) other (4D-FU2)
Source Setup:	src hash: < 888E2E7F7AD237DC7A732281DD93F325065E5871 > 78125000 total sectors (40000000000 bytes) Model (0BB-75JHC0) serial # (WD-WMAMC46588) N Start LBA Length Start C/H/S End C/H/S boot Partition type 1 P 000000063 020980827 0000/001/01 1023/254/63 0C Fat32X 2 X 020980890 057143205 1023/000/01 1023/254/63 0F extended 3 S 000000063 000032067 1023/001/01 1023/254/63 01 Fat12 4 x 000032130 002104515 1023/000/01 1023/254/63 05 extended 5 S 000000063 002104452 1023/001/01 1023/254/63 06 Fat16 6 x 002136645 004192965 1023/000/01 1023/254/63 05 extended 7 S 000000063 004192902 1023/001/01 1023/254/63 16 other 8 x 006329610 008401995 1023/000/01 1023/254/63 05 extended 9 S 000000063 008401932 1023/001/01 1023/254/63 0B Fat32 10 x 014731605 010490445 1023/000/01 1023/254/63 05 extended 11 S 000000063 010490382 1023/001/01 1023/254/63 83 Linux 12 x 025222050 004209030 1023/000/01 1023/254/63 05 extended 13 S 000000063 004208967 1023/001/01 1023/254/63 82 Linux swap 14 x 029431080 027712125 1023/000/01 1023/254/63 05 extended 15 S 000000063 027712062 1023/001/01 1023/254/63 07 NTFS 16 S 000000000 000000000 0000/000/00 0000/000/00 00 empty entry 17 P 000000000 000000000 0000/000/00 0000/000/00 00 empty entry 18 P 000000000 000000000 0000/000/00 0000/000/00 00 empty entry 1 020980827 sectors 10742183424 bytes 3 000032067 sectors 16418304 bytes 5 002104452 sectors 1077479424 bytes 7 004192902 sectors 2146765824 bytes 9 008401932 sectors 4301789184 bytes 11 010490382 sectors 5371075584 bytes 13 004208967 sectors 2154991104 bytes 15 027712062 sectors 14188575744 bytes
Log Highlights:	IXImager Log file SCSI device sdb: 17783249 512-byte hdwr sectors (9105 MB) SCSI device sdc: 78125000 512-byte hdwr sectors (40000 MB) SCSI device sdd: 781443888 512-byte hdwr sectors (400099 MB) SCSI device sdb: 17783249 512-byte hdwr sectors (9105 MB) Initializing... Opened output device '/dev/sdb' Beginning Restore operation for 4301789184 bytes Beginning Restore operation Beginning Restore operation Restore Complete Restore was completed successfully. Read : 98.98 MB (98984710 bytes) Written : 4.302 GB (4301789184 bytes) Total Processed: 4.302 GB (4301789184 bytes) Restore Speed : 13.04 MB/sec Elapsed Time : 0h 5m 30s Bad Sectors : 0 Clearing computer memory...

Test Case DA-14-F32 ILook IXimager Version 2.0, Feb 01 2006		
Results:	Hashes of src and dst partitions Src SHA1 Hash: 72462489BCF79A98B59B6A8CD938FEB46FA2A781 - Dst SHA1 Hash: 72462489BCF79A98B59B6A8CD938FEB46FA2A781 -	
	Assertion & Expected Result	Actual Result
	AM-03 Execution environment is XE.	as expected
	AO-12 A clone is created from an image file.	as expected
	AO-13 Clone created using interface AI.	as expected
	AO-14 An unaligned clone is created.	as expected
	AO-17 Excess sectors are unchanged.	as expected
	AO-23 Logged information is correct.	as expected
Analysis:	Expected results achieved	

5.2.54   DA-14-F32X

Test Case DA-14-F32X ILook IXimager Version 2.0, Feb 01 2006	
Description:	DA-14 Create an unaligned clone from an image file.
Assertions:	AM-03 The tool executes in execution environment XE. AO-12 If requested, a clone is created from an image file. AO-13 A clone is created using access interface DST-AI to write to the clone device. AO-14 If an unaligned clone is created, each sector written to the clone is accurately written to the same disk address on the clone that the sector occupied on the digital source. AO-17 If requested, any excess sectors on a clone destination device are not modified. AO-23 If the tool logs any log significant information, the information is accurately recorded in the log file.
Tester Name:	brl
Test Host:	Max
Test Date:	Mon Apr 24 14:19:41 2006
Drives:	src(44) dst (E6) other (4D-FU2)
Source Setup:	src hash: < E196D36E7B322C0EF83923112AD1800581742B6E > 78165360 total sectors (40020664320 bytes) 65534/015/63 (max cyl/hd values) 65535/016/63 (number of cyl/hd) IDE disk: Model (WDC WD400JB-00FMA0) serial # (WD-WMAJC1011319) N Start LBA Length Start C/H/S End C/H/S boot Partition type 1 P 000000063 020980827 0000/001/01 1023/254/63 0C Fat32X 2 X 020980890 057175335 1023/000/01 1023/254/63 0F extended 3 S 000000063 000032067 1023/001/01 1023/254/63 01 Fat12 4 x 000032130 002104515 1023/000/01 1023/254/63 05 extended 5 S 000000063 002104452 1023/001/01 1023/254/63 06 Fat16 6 x 002136645 004192965 1023/000/01 1023/254/63 05 extended 7 S 000000063 004192902 1023/001/01 1023/254/63 16 other 8 x 006329610 008401995 1023/000/01 1023/254/63 05 extended 9 S 000000063 008401932 1023/001/01 1023/254/63 0B Fat32 10 x 014731605 010490445 1023/000/01 1023/254/63 05 extended 11 S 000000063 010490382 1023/001/01 1023/254/63 83 Linux 12 x 025222050 004209030 1023/000/01 1023/254/63 05 extended 13 S 000000063 004208967 1023/001/01 1023/254/63 82 Linux swap 14 x 029431080 027744255 1023/000/01 1023/254/63 05 extended 15 S 000000063 027744192 1023/001/01 1023/254/63 07 NTFS 16 S 000000000 000000000 0000/000/00 0000/000/00 00 empty entry 17 P 000000000 000000000 0000/000/00 0000/000/00 00 empty entry 18 P 000000000 000000000 0000/000/00 0000/000/00 00 empty entry 1 020980827 sectors 10742183424 bytes 3 000032067 sectors 16418304 bytes 5 002104452 sectors 1077479424 bytes 7 004192902 sectors 2146765824 bytes 9 008401932 sectors 4301789184 bytes 11 010490382 sectors 5371075584 bytes 13 004208967 sectors 2154991104 bytes 15 027744192 sectors 14205026304 bytes

Test Case DA-14-F32X ILook IXimager Version 2.0, Feb 01 2006	
Log Highlights:	IXImager Log file SCSI device sdb: 35843670 512-byte hdwr sectors (18352 MB) SCSI device sdc: 78165360 512-byte hdwr sectors (40021 MB) SCSI device sdd: 781443888 512-byte hdwr sectors (400099 MB) SCSI device sdb: 35843670 512-byte hdwr sectors (18352 MB) Initializing... Opened output device '/dev/sdb' Beginning Restore operation for 10742183424 bytes Beginning Restore operation Beginning Restore operation Restore Complete Restore was completed successfully. Read : 247.0 MB (247043065 bytes) Written : 10.74 GB (10742183424 bytes) Total Processed : 10.74 GB (10742183424 bytes) Restore Speed : 31.59 MB/sec Elapsed Time : 0h 5m 40s Bad Sectors : 0 Clearing computer memory... Hashes of src and dst partitions Src SHA1 Hash: D190A47B60A17FE6912CA26BE237E923AD592FAE - Dst SHA1 Hash: D190A47B60A17FE6912CA26BE237E923AD592FAE -
Results:	

Assertion & Expected Result	Actual Result
AM-03 Execution environment is XE.	as expected
AO-12 A clone is created from an image file.	as expected
AO-13 Clone created using interface AI.	as expected
AO-14 An unaligned clone is created.	as expected
AO-17 Excess sectors are unchanged.	as expected
AO-23 Logged information is correct.	as expected

Analysis:	Expected results achieved

5.2.55 DA-14-FIREWIRE

Test Case DA-14-FIREWIRE ILook IXimager Version 2.0, Feb 01 2006	
Description:	DA-14 Create an unaligned clone from an image file.
Assertions:	AM-03 The tool executes in execution environment XE. AO-12 If requested, a clone is created from an image file. AO-13 A clone is created using access interface DST-AI to write to the clone device. AO-14 If an unaligned clone is created, each sector written to the clone is accurately written to the same disk address on the clone that the sector occupied on the digital source. AO-17 If requested, any excess sectors on a clone destination device are not modified. AO-23 If the tool logs any log significant information, the information is accurately recorded in the log file.
Tester Name:	brl
Test Host:	JohnSteed
Test Date:	Tue Apr 4 13:45:04 2006
Drives:	src(83-FU2) dst (84-FU2) other (4D-FU2)
Source Setup:	src hash: < 9B0D0FEA3023476FA5D24436C0CEFCB585EB8695 > 160836480 total sectors (82348277760 bytes) 10010/254/63 (max cyl/hd values) 10011/255/63 (number of cyl/hd) Model (HDS722580VLAT20) serial # ()
Log Highlights:	Comparision of original to clone Sectors compared: 160836480 Sectors match: 160836480 Sectors differ: 0 Bytes differ: 0

	Test Case DA-14-FIREWIRE ILook IXimager Version 2.0, Feb 01 2006
	Diffs range 0 source read errors, 0 destination read errors IXImager Log file hda: 156301488 sectors (80026 MB) w/8192KiB Cache, CHS=9729/255/63, UDMA(100) SCSI device sda: 160836480 512-byte hdwr sectors (82348 MB) SCSI device sdb: 781443888 512-byte hdwr sectors (400099 MB) SCSI device sda: 160836480 512-byte hdwr sectors (82348 MB) Initializing... Opened output device '/dev/sda' Beginning Restore operation for 82348277760 bytes Beginning Restore operation Beginning Restore operation Opened input file '/ILookImager/ILook.009/DA06FIREWIRE002.asb' continuing at byte 28172419072 Restoring from /ILook.009/DA06FIREWIRE002.asb Opened input file '/ILookImager/ILook.009/DA06FIREWIRE003.asb' continuing at byte 56340840448 Restoring from /ILook.009/DA06FIREWIRE003.asb Restore Complete Restore was completed successfully. Read : 1.894 GB (1894487827 bytes) Written : 82.35 GB (82348277760 bytes) Total Processed: 82.35 GB (82348277760 bytes) Restore Speed : 20.92 MB/sec Elapsed Time : 1h 5m 37s Bad Sectors : 0 Clearing computer memory...
Results:	<table><tr><th>Assertion & Expected Result</th><th>Actual Result</th></tr><tr><td>AM-03 Execution environment is XE.</td><td>as expected</td></tr><tr><td>AO-12 A clone is created from an image file.</td><td>as expected</td></tr><tr><td>AO-13 Clone created using interface AI.</td><td>as expected</td></tr><tr><td>AO-14 An unaligned clone is created.</td><td>as expected</td></tr><tr><td>AO-17 Excess sectors are unchanged.</td><td>as expected</td></tr><tr><td>AO-23 Logged information is correct.</td><td>as expected</td></tr></table>
Analysis:	Expected results achieved

5.2.56 DA-14-FLOPPY

	Test Case DA-14-FLOPPY ILook IXimager Version 2.0, Feb 01 2006
Description:	DA-14 Create an unaligned clone from an image file.
Assertions:	AM-03 The tool executes in execution environment XE. AO-12 If requested, a clone is created from an image file. AO-13 A clone is created using access interface DST-AI to write to the clone device. AO-14 If an unaligned clone is created, each sector written to the clone is accurately written to the same disk address on the clone that the sector occupied on the digital source. AO-17 If requested, any excess sectors on a clone destination device are not modified. AO-23 If the tool logs any log significant information, the information is accurately recorded in the log file.
Tester Name:	brl
Test Host:	JohnSteed
Test Date:	Wed May 3 13:47:57 2006
Drives:	src(floppy) dst (destination-floppy) other (4D-FU2)
Source Setup:	src hash: < E2863334AC7EAABC7C8A0D62EB0D3B3AF29F2C40 > Floppy disk
Log Highlights:	IXImager Log file hda: 156301488 sectors (80026 MB) w/8192KiB Cache, CHS=9729/255/63, UDMA(100) SCSI device sda: 781443888 512-byte hdwr sectors (400099 MB)

	Test Case DA-14-FLOPPY ILook IXimager Version 2.0, Feb 01 2006
	Initializing... Checking ILook IXimager file header... Opened output device '/dev/fd0' Beginning Restore operation for 1474560 bytes Beginning Restore operation Beginning Restore operation Restore Complete Restore was completed successfully. Read : 141.8 kB (141815 bytes) Written : 1.475 MB (1474560 bytes) Total Processed: 1.475 MB (1474560 bytes) Restore Speed : 27.82 kB/sec Elapsed Time : 0h 0m 53s Bad Sectors : 0 Clearing computer memory... Source SHA1 Hash: E2863334AC7EAABC7C8A0D62EB0D3B3AF29F2C40
Results:	<table><tr><th>Assertion & Expected Result</th><th>Actual Result</th></tr><tr><td>AM-03 Execution environment is XE.</td><td>as expected</td></tr><tr><td>AO-12 A clone is created from an image file.</td><td>as expected</td></tr><tr><td>AO-13 Clone created using interface AI.</td><td>as expected</td></tr><tr><td>AO-14 An unaligned clone is created.</td><td>as expected</td></tr><tr><td>AO-17 Excess sectors are unchanged.</td><td>as expected</td></tr><tr><td>AO-23 Logged information is correct.</td><td>as expected</td></tr></table>
Analysis:	Expected results achieved

5.2.57 DA-14-HIDDEN

	Test Case DA-14-HIDDEN ILook IXimager Version 2.0, Feb 01 2006
Description:	DA-14 Create an unaligned clone from an image file.
Assertions:	AM-03 The tool executes in execution environment XE. AO-12 If requested, a clone is created from an image file. AO-13 A clone is created using access interface DST-AI to write to the clone device. AO-14 If an unaligned clone is created, each sector written to the clone is accurately written to the same disk address on the clone that the sector occupied on the digital source. AO-17 If requested, any excess sectors on a clone destination device are not modified. AO-23 If the tool logs any log significant information, the information is accurately recorded in the log file.
Tester Name:	brl
Test Host:	Max
Test Date:	Mon Apr 24 17:25:31 2006
Drives:	src(44) dst (2C) other (4D-FU2)
Source Setup:	src hash: < E196D36E7B322C0EF83923112AD1800581742B6E > 78165360 total sectors (40020664320 bytes) 65534/015/63 (max cyl/hd values) 65535/016/63 (number of cyl/hd) IDE disk: Model (WDC WD400JB-00FMA0) serial # (WD-WMAJC1011319) N Start LBA Length Start C/H/S End C/H/S boot Partition type 1 P 000000063 020980827 0000/001/01 1023/254/63 0C Fat32X 2 X 020980890 057175335 1023/000/01 1023/254/63 0F extended 3 S 000000063 000032067 1023/001/01 1023/254/63 01 Fat12 4 x 000032130 002104515 1023/000/01 1023/254/63 05 extended 5 S 000000063 002104452 1023/001/01 1023/254/63 06 Fat16 6 x 002136645 004192965 1023/000/01 1023/254/63 05 extended 7 S 000000063 004192902 1023/001/01 1023/254/63 16 other 8 x 006329610 008401995 1023/000/01 1023/254/63 05 extended 9 S 000000063 008401932 1023/001/01 1023/254/63 0B Fat32 10 x 014731605 010490445 1023/000/01 1023/254/63 05 extended 11 S 000000063 010490382 1023/001/01 1023/254/63 83 Linux 12 x 025222050 004209030 1023/000/01 1023/254/63 05 extended 13 S 000000063 004208967 1023/001/01 1023/254/63 82 Linux swap

Test Case DA-14-HIDDEN ILook IXimager Version 2.0, Feb 01 2006	
| | ```
14 x 029431080 027744255 1023/000/01 1023/254/63   05 extended
15 S 000000063 027744192 1023/001/01 1023/254/63   07 NTFS
16 S 000000000 000000000 0000/000/00 0000/000/00   00 empty entry
17 P 000000000 000000000 0000/000/00 0000/000/00   00 empty entry
18 P 000000000 000000000 0000/000/00 0000/000/00   00 empty entry
 1 020980827 sectors 10742183424 bytes
 3 000032067 sectors 16418304 bytes
 5 002104452 sectors 1077479424 bytes
 7 004192902 sectors 2146765824 bytes
 9 008401932 sectors 4301789184 bytes
11 010490382 sectors 5371075584 bytes
13 004208967 sectors 2154991104 bytes
15 027744192 sectors 14205026304 bytes
``` |
| Log Highlights: | ```
IXImager Log file
SCSI device sdb: 17783249 512-byte hdwr sectors (9105 MB)
SCSI device sdc: 78165360 512-byte hdwr sectors (40021 MB)
SCSI device sdd: 781443888 512-byte hdwr sectors (400099 MB)
SCSI device sdb: 17783249 512-byte hdwr sectors (9105 MB)
Initializing...
Opened output device '/dev/sdb'
Beginning Restore operation for 2146765824 bytes
Beginning Restore operation
Beginning Restore operation
Restore Complete
Restore was completed successfully.

Read            : 49.54 MB (49537184 bytes)
Written         : 2.147 GB (2146765824 bytes)
Total Processed : 2.147 GB (2146765824 bytes)
Restore Speed   : 13.25 MB/sec
Elapsed Time    : 0h  2m 42s
Bad Sectors     : 0
Clearing computer memory...

Hashes of src and dst partitions
Src SHA1 Hash: 0893C80EDC0E9074FD139B67FB6DE3CE9390C550  -
Dst SHA1 Hash: 0893C80EDC0E9074FD139B67FB6DE3CE9390C550  -
``` |
| Results: | |

Assertion & Expected Result	Actual Result
AM-03 Execution environment is XE.	as expected
AO-12 A clone is created from an image file.	as expected
AO-13 Clone created using interface AI.	as expected
AO-14 An unaligned clone is created.	as expected
AO-17 Excess sectors are unchanged.	as expected
AO-23 Logged information is correct.	as expected

Analysis:	Expected results achieved

5.2.58 DA-14-HOT

Test Case DA-14-HOT ILook IXimager Version 2.0, Feb 01 2006	
Description:	DA-14 Create an unaligned clone from an image file.
Assertions:	AM-03 The tool executes in execution environment XE. AO-12 If requested, a clone is created from an image file. AO-13 A clone is created using access interface DST-AI to write to the clone device. AO-14 If an unaligned clone is created, each sector written to the clone is accurately written to the same disk address on the clone that the sector occupied on the digital source. AO-17 If requested, any excess sectors on a clone destination device are not modified. AO-23 If the tool logs any log significant information, the information is accurately recorded in the log file.
Tester Name:	brl
Test Host:	Joe

Test Case DA-14-HOT ILook IXimager Version 2.0, Feb 01 2006	
Test Date:	Wed May 10 13:05:37 2006
Drives:	src(07) dst (17) other (8F-FU2+8D-FU2)
Source Setup:	src hash: < 655E9BDDB36A3F9C5C4CC8BF32B8C5B41AF9F52E> 156301488 total sectors (80026361856 bytes) Model (WDC WD800JD-32HK) serial # (WD-WMAJ91510044) N Start LBA Length Start C/H/S End C/H/S boot Partition type 1 P 000000063 156280257 0000/001/01 1023/254/63 Boot 07 NTFS 2 P 000000000 000000000 0000/000/00 0000/000/00 00 empty entry 3 P 000000000 000000000 0000/000/00 0000/000/00 00 empty entry 4 P 000000000 000000000 0000/000/00 0000/000/00 00 empty entry 1 156280257 sectors 80015491584 bytes
Log Highlights:	Comparision of original to clone Sectors compared: 156301488 Sectors match: 156301488 Sectors differ: 0 Bytes differ: 0 Diffs range Source (156301488) has 78140160 fewer sectors than destination (234441648) Zero fill: 0 Src Byte fill (07): 0 Dst Byte fill (17): 78140160 Other fill: 0 Other no fill: 0 Zero fill range: Src fill range: Dst fill range: 156301488-234441647 Other fill range: Other not filled range: 0 source read errors, 0 destination read errors IXImager Log file ata1: dev 0 ATA-6, max UDMA/100, 234441648 sectors: LBA48 SCSI device sdb: 234441648 512-byte hdwr sectors (120034 MB) SCSI device sdc: 78140160 512-byte hdwr sectors (40008 MB) SCSI device sdd: 781422768 512-byte hdwr sectors (400088 MB) SCSI device sdb: 234441648 512-byte hdwr sectors (120034 MB) Initializing... Opened output device '/dev/sdb' Beginning Restore operation for 80026361856 bytes Beginning Restore operation Beginning Restore operation Opened input file '/ILookImager/ILook.001/DA13002.asb' continuing at byte 1285554176 Restoring from /ILook.001/DA13002.asb Opened input file '/ILookImager/ILook.001/DA13003.asb' continuing at byte 22492741632 Restoring from /ILook.001/DA13003.asb Searching for files. Please wait... Scanning for devices. Please wait... User entered the Select Next Input Device Menu Please wait while I check for media... Checking source device... User selected device '/dev/sdd' for input Restoring from /dev/sdd1 A 400.1 GB Win95 FAT32 (LBA) Partition on Firewire0,1 Restoring to /dev/sdb A 120.0 GB WDC WD1200JD-00G Hard Drive Searching for files. Please wait... User entered the Select Image menu User selected 'ILook.003' User exited the Select Image Menu Opened input file '/ILookImager/ILook.003/DA13004.asb' continuing at byte 50655920128 Restoring from /ILook.003/DA13004.asb Opened input file '/ILookImager/ILook.003/DA13005.asb' continuing at byte 78820933632 Restoring from /ILook.003/DA13005.asb Restore Complete Restore was completed successfully. Read : 2.620 GB (2619912273 bytes)

	Test Case DA-14-HOT ILook IXimager Version 2.0, Feb 01 2006
	Written : 80.03 GB (80026361856 bytes) Total Processed: 80.03 GB (80026361856 bytes) Restore Speed : 21.25 MB/sec Elapsed Time : 1h 2m 46s Bad Sectors : 0 Clearing computer memory...
Results:	

Assertion & Expected Result	Actual Result
AM-03 Execution environment is XE.	as expected
AO-12 A clone is created from an image file.	as expected
AO-13 Clone created using interface AI.	as expected
AO-14 An unaligned clone is created.	as expected
AO-17 Excess sectors are unchanged.	as expected
AO-23 Logged information is correct.	as expected

Analysis:	Expected results achieved

5.2.59   DA-14-NT

	Test Case DA-14-NT ILook IXimager Version 2.0, Feb 01 2006
Description:	DA-14 Create an unaligned clone from an image file.
Assertions:	AM-03 The tool executes in execution environment XE. AO-12 If requested, a clone is created from an image file. AO-13 A clone is created using access interface DST-AI to write to the clone device. AO-14 If an unaligned clone is created, each sector written to the clone is accurately written to the same disk address on the clone that the sector occupied on the digital source. AO-17 If requested, any excess sectors on a clone destination device are not modified. AO-23 If the tool logs any log significant information, the information is accurately recorded in the log file.
Tester Name:	brl
Test Host:	Joe
Test Date:	Tue Apr 25 09:42:25 2006
Drives:	src(43) dst (E6) other (4D-FU2)

Source Setup:	src hash: < 888E2E7F7AD237DC7A732281DD93F325065E5871 >
	78125000 total sectors (40000000000 bytes)
	Model (0BB-75JHC0) serial # (WD-WMAMC46588)
	  N Start LBA Length Start C/H/S End C/H/S boot Partition type
	  1 P 000000063 020980827 0000/001/01 1023/254/63 0C Fat32X
	  2 X 020980890 057143205 1023/000/01 1023/254/63 0F extended
	  3 S 000000063 000032067 1023/001/01 1023/254/63 01 Fat12
	  4 x 000032130 002104515 1023/000/01 1023/254/63 05 extended
	  5 S 000000063 002104452 1023/001/01 1023/254/63 06 Fat16
	  6 x 002136645 004192965 1023/000/01 1023/254/63 05 extended
	  7 S 000000063 004192902 1023/001/01 1023/254/63 16 other
	  8 x 006329610 008401995 1023/000/01 1023/254/63 05 extended
	  9 S 000000063 008401932 1023/001/01 1023/254/63 0B Fat32
	 10 x 014731605 010490445 1023/000/01 1023/254/63 05 extended
	 11 S 000000063 010490382 1023/001/01 1023/254/63 83 Linux
	 12 x 025222050 004209030 1023/000/01 1023/254/63 05 extended
	 13 S 000000063 004208967 1023/001/01 1023/254/63 82 Linux swap
	 14 x 029431080 027712125 1023/000/01 1023/254/63 05 extended
	 15 S 000000063 027712062 1023/001/01 1023/254/63 07 NTFS
	 16 S 000000000 000000000 0000/000/00 0000/000/00 00 empty entry
	 17 P 000000000 000000000 0000/000/00 0000/000/00 00 empty entry
	 18 P 000000000 000000000 0000/000/00 0000/000/00 00 empty entry
	  1 020980827 sectors 10742183424 bytes
	  3 000032067 sectors 16418304 bytes
	  5 002104452 sectors 1077479424 bytes
	  7 004192902 sectors 2146765824 bytes
	  9 008401932 sectors 4301789184 bytes
	 11 010490382 sectors 5371075584 bytes
	 13 004208967 sectors 2154991104 bytes
	 15 027712062 sectors 14188575744 bytes

Test Case DA-14-NT ILook IXimager Version 2.0, Feb 01 2006	
Log Highlights:	IXImager Log file SCSI device sdb: 35843670 512-byte hdwr sectors (18352 MB) SCSI device sdc: 78125000 512-byte hdwr sectors (40000 MB) SCSI device sdd: 781443888 512-byte hdwr sectors (400099 MB) SCSI device sdb: 35843670 512-byte hdwr sectors (18352 MB) Initializing... Opened output device '/dev/sdb' Beginning Restore operation for 14188575744 bytes Beginning Restore operation Beginning Restore operation Restore Complete Restore was completed successfully. Read : 324.5 MB (324528081 bytes) Written : 14.19 GB (14188575744 bytes) Total Processed: 14.19 GB (14188575744 bytes) Restore Speed : 31.88 MB/sec Elapsed Time : 0h 7m 25s Bad Sectors : 0 Clearing computer memory... Hashes of src and dst partitions Src SHA1 Hash: 73EB2D27564B060DB796EFB78694A10E6B43D23F - Dst SHA1 Hash: 73EB2D27564B060DB796EFB78694A10E6B43D23F -
Results:	<table><tr><th>Assertion & Expected Result</th><th>Actual Result</th></tr><tr><td>AM-03 Execution environment is XE.</td><td>as expected</td></tr><tr><td>AO-12 A clone is created from an image file.</td><td>as expected</td></tr><tr><td>AO-13 Clone created using interface AI.</td><td>as expected</td></tr><tr><td>AO-14 An unaligned clone is created.</td><td>as expected</td></tr><tr><td>AO-17 Excess sectors are unchanged.</td><td>as expected</td></tr><tr><td>AO-23 Logged information is correct.</td><td>as expected</td></tr></table>
Analysis:	Expected results achieved

5.2.60 DA-14-RAW

Test Case DA-14-RAW ILook IXimager Version 2.0, Feb 01 2006	
Description:	DA-14 Create an unaligned clone from an image file.
Assertions:	AM-03 The tool executes in execution environment XE. AO-12 If requested, a clone is created from an image file. AO-13 A clone is created using access interface DST-AI to write to the clone device. AO-14 If an unaligned clone is created, each sector written to the clone is accurately written to the same disk address on the clone that the sector occupied on the digital source. AO-17 If requested, any excess sectors on a clone destination device are not modified. AO-23 If the tool logs any log significant information, the information is accurately recorded in the log file.
Tester Name:	brl
Test Host:	Joe
Test Date:	Thu May 4 09:55:27 2006
Drives:	src(2A) dst (E6) other (4D-FU2)
Source Setup:	src hash: < F5F9F2903DCAB895F36E270FB22A722E27918125 > 17783249 total sectors (9105023488 bytes) Model (QM39100TD-SCA) serial # (PCB=20-116711-06 HDAQM39100TD-SCA) N Start LBA Length Start C/H/S End C/H/S boot Partition type 1 P 000000063 017751762 0000/001/01 1023/254/63 Boot 07 NTFS 2 P 000000000 000000000 0000/000/00 0000/000/00 00 empty entry 3 P 000000000 000000000 0000/000/00 0000/000/00 00 empty entry 4 P 000000000 000000000 0000/000/00 0000/000/00 00 empty entry 1 017751762 sectors 9088902144 bytes
Log Highlights:	Comparision of original to clone

```
Test Case DA-14-RAW ILook IXimager Version 2.0, Feb 01 2006
                Sectors compared: 17783249
                Sectors match:    17783249
                Sectors differ:          0
                Bytes differ:            0
                Diffs range
                Source (17783249) has 18060421 fewer sectors than destination (35843670)
                Zero fill:               0
                Src Byte fill (2A):      0
                Dst Byte fill (E6): 18060421
                Other fill:              0
                Other no fill:           0
                Zero fill range:
                Src fill range:
                Dst fill range:   17783249-35843669
                Other fill range:
                Other not filled range:
                0 source read errors, 0 destination read errors

                IXImager Log file
                SCSI device sdb: 17783249 512-byte hdwr sectors (9105 MB)
                SCSI device sdc: 35843670 512-byte hdwr sectors (18352 MB)
                SCSI device sdd: 781443888 512-byte hdwr sectors (400099 MB)
                SCSI device sdc: 35843670 512-byte hdwr sectors (18352 MB)
                Initializing...
                Opened output device '/dev/sdc'
                Beginning Restore operation for 9105023488 bytes
                Beginning Restore operation
                Beginning Restore operation
                Opened input file '/ILookImager/ILook.022/DA10RAW002.asb'
                continuing at byte 646709248
                Restoring from /ILook.022/DA10RAW002.asb
                Opened input file '/ILookImager/ILook.022/DA10RAW003.asb'
                continuing at byte 1293418496
                Restoring from /ILook.022/DA10RAW003.asb
                Opened input file '/ILookImager/ILook.022/DA10RAW004.asb'
                continuing at byte 1940127744
                Restoring from /ILook.022/DA10RAW004.asb
                Opened input file '/ILookImager/ILook.022/DA10RAW005.asb'
                continuing at byte 2586836992
                Restoring from /ILook.022/DA10RAW005.asb
                Opened input file '/ILookImager/ILook.022/DA10RAW006.asb'
                continuing at byte 3233546240
                Restoring from /ILook.022/DA10RAW006.asb
                Opened input file '/ILookImager/ILook.022/DA10RAW007.asb'
                continuing at byte 3880255488
                Restoring from /ILook.022/DA10RAW007.asb
                Opened input file '/ILookImager/ILook.022/DA10RAW008.asb'
                continuing at byte 4526964736
                Restoring from /ILook.022/DA10RAW008.asb
                Opened input file '/ILookImager/ILook.022/DA10RAW009.asb'
                continuing at byte 5173673984
                Restoring from /ILook.022/DA10RAW009.asb
                Opened input file '/ILookImager/ILook.022/DA10RAW010.asb'
                continuing at byte 5820383232
                Restoring from /ILook.022/DA10RAW010.asb
                Opened input file '/ILookImager/ILook.022/DA10RAW011.asb'
                continuing at byte 6467092480
                Restoring from /ILook.022/DA10RAW011.asb
                Opened input file '/ILookImager/ILook.022/DA10RAW012.asb'
                continuing at byte 7113801728
                Restoring from /ILook.022/DA10RAW012.asb
                Opened input file '/ILookImager/ILook.022/DA10RAW013.asb'
                continuing at byte 7760510976
                Restoring from /ILook.022/DA10RAW013.asb
                Opened input file '/ILookImager/ILook.022/DA10RAW014.asb'
                continuing at byte 8407220224
                Restoring from /ILook.022/DA10RAW014.asb
                Opened input file '/ILookImager/ILook.022/DA10RAW015.asb'
                continuing at byte 9053929472
                Restoring from /ILook.022/DA10RAW015.asb
                Restore Complete
                Restore was completed successfully.
```

	Test Case DA-14-RAW ILook IXimager Version 2.0, Feb 01 2006
	Read : 9.123 GB (9122743904 bytes) Written : 9.105 GB (9105023488 bytes) Total Processed: 9.105 GB (9105023488 bytes) Restore Speed : 15.12 MB/sec Elapsed Time : 0h 10m 2s Bad Sectors : 0 Clearing computer memory...
Results:	

Assertion & Expected Result	Actual Result
AM-03 Execution environment is XE.	as expected
AO-12 A clone is created from an image file.	as expected
AO-13 Clone created using interface AI.	as expected
AO-14 An unaligned clone is created.	as expected
AO-17 Excess sectors are unchanged.	as expected
AO-23 Logged information is correct.	as expected

Analysis:	Expected results achieved

5.2.61 DA-14-SATA28

	Test Case DA-14-SATA28 ILook IXimager Version 2.0, Feb 01 2006
Description:	DA-14 Create an unaligned clone from an image file.
Assertions:	AM-03 The tool executes in execution environment XE. AO-12 If requested, a clone is created from an image file. AO-13 A clone is created using access interface DST-AI to write to the clone device. AO-14 If an unaligned clone is created, each sector written to the clone is accurately written to the same disk address on the clone that the sector occupied on the digital source. AO-17 If requested, any excess sectors on a clone destination device are not modified. AO-23 If the tool logs any log significant information, the information is accurately recorded in the log file.
Tester Name:	brl
Test Host:	Freddy
Test Date:	Fri Mar 31 11:10:05 2006
Drives:	src(07) dst (17) other (4D-FU2)
Source Setup:	src hash: < 655E9BDDB36A3F9C5C4CC8BF32B8C5B41AF9F52E> 156301488 total sectors (80026361856 bytes) Model (WDC WD800JD-32HK) serial # (WD-WMAJ91510044) N Start LBA Length Start C/H/S End C/H/S boot Partition type 1 P 000000063 156280257 0000/001/01 1023/254/63 Boot 07 NTFS 2 P 000000000 000000000 0000/000/00 0000/000/00 00 empty entry 3 P 000000000 000000000 0000/000/00 0000/000/00 00 empty entry 4 P 000000000 000000000 0000/000/00 0000/000/00 00 empty entry 1 156280257 sectors 80015491584 bytes
Log Highlights:	Comparision of original to clone Sectors compared: 156301488 Sectors match: 156301488 Sectors differ: 0 Bytes differ: 0 Diffs range Source (156301488) has 78140160 fewer sectors than destination (234441648) Zero fill: 0 Src Byte fill (07): 0 Dst Byte fill (17): 78140160 Other fill: 0 Other no fill: 0 Zero fill range: Src fill range: Dst fill range: 156301488-234441647 Other fill range: Other not filled range: 0 source read errors, 0 destination read errors

	Test Case DA-14-SATA28 ILook IXimager Version 2.0, Feb 01 2006
	IXImager Log file SCSI device sdb: 781443888 512-byte hdwr sectors (400099 MB) ata1: dev 0 ATA-6, max UDMA/100, 234441648 sectors: LBA48 SCSI device sdc: 234441648 512-byte hdwr sectors (120034 MB) SCSI device sdc: 234441648 512-byte hdwr sectors (120034 MB) Initializing... Opened output device '/dev/sdc' Beginning Restore operation for 80026361856 bytes Beginning Restore operation Beginning Restore operation Opened input file '/ILookImager/ILook.007/DA06SATA48002.asb' continuing at byte 1284833280 Restoring from /ILook.007/DA06SATA48002.asb Opened input file '/ILookImager/ILook.007/DA06SATA48003.asb' continuing at byte 22479896576 Restoring from /ILook.007/DA06SATA48003.asb Opened input file '/ILookImager/ILook.007/DA06SATA48004.asb' continuing at byte 50644058112 Restoring from /ILook.007/DA06SATA48004.asb Opened input file '/ILookImager/ILook.007/DA06SATA48005.asb' continuing at byte 78810251264 Restoring from /ILook.007/DA06SATA48005.asb Restore Complete Restore was completed successfully. Read : 2.620 GB (2620183743 bytes) Written : 80.03 GB (80026361856 bytes) Total Processed: 80.03 GB (80026361856 bytes) Restore Speed : 47.83 MB/sec Elapsed Time : 0h 27m 53s Bad Sectors : 0 Clearing computer memory...
Results:	<table><tr><th>Assertion & Expected Result</th><th>Actual Result</th></tr><tr><td>AM-03 Execution environment is XE.</td><td>as expected</td></tr><tr><td>AO-12 A clone is created from an image file.</td><td>as expected</td></tr><tr><td>AO-13 Clone created using interface AI.</td><td>as expected</td></tr><tr><td>AO-14 An unaligned clone is created.</td><td>as expected</td></tr><tr><td>AO-17 Excess sectors are unchanged.</td><td>as expected</td></tr><tr><td>AO-23 Logged information is correct.</td><td>as expected</td></tr></table>
Analysis:	Expected results achieved

5.2.62 DA-14-SATA48

Test Case DA-14-SATA48 ILook IXimager Version 2.0, Feb 01 2006	
Description:	DA-14 Create an unaligned clone from an image file.
Assertions:	AM-03 The tool executes in execution environment XE. AO-12 If requested, a clone is created from an image file. AO-13 A clone is created using access interface DST-AI to write to the clone device. AO-14 If an unaligned clone is created, each sector written to the clone is accurately written to the same disk address on the clone that the sector occupied on the digital source. AO-17 If requested, any excess sectors on a clone destination device are not modified. AO-23 If the tool logs any log significant information, the information is accurately recorded in the log file.
Tester Name:	brl
Test Host:	Joe
Test Date:	Tue Apr 4 15:36:46 2006
Drives:	src(16) dst (0E) other (4D-FU2)
Source Setup:	src hash: < F82982A9C63133988C1D2B4DA7C9C25CCA2D77A5 > 312581808 total sectors (160041885696 bytes) 19456/254/63 (max cyl/hd values) 19457/255/63 (number of cyl/hd) Model (WDC WD1600JD-00G) serial # (WD-WMAES2058252)

Test Case DA-14-SATA48 ILook IXimager Version 2.0, Feb 01 2006

| | ``` 
  N   Start LBA  Length      Start C/H/S  End C/H/S   boot  Partition type
  1 P 000000063  312560577   0000/001/01  1023/254/63 Boot  07 NTFS
  2 P 000000000  000000000   0000/000/00  0000/000/00       00 empty entry
  3 P 000000000  000000000   0000/000/00  0000/000/00       00 empty entry
  4 P 000000000  000000000   0000/000/00  0000/000/00       00 empty entry
  1 312560577 sectors 160031015424 bytes
``` |
| Log Highlights: | ```
Comparision of original to clone
Sectors compared: 312581808
Sectors match:    312581808
Sectors differ:           0
Bytes differ:             0
Diffs range
Source (312581808) has 175815360 fewer sectors than destination (488397168)
Zero fill:                 0
Src Byte fill (16):        0
Dst Byte fill (0E): 175815360
Other fill:                0
Other no fill:             0
Zero fill range:
Src fill range:
Dst fill range:   312581808-488397167
Other fill range:
Other not filled range:
0 source read errors, 0 destination read errors

IXImager Log file
ata2: dev 0 ATA-6, max UDMA/100, 488397168 sectors: LBA48
SCSI device sdb: 488397168 512-byte hdwr sectors (250059 MB)
SCSI device sdc: 781443888 512-byte hdwr sectors (400099 MB)
SCSI device sdb: 488397168 512-byte hdwr sectors (250059 MB)
Initializing...
Opened output device '/dev/sdb'
Beginning Restore operation for 160041885696 bytes
Beginning Restore operation
Beginning Restore operation
Opened input file '/ILookImager/ILook.010/DA06SATA48002.asb'
continuing at byte 1265631232
Restoring from /ILook.010/DA06SATA48002.asb
Opened input file '/ILookImager/ILook.010/DA06SATA48003.asb'
continuing at byte 22619160576
Restoring from /ILook.010/DA06SATA48003.asb
Opened input file '/ILookImager/ILook.010/DA06SATA48004.asb'
continuing at byte 50721521664
Restoring from /ILook.010/DA06SATA48004.asb
Opened input file '/ILookImager/ILook.010/DA06SATA48005.asb'
continuing at byte 78887649280
Restoring from /ILook.010/DA06SATA48005.asb
Opened input file '/ILookImager/ILook.010/DA06SATA48006.asb'
continuing at byte 107050106880
Restoring from /ILook.010/DA06SATA48006.asb
Opened input file '/ILookImager/ILook.010/DA06SATA48007.asb'
continuing at byte 135216234496
Restoring from /ILook.010/DA06SATA48007.asb
Restore Complete
Restore was completed successfully.

Read            : 4.459 GB (4459320703 bytes)
Written         : 160.0 GB (160041885696 bytes)
Total Processed : 160.0 GB (160041885696 bytes)
Restore Speed   : 53.94 MB/sec
Elapsed Time    : 0h 49m 27s
Bad Sectors     : 0
Clearing computer memory...
``` |
| Results: | |

Assertion & Expected Result	Actual Result
AM-03 Execution environment is XE.	as expected
AO-12 A clone is created from an image file.	as expected
AO-13 Clone created using interface AI.	as expected
AO-14 An unaligned clone is created.	as expected
AO-17 Excess sectors are unchanged.	as expected

Test Case DA-14-SATA48 ILook IXimager Version 2.0, Feb 01 2006		
	AO-23 Logged information is correct.	as expected
Analysis:	Expected results achieved	

5.2.63 DA-14-SCSI

Test Case DA-14-SCSI ILook IXimager Version 2.0, Feb 01 2006	
Description:	DA-14 Create an unaligned clone from an image file.
Assertions:	AM-03 The tool executes in execution environment XE. AO-12 If requested, a clone is created from an image file. AO-13 A clone is created using access interface DST-AI to write to the clone device. AO-14 If an unaligned clone is created, each sector written to the clone is accurately written to the same disk address on the clone that the sector occupied on the digital source. AO-17 If requested, any excess sectors on a clone destination device are not modified. AO-23 If the tool logs any log significant information, the information is accurately recorded in the log file.
Tester Name:	brl
Test Host:	Joe
Test Date:	Fri Mar 31 11:05:11 2006
Drives:	src(2A) dst (24) other (4D-FU2)

Source Setup:	src hash: < F5F9F2903DCAB895F36E270FB22A722E27918125 >
	17783249 total sectors (9105023488 bytes)
	Model (QM39100TD-SCA) serial # (PCB=20-116711-06 HDAQM39100TD-SCA)
	  N Start LBA Length Start C/H/S End C/H/S boot Partition type
	  1 P 000000063 017751762 0000/001/01 1023/254/63 Boot 07 NTFS
	  2 P 000000000 000000000 0000/000/00 0000/000/00 00 empty entry
	  3 P 000000000 000000000 0000/000/00 0000/000/00 00 empty entry
	  4 P 000000000 000000000 0000/000/00 0000/000/00 00 empty entry
	1 017751762 sectors 9088902144 bytes

Log Highlights:	Comparision of original to clone Sectors compared: 17783249 Sectors match: 17783249 Sectors differ: 0 Bytes differ: 0 Diffs range Source (17783249) has 125591492 fewer sectors than destination (143374741) Zero fill: 0 Src Byte fill (2A): 0 Dst Byte fill (24): 125591492 Other fill: 0 Other no fill: 0 Zero fill range: Src fill range: Dst fill range: 17783249-143374740 Other fill range: Other not filled range: 0 source read errors, 0 destination read errors IXImager Log file SCSI device sdb: 143374741 512-byte hdwr sectors (73408 MB) SCSI device sdc: 781443888 512-byte hdwr sectors (400099 MB) SCSI device sdb: 143374741 512-byte hdwr sectors (73408 MB) Initializing... Opened output device '/dev/sdb' Beginning Restore operation for 9105023488 bytes Beginning Restore operation Beginning Restore operation Restore Complete Restore was completed successfully. Read : 606.9 MB (606900616 bytes) Written : 9.105 GB (9105023488 bytes) Total Processed: 9.105 GB (9105023488 bytes)

Test Case DA-14-SCSI ILook IXimager Version 2.0, Feb 01 2006		
	Restore Speed : 53.88 MB/sec Elapsed Time : 0h 2m 49s Bad Sectors : 0 Clearing computer memory...	
Results:	Assertion & Expected Result	Actual Result
	AM-03 Execution environment is XE.	as expected
	AO-12 A clone is created from an image file.	as expected
	AO-13 Clone created using interface AI.	as expected
	AO-14 An unaligned clone is created.	as expected
	AO-17 Excess sectors are unchanged.	as expected
	AO-23 Logged information is correct.	as expected
Analysis:	Expected results achieved	

5.2.64 DA-14-SWAP

Test Case DA-14-SWAP ILook IXimager Version 2.0, Feb 01 2006	
Description:	DA-14 Create an unaligned clone from an image file.
Assertions:	AM-03 The tool executes in execution environment XE. AO-12 If requested, a clone is created from an image file. AO-13 A clone is created using access interface DST-AI to write to the clone device. AO-14 If an unaligned clone is created, each sector written to the clone is accurately written to the same disk address on the clone that the sector occupied on the digital source. AO-17 If requested, any excess sectors on a clone destination device are not modified. AO-23 If the tool logs any log significant information, the information is accurately recorded in the log file.
Tester Name:	brl
Test Host:	Max
Test Date:	Tue Apr 25 09:20:35 2006
Drives:	src(44) dst (2C) other (4D-FU2)
Source Setup:	src hash: < E196D36E7B322C0EF83923112AD1800581742B6E > 78165360 total sectors (40020664320 bytes) 65534/015/63 (max cyl/hd values) 65535/016/63 (number of cyl/hd) IDE disk: Model (WDC WD400JB-00FMA0) serial # (WD-WMAJC1011319) N Start LBA Length Start C/H/S End C/H/S boot Partition type 1 P 000000063 020980827 0000/001/01 1023/254/63 0C Fat32X 2 X 020980890 057175335 1023/000/01 1023/254/63 0F extended 3 S 000000063 000032067 1023/001/01 1023/254/63 01 Fat12 4 x 000032130 002104515 1023/000/01 1023/254/63 05 extended 5 S 000000063 002104452 1023/001/01 1023/254/63 06 Fat16 6 x 002136645 004192965 1023/000/01 1023/254/63 05 extended 7 S 000000063 004192902 1023/001/01 1023/254/63 16 other 8 x 006329610 008401995 1023/000/01 1023/254/63 05 extended 9 S 000000063 008401932 1023/001/01 1023/254/63 0B Fat32 10 x 014731605 010490445 1023/000/01 1023/254/63 05 extended 11 S 000000063 010490382 1023/001/01 1023/254/63 83 Linux 12 x 025222050 004209030 1023/000/01 1023/254/63 05 extended 13 S 000000063 004208967 1023/001/01 1023/254/63 82 Linux swap 14 x 029431080 027744255 1023/000/01 1023/254/63 05 extended 15 S 000000063 027744192 1023/001/01 1023/254/63 07 NTFS 16 S 000000000 000000000 0000/000/00 0000/000/00 00 empty entry 17 P 000000000 000000000 0000/000/00 0000/000/00 00 empty entry 18 P 000000000 000000000 0000/000/00 0000/000/00 00 empty entry 1 020980827 sectors 10742183424 bytes 3 000032067 sectors 16418304 bytes 5 002104452 sectors 1077479424 bytes 7 004192902 sectors 2146765824 bytes 9 008401932 sectors 4301789184 bytes 11 010490382 sectors 5371075584 bytes 13 004208967 sectors 2154991104 bytes 15 027744192 sectors 14205026304 bytes

Test Case DA-14-SWAP ILook IXimager Version 2.0, Feb 01 2006	
Log Highlights:	IXImager Log file SCSI device sdb: 17783249 512-byte hdwr sectors (9105 MB) SCSI device sdc: 78165360 512-byte hdwr sectors (40021 MB) SCSI device sdd: 781443888 512-byte hdwr sectors (400099 MB) SCSI device sdb: 17783249 512-byte hdwr sectors (9105 MB) Initializing... Opened output device '/dev/sdb' Beginning Restore operation for 2154991104 bytes Beginning Restore operation Beginning Restore operation Restore Complete Restore was completed successfully. Read : 49.74 MB (49737188 bytes) Written : 2.155 GB (2154991104 bytes) Total Processed: 2.155 GB (2154991104 bytes) Restore Speed : 13.22 MB/sec Elapsed Time : 0h 2m 43s Bad Sectors : 0 Clearing computer memory... Hashes of src and dst partitions Src SHA1 Hash: 7BDD19B23E43AB62042FBF47FAD69BB878F1EC6A - Dst SHA1 Hash: 7BDD19B23E43AB62042FBF47FAD69BB878F1EC6A -
Results:	

Assertion & Expected Result	Actual Result
AM-03 Execution environment is XE.	as expected
AO-12 A clone is created from an image file.	as expected
AO-13 Clone created using interface AI.	as expected
AO-14 An unaligned clone is created.	as expected
AO-17 Excess sectors are unchanged.	as expected
AO-23 Logged information is correct.	as expected

Analysis:	Expected results achieved

5.2.65 DA-14-THUMB

Test Case DA-14-THUMB ILook IXimager Version 2.0, Feb 01 2006	
Description:	DA-14 Create an unaligned clone from an image file.
Assertions:	AM-03 The tool executes in execution environment XE. AO-12 If requested, a clone is created from an image file. AO-13 A clone is created using access interface DST-AI to write to the clone device. AO-14 If an unaligned clone is created, each sector written to the clone is accurately written to the same disk address on the clone that the sector occupied on the digital source. AO-17 If requested, any excess sectors on a clone destination device are not modified. AO-23 If the tool logs any log significant information, the information is accurately recorded in the log file.
Tester Name:	brl
Test Host:	JohnSteed
Test Date:	Wed May 10 11:01:08 2006
Drives:	src(D2-THUMB) dst (D4-THUMB) other (4D-FU2)
Source Setup:	src hash: < 712C9F59F598745977E4E19F235F83CE8F4EC7BA > 253400 total sectors (129740800 bytes) Model (TS128MJFLASHA) serial # () Removable media, no partition table.
Log Highlights:	Comparision of original to clone Sectors compared: 253400 Sectors match: 253400 Sectors differ: 0 Bytes differ: 0 Diffs range

Test Case DA-14-THUMB ILook IXimager Version 2.0, Feb 01 2006

```
                Source (253400) has 252456 fewer sectors than destination (505856)
                Zero fill:                 0
                Src Byte fill (D2):        0
                Dst Byte fill (D4):   252456
                Other fill:                0
                Other no fill:             0
                Zero fill range:
                Src fill range:
                Dst fill range:   253400-505855
                Other fill range:
                Other not filled range:
                0 source read errors, 0 destination read errors

                IXImager Log file
                hda: 156301488 sectors (80026 MB) w/8192KiB Cache, CHS=9729/255/63,
                UDMA(100)
                /dev/sda: I/O error reading 8 sectors, sector 0
                /dev/sda: I/O error reading 8 sectors, sector 0
                SCSI device sda: 505856 512-byte hdwr sectors (259 MB)
                SCSI device sdb: 781443888 512-byte hdwr sectors (400099 MB)
                SCSI device sda: 505856 512-byte hdwr sectors (259 MB)
                Initializing...
                Opened output device '/dev/sda'
                Beginning Restore operation for 129740800 bytes
                Beginning Restore operation
                Beginning Restore operation
                Restore Complete
                Restore was completed successfully.

                Read             :  3.095 MB (3094822 bytes)
                Written          :  129.7 MB (129740800 bytes)
                Total Processed:   129.7 MB (129740800 bytes)
                Restore Speed    :  6.828 MB/sec
                Elapsed Time     :  0h  0m 19s
                Bad Sectors      :  0
                Clearing computer memory...
```

Results:	Assertion & Expected Result	Actual Result
	AM-03 Execution environment is XE.	as expected
	AO-12 A clone is created from an image file.	as expected
	AO-13 Clone created using interface AI.	as expected
	AO-14 An unaligned clone is created.	as expected
	AO-17 Excess sectors are unchanged.	as expected
	AO-23 Logged information is correct.	as expected
Analysis:	Expected results achieved	

5.2.66 DA-14-USB

Test Case DA-14-USB ILook IXimager Version 2.0, Feb 01 2006

Description:	DA-14 Create an unaligned clone from an image file.
Assertions:	AM-03 The tool executes in execution environment XE. AO-12 If requested, a clone is created from an image file. AO-13 A clone is created using access interface DST-AI to write to the clone device. AO-14 If an unaligned clone is created, each sector written to the clone is accurately written to the same disk address on the clone that the sector occupied on the digital source. AO-17 If requested, any excess sectors on a clone destination device are not modified. AO-23 If the tool logs any log significant information, the information is accurately recorded in the log file.
Tester Name:	brl
Test Host:	Freddy
Test Date:	Mon Apr 3 15:57:26 2006
Drives:	src (63-FU2) dst (85-FU2) other (4D-FU2)
Source	src hash: < F7069EDCBEAC863C88DECED82159F22DA96BE99B >

Test Case	DA-14-USB ILook IXimager Version 2.0, Feb 01 2006
| Setup: | 117304992 total sectors (60060155904 bytes)<br>Model (SP0612N          ) serial # ()<br>```
N    Start LBA Length      Start C/H/S End C/H/S   boot Partition type
1 P  000000063 004192902   0000/001/01 0260/254/63 Boot 06 Fat16
2 X  004192965 113097600   0261/000/01 1023/254/63      0F extended
3 S  000000063 113097537   0261/001/01 1023/254/63      0B Fat32
4 S  000000000 000000000   0000/000/00 0000/000/00      00 empty entry
5 P  000000000 000000000   0000/000/00 0000/000/00      00 empty entry
6 P  000000000 000000000   0000/000/00 0000/000/00      00 empty entry
1 004192902 sectors 2146765824 bytes
3 113097537 sectors 57905938944 bytes
``` |
Log Highlights:	Comparision of original to clone Sectors compared: 117304992 Sectors match: 117304992 Sectors differ: 0 Bytes differ: 0 Diffs range Source (117304992) has 43531488 fewer sectors than destination (160836480) Zero fill: 0 Src Byte fill (63): 0 Dst Byte fill (85): 43531488 Other fill: 0 Other no fill: 0 Zero fill range: Src fill range: Dst fill range: 117304992-160836479 Other fill range: Other not filled range: 0 source read errors, 0 destination read errors IXImager Log file SCSI device sda: 160836480 512-byte hdwr sectors (82348 MB) SCSI device sdc: 781443888 512-byte hdwr sectors (400099 MB) SCSI device sda: 160836480 512-byte hdwr sectors (82348 MB) Initializing... Opened output device '/dev/sda' Beginning Restore operation for 60060155904 bytes Beginning Restore operation Beginning Restore operation Opened input file '/ILookImager/ILook.004/DA06USB002.asb' continuing at byte 28178251776 Restoring from /ILook.004/DA06USB002.asb Opened input file '/ILookImager/ILook.004/DA06USB003.asb' continuing at byte 56341823488 Restoring from /ILook.004/DA06USB003.asb Restore Complete Restore was completed successfully. Read : 1.382 GB (1381727236 bytes) Written : 60.06 GB (60060155904 bytes) Total Processed : 60.06 GB (60060155904 bytes) Restore Speed : 14.99 MB/sec Elapsed Time : 1h 6m 46s Bad Sectors : 0 Clearing computer memory...
Results:	<table><tr><th>Assertion & Expected Result</th><th>Actual Result</th></tr><tr><td>AM-03 Execution environment is XE.</td><td>as expected</td></tr><tr><td>AO-12 A clone is created from an image file.</td><td>as expected</td></tr><tr><td>AO-13 Clone created using interface AI.</td><td>as expected</td></tr><tr><td>AO-14 An unaligned clone is created.</td><td>as expected</td></tr><tr><td>AO-17 Excess sectors are unchanged.</td><td>as expected</td></tr><tr><td>AO-23 Logged information is correct.</td><td>as expected</td></tr></table>
Analysis:	Expected results achieved
```

5.2.67 DA-14-X2

Test Case DA-14-X2 ILook IXimager Version 2.0, Feb 01 2006	
Description:	DA-14 Create an unaligned clone from an image file.
Assertions:	AM-03 The tool executes in execution environment XE. AO-12 If requested, a clone is created from an image file. AO-13 A clone is created using access interface DST-AI to write to the clone device. AO-14 If an unaligned clone is created, each sector written to the clone is accurately written to the same disk address on the clone that the sector occupied on the digital source. AO-17 If requested, any excess sectors on a clone destination device are not modified. AO-23 If the tool logs any log significant information, the information is accurately recorded in the log file.
Tester Name:	brl
Test Host:	Joe
Test Date:	Mon Apr 24 15:56:52 2006
Drives:	src(43) dst (2F) other (4D-FU2)
Source Setup:	src hash: < 888E2E7F7AD237DC7A732281DD93F325065E5871 > 78125000 total sectors (40000000000 bytes) Model (0BB-75JHC0) serial # (WD-WMAMC46588) N Start LBA Length Start C/H/S End C/H/S boot Partition type 1 P 000000063 020980827 0000/001/01 1023/254/63 0C Fat32X 2 X 020980890 057143205 1023/000/01 1023/254/63 0F extended 3 S 000000063 000032067 1023/001/01 1023/254/63 01 Fat12 4 x 000032130 002104515 1023/000/01 1023/254/63 05 extended 5 S 000000063 002104452 1023/001/01 1023/254/63 06 Fat16 6 x 002136645 004192965 1023/000/01 1023/254/63 05 extended 7 S 000000063 004192902 1023/001/01 1023/254/63 16 other 8 x 006329610 008401995 1023/000/01 1023/254/63 05 extended 9 S 000000063 008401932 1023/001/01 1023/254/63 0B Fat32 10 x 014731605 010490445 1023/000/01 1023/254/63 05 extended 11 S 000000063 010490382 1023/001/01 1023/254/63 83 Linux 12 x 025222050 004209030 1023/000/01 1023/254/63 05 extended 13 S 000000063 004208967 1023/001/01 1023/254/63 82 Linux swap 14 x 029431080 027712125 1023/000/01 1023/254/63 05 extended 15 S 000000063 027712062 1023/001/01 1023/254/63 07 NTFS 16 S 000000000 000000000 0000/000/00 0000/000/00 00 empty entry 17 P 000000000 000000000 0000/000/00 0000/000/00 00 empty entry 18 P 000000000 000000000 0000/000/00 0000/000/00 00 empty entry 1 020980827 sectors 10742183424 bytes 3 000032067 sectors 16418304 bytes 5 002104452 sectors 1077479424 bytes 7 004192902 sectors 2146765824 bytes 9 008401932 sectors 4301789184 bytes 11 010490382 sectors 5371075584 bytes 13 004208967 sectors 2154991104 bytes 15 027712062 sectors 14188575744 bytes
Log Highlights:	IXImager Log file SCSI device sdb: 17783249 512-byte hdwr sectors (9105 MB) SCSI device sdc: 78125000 512-byte hdwr sectors (40000 MB) SCSI device sdd: 781443888 512-byte hdwr sectors (400099 MB) SCSI device sdb: 17783249 512-byte hdwr sectors (9105 MB) Initializing... Opened output device '/dev/sdb' Beginning Restore operation for 5371075584 bytes Beginning Restore operation Beginning Restore operation Restore Complete Restore was completed successfully. Read : 125.1 MB (125099895 bytes) Written : 5.371 GB (5371075584 bytes) Total Processed: 5.371 GB (5371075584 bytes) Restore Speed : 12.91 MB/sec Elapsed Time : 0h 6m 56s Bad Sectors : 0 Clearing computer memory...

Test Case DA-14-X2 ILook IXimager Version 2.0, Feb 01 2006		
	Hashes of src and dst partitions Src SHA1 Hash: 283BCC32DE892C12C37698AF7E38703619E57F57 - Dst SHA1 Hash: 283BCC32DE892C12C37698AF7E38703619E57F57 -	
Results:	Assertion & Expected Result	Actual Result
	AM-03 Execution environment is XE.	as expected
	AO-12 A clone is created from an image file.	as expected
	AO-13 Clone created using interface AI.	as expected
	AO-14 An unaligned clone is created.	as expected
	AO-17 Excess sectors are unchanged.	as expected
	AO-23 Logged information is correct.	as expected
Analysis:	Expected results achieved	

5.2.68 DA-14-ZIP

Test Case DA-14-ZIP ILook IXimager Version 2.0, Feb 01 2006	
Description:	DA-14 Create an unaligned clone from an image file.
Assertions:	AM-03 The tool executes in execution environment XE. AO-12 If requested, a clone is created from an image file. AO-13 A clone is created using access interface DST-AI to write to the clone device. AO-14 If an unaligned clone is created, each sector written to the clone is accurately written to the same disk address on the clone that the sector occupied on the digital source. AO-17 If requested, any excess sectors on a clone destination device are not modified. AO-23 If the tool logs any log significant information, the information is accurately recorded in the log file.
Tester Name:	brl
Test Host:	Nick
Test Date:	Thu May 11 10:52:02 2006
Drives:	src(E2-ZIP) dst (E1-ZIP) other (4D-FU2)
Source Setup:	src hash: < AFEA6483060C6FAD1026B7094810674E91AEA5D7 > 196608 total sectors (100663296 bytes) Model (ZIP 250) serial # () Removable media, no partition table.
Log Highlights:	Comparision of original to clone Sectors compared: 196608 Sectors match: 196608 Sectors differ: 0 Bytes differ: 0 Diffs range Source (196608) has 292864 fewer sectors than destination (489472) Zero fill: 0 Src Byte fill (E2): 0 Dst Byte fill (E1): 292864 Other fill: 0 Other no fill: 0 Zero fill range: Src fill range: Dst fill range: 196608-489471 Other fill range: Other not filled range: 0 source read errors, 0 destination read errors IXImager Log file hda: 156250000 sectors (80000 MB) w/1821KiB Cache, CHS=9726/255/63, UDMA(100) SCSI device sda: 781443888 512-byte hdwr sectors (400099 MB) SCSI device sdb: 196608 512-byte hdwr sectors (101 MB) Initializing... Opened output device '/dev/hdb' Beginning Restore operation for 100663296 bytes

Test Case DA-14-ZIP ILook IXimager Version 2.0, Feb 01 2006	
	Beginning Restore operation Beginning Restore operation Restore Complete Restore was completed successfully. Read : 2.432 MB (2432402 bytes) Written : 100.7 MB (100663296 bytes) Total Processed: 100.7 MB (100663296 bytes) Restore Speed : 1.213 MB/sec Elapsed Time : 0h 1m 23s Bad Sectors : 0 Clearing computer memory...
Results:	<table><tr><th>Assertion & Expected Result</th><th>Actual Result</th></tr><tr><td>AM-03 Execution environment is XE.</td><td>as expected</td></tr><tr><td>AO-12 A clone is created from an image file.</td><td>as expected</td></tr><tr><td>AO-13 Clone created using interface AI.</td><td>as expected</td></tr><tr><td>AO-14 An unaligned clone is created.</td><td>as expected</td></tr><tr><td>AO-17 Excess sectors are unchanged.</td><td>as expected</td></tr><tr><td>AO-23 Logged information is correct.</td><td>as expected</td></tr></table>
Analysis:	Expected results achieved

5.2.69   DA-17

Test Case DA-17 ILook IXimager Version 2.0, Feb 01 2006	
Description:	DA-17 Create a truncated clone from an image file.
Assertions:	AM-03 The tool executes in execution environment XE. AO-12 If requested, a clone is created from an image file. AO-13 A clone is created using access interface DST-AI to write to the clone device. AO-19 If there is insufficient space to create a complete clone, a truncated clone is created using all available sectors of the clone device. AO-20 If a truncated clone is created, the tool notifies the user. AO-23 If the tool logs any log significant information, the information is accurately recorded in the log file.
Tester Name:	brl
Test Host:	Joe
Test Date:	Fri May 26 14:50:36 2006
Drives:	src(41) dst (5A) other (4D-FU2)
Source Setup:	src hash: < 15CAA1A307271160D8372668BF8A03FC45A51CC9 > 78125000 total sectors (40000000000 bytes) 65534/015/63 (max cyl/hd values) 65535/016/63 (number of cyl/hd) IDE disk: Model (WDC WD400BB-75JHC0) serial # (WD-WMAMC4658355) N Start LBA Length Start C/H/S End C/H/S boot Partition type 1 P 000000063 078107967 0000/001/01 1023/254/63 Boot 07 NTFS 2 P 000000000 000000000 0000/000/00 0000/000/00 00 empty entry 3 P 000000000 000000000 0000/000/00 0000/000/00 00 empty entry 4 P 000000000 000000000 0000/000/00 0000/000/00 00 empty entry 1 078107967 sectors 39991279104 bytes
Log Highlights:	Comparision of original to clone Sectors compared: 12692736 Sectors match: 12692736 Sectors differ: 0 Bytes differ: 0 Diffs range Source (78125000) has 65432264 more sectors than destination (12692736) 0 source read errors, 0 destination read errors IXImager Log file hda: 12692736 sectors (6498 MB) w/468KiB Cache, CHS=13431/15/63, UDMA(33) SCSI device sdb: 781443888 512-byte hdwr sectors (400099 MB) Initializing... Opened output device '/dev/hda'

	Test Case DA-17 ILook IXimager Version 2.0, Feb 01 2006
	Beginning Restore operation for 40000000000 bytes Beginning Restore operation Beginning Restore operation Your target device has run out of free space! Restore Aborted Restore was aborted. Read : 150.1 MB (150142976 bytes) Written : 6.499 GB (6498680832 bytes) Total Processed : 6.501 GB (6500712448 bytes) Expected Size : 40.00 GB (40000000000 bytes) Restore Speed : 1.700 MB/sec Elapsed Time : 1h 3m 43s Bad Sectors : 0 Clearing computer memory...
Results:	<table><tr><th>Assertion & Expected Result</th><th>Actual Result</th></tr><tr><td>AM-03 Execution environment is XE.</td><td>as expected</td></tr><tr><td>AO-12 A clone is created from an image file.</td><td>as expected</td></tr><tr><td>AO-13 Clone created using interface AI.</td><td>as expected</td></tr><tr><td>AO-19 Truncated clone is created.</td><td>as expected</td></tr><tr><td>AO-20 User notified that clone is truncated.</td><td>as expected</td></tr><tr><td>AO-23 Logged information is correct.</td><td>as expected</td></tr></table>
Analysis:	Expected results achieved

5.2.70   DA-24

	Test Case DA-24 ILook IXimager Version 2.0, Feb 01 2006
Description:	DA-24 Verify a valid image.
Assertions:	AM-03 The tool executes in execution environment XE. AO-06 If the tool performs an image file integrity check on an image file that has not been changed since the file was created, the tool shall notify the user that the image file has not been changed. AO-23 If the tool logs any log significant information, the information is accurately recorded in the log file.
Tester Name:	Brl
Test Host:	JohnSteed
Test Date:	Tue May 16 11:02:54 2006
Drives:	src(4D-FU2) dst (4D-FU2) other (none)

Source Setup:	src hash: < F5F9F2903DCAB895F36E270FB22A722E27918125 >
	17783249 total sectors (9105023488 bytes)
	Model (QM39100TD-SCA) serial # (PCB=20-116711-06 HDAQM39100TD-SCA)
	  N Start LBA Length Start C/H/S End C/H/S boot Partition type
	  1 P 000000063 017751762 0000/001/01 1023/254/63 Boot 07 NTFS
	  2 P 000000000 000000000 0000/000/00 0000/000/00 00 empty entry
	  3 P 000000000 000000000 0000/000/00 0000/000/00 00 empty entry
	  4 P 000000000 000000000 0000/000/00 0000/000/00 00 empty entry
	1 017751762 sectors 9088902144 bytes

Log Highlights:	IXImager Log file hda: 156301488 sectors (80026 MB) w/8192KiB Cache, CHS=9729/255/63, UDMA(100) SCSI device sda: 781443888 512-byte hdwr sectors (400099 MB) Initializing... Beginning Verify operation for 9105023488 bytes Beginning Verify operation Beginning Verify operation Verify Complete Verify was completed successfully. Read : 606.9 MB (606900616 bytes) Written : 0.000 MB (0 bytes) Total Processed : 9.105 GB (9105023488 bytes) Verify Speed : 31.84 MB/sec Elapsed Time : 0h 4m 46s

Test Case DA-24 ILook IXimager Version 2.0, Feb 01 2006		
	Bad Sectors : 0 SHA-1 Value : f5f9f2903dcab895f36e270fb22a722e27918125 : for 9105023488 bytes Clearing computer memory...	
Results:	Assertion & Expected Result	Actual Result
	AM-03 Execution environment is XE.	as expected
	AO-06 Tool verifies image file unchanged.	as expected
	AO-23 Logged information is correct.	as expected
Analysis:	Expected results achieved	

5.2.71 DA-25

Test Case DA-25 ILook IXimager Version 2.0, Feb 01 2006	
Description:	DA-25 Detect a corrupted image.
Assertions:	AM-03 The tool executes in execution environment XE. AO-07 If the tool performs an image file integrity check on an image file that has been changed since the file was created, the tool shall notify the user that the image file has been changed. AO-08 If the tool performs an image file integrity check on an image file that has been changed since the file was created, the tool shall notify the user of the affected locations. AO-23 If the tool logs any log significant information, the information is accurately recorded in the log file.
Tester Name:	Brl
Test Host:	JohnSteed
Test Date:	Tue May 16 11:05:04 2006
Drives:	src(4D-FU2) dst (4D-FU2) other (none)
Source Setup:	src hash: < F5F9F2903DCAB895F36E270FB22A722E27918125 > 17783249 total sectors (9105023488 bytes) Model (QM39100TD-SCA) serial # (PCB=20-116711-06 HDAQM39100TD-SCA) N Start LBA Length Start C/H/S End C/H/S boot Partition type 1 P 000000063 017751762 0000/001/01 1023/254/63 Boot 07 NTFS 2 P 000000000 000000000 0000/000/00 0000/000/00 00 empty entry 3 P 000000000 000000000 0000/000/00 0000/000/00 00 empty entry 4 P 000000000 000000000 0000/000/00 0000/000/00 00 empty entry 1 017751762 sectors 9088902144 bytes
Log Highlights:	IXImager Log file hda: 156301488 sectors (80026 MB) w/8192KiB Cache, CHS=9729/255/63, UDMA(100) SCSI device sda: 781443888 512-byte hdwr sectors (400099 MB) Initializing... Beginning Verify operation for 9105023488 bytes Beginning Verify operation Beginning Verify operation Opened input file '/ILookImager/ILook.022/DA10RAW002.asb' continuing at byte 646709248 Calculating SHA-1 hash of /ILook.022/DA10RAW002.asb Opened input file '/ILookImager/ILook.022/DA10RAW003.asb' continuing at byte 1293418496 Calculating SHA-1 hash of /ILook.022/DA10RAW003.asb Opened input file '/ILookImager/ILook.022/DA10RAW004.asb' continuing at byte 1940127744 Calculating SHA-1 hash of /ILook.022/DA10RAW004.asb Opened input file '/ILookImager/ILook.022/DA10RAW005.asb' continuing at byte 2586836992 Calculating SHA-1 hash of /ILook.022/DA10RAW005.asb Opened input file '/ILookImager/ILook.022/DA10RAW006.asb' continuing at byte 3233546240 Calculating SHA-1 hash of /ILook.022/DA10RAW006.asb Opened input file '/ILookImager/ILook.022/DA10RAW007.asb' continuing at byte 3880255488 Calculating SHA-1 hash of /ILook.022/DA10RAW007.asb Opened input file '/ILookImager/ILook.022/DA10RAW008.asb'

Test Case DA-25 ILook IXimager Version 2.0, Feb 01 2006	
	continuing at byte 4526964736 Calculating SHA-1 hash of /ILook.022/DA10RAW008.asb Opened input file '/ILookImager/ILook.022/DA10RAW009.asb' continuing at byte 5173673984 Calculating SHA-1 hash of /ILook.022/DA10RAW009.asb Opened input file '/ILookImager/ILook.022/DA10RAW010.asb' continuing at byte 5820383232 Calculating SHA-1 hash of /ILook.022/DA10RAW010.asb An error occurred while trying to verify the data at offset 5821235200 from the original source device. The checksum for the 88826 bytes of data currently stored at this position does not match the checksum that was archived as part of segment -4691104391841710080 when the image file was created. This generally indicates that your image file has become corrupted. Would you like to continue this operation anyways? User selected: Continue Opened input file '/ILookImager/ILook.022/DA10RAW011.asb' continuing at byte 6467092480 Calculating SHA-1 hash of /ILook.022/DA10RAW011.asb Opened input file '/ILookImager/ILook.022/DA10RAW012.asb' continuing at byte 7113801728 Calculating SHA-1 hash of /ILook.022/DA10RAW012.asb Opened input file '/ILookImager/ILook.022/DA10RAW013.asb' continuing at byte 7760510976 Calculating SHA-1 hash of /ILook.022/DA10RAW013.asb Opened input file '/ILookImager/ILook.022/DA10RAW014.asb' continuing at byte 8407220224 Calculating SHA-1 hash of /ILook.022/DA10RAW014.asb Opened input file '/ILookImager/ILook.022/DA10RAW015.asb' continuing at byte 9053929472 Calculating SHA-1 hash of /ILook.022/DA10RAW015.asb Verify Complete Verify was completed successfully. Read : 9.123 GB (9122743904 bytes) Written : 0.000 MB (0 bytes) Total Processed: 9.105 GB (9105023488 bytes) Verify Speed : 9.635 MB/sec Elapsed Time : 0h 15m 45s Bad Sectors : 0 SHA-1 Value : 70a130944f45a41c23b0ffaae01958ae348491e3 : for 9105023488 bytes Clearing computer memory...
Results:	<table><tr><th>Assertion & Expected Result</th><th>Actual Result</th></tr><tr><td>AM-03 Execution environment is XE.</td><td>as expected</td></tr><tr><td>AO-07 User notified if image file has changed.</td><td>as expected</td></tr><tr><td>AO-08 User notified of changed locations.</td><td>as expected</td></tr><tr><td>AO-23 Logged information is correct.</td><td>as expected</td></tr></table>
Analysis:	Expected results achieved

5.2.72 DA-26-d2dd

Test Case DA-26-d2dd ILook IXimager Version 2.0, Feb 01 2006	
Description:	DA-26 Convert an image to an alternate image file format.
Assertions:	AM-03 The tool executes in execution environment XE. AO-09 If the tool converts a source image file from one format to a target image file in another format, the acquired data represented in the target image file is the same as the acquired data in the source image file. AO-23 If the tool logs any log significant information, the information is accurately recorded in the log file.
Tester Name:	Brl
Test Host:	JohnSteed
Test Date:	Tue May 16 11:07:57 2006
Drives:	src(4D-FU2) dst (4D-FU2) other (none)

```
Test Case DA-26-d2dd ILook IXimager Version 2.0, Feb 01 2006
```

| Source Setup: | ```
src hash: < F5F9F2903DCAB895F36E270FB22A722E27918125 >
17783249 total sectors (9105023488 bytes)
Model (QM39100TD-SCA   ) serial # (PCB=20-116711-06 HDAQM39100TD-SCA   )
 N   Start LBA Length      Start C/H/S End C/H/S   boot Partition type
 1 P 000000063 017751762   0000/001/01 1023/254/63 Boot 07 NTFS
 2 P 000000000 000000000   0000/000/00 0000/000/00      00 empty entry
 3 P 000000000 000000000   0000/000/00 0000/000/00      00 empty entry
 4 P 000000000 000000000   0000/000/00 0000/000/00      00 empty entry
1 017751762 sectors 9088902144 bytes
``` |
|---|---|
| Log Highlights: | ```
IXImager Log file
hda: 156301488 sectors (80026 MB) w/8192KiB Cache, CHS=9729/255/63,
UDMA(100)
SCSI device sda: 781443888 512-byte hdwr sectors (400099 MB)
Initializing...
Opened output file '/ILookImager/ILook.032/DA06SCSI001.asb'
Beginning Copy operation for 9105023488 bytes
Beginning Copy operation
Beginning Copy operation
Opened output file '/ILookImager/ILook.032/DA06SCSI002.asb'
continuing at byte 649986048
Copy is being stored to /ILook.032/DA06SCSI002.asb
Opened output file '/ILookImager/ILook.032/DA06SCSI003.asb'
continuing at byte 1297940480
Copy is being stored to /ILook.032/DA06SCSI003.asb
Opened output file '/ILookImager/ILook.032/DA06SCSI004.asb'
continuing at byte 1945894912
Copy is being stored to /ILook.032/DA06SCSI004.asb
Opened output file '/ILookImager/ILook.032/DA06SCSI005.asb'
continuing at byte 2593849344
Copy is being stored to /ILook.032/DA06SCSI005.asb
Opened output file '/ILookImager/ILook.032/DA06SCSI006.asb'
continuing at byte 3241803776
Copy is being stored to /ILook.032/DA06SCSI006.asb
Opened output file '/ILookImager/ILook.032/DA06SCSI007.asb'
continuing at byte 3889758208
Copy is being stored to /ILook.032/DA06SCSI007.asb
Opened output file '/ILookImager/ILook.032/DA06SCSI008.asb'
continuing at byte 4537712640
Copy is being stored to /ILook.032/DA06SCSI008.asb
Opened output file '/ILookImager/ILook.032/DA06SCSI009.asb'
continuing at byte 5185667072
Copy is being stored to /ILook.032/DA06SCSI009.asb
Opened output file '/ILookImager/ILook.032/DA06SCSI010.asb'
continuing at byte 5833621504
Copy is being stored to /ILook.032/DA06SCSI010.asb
Opened output file '/ILookImager/ILook.032/DA06SCSI011.asb'
continuing at byte 6481575936
Copy is being stored to /ILook.032/DA06SCSI011.asb
Opened output file '/ILookImager/ILook.032/DA06SCSI012.asb'
continuing at byte 7129530368
Copy is being stored to /ILook.032/DA06SCSI012.asb
Opened output file '/ILookImager/ILook.032/DA06SCSI013.asb'
continuing at byte 7777484800
Copy is being stored to /ILook.032/DA06SCSI013.asb
Opened output file '/ILookImager/ILook.032/DA06SCSI014.asb'
continuing at byte 8425439232
Copy is being stored to /ILook.032/DA06SCSI014.asb
Opened output file '/ILookImager/ILook.032/DA06SCSI015.asb'
continuing at byte 9073393664
Copy is being stored to /ILook.032/DA06SCSI015.asb
Copy Complete
Copy was completed successfully.

Read            : 606.9 MB (606900616 bytes)
Written         : 9.105 GB (9105023488 bytes)
Total Processed : 9.105 GB (9105023488 bytes)
Copy Speed      : 21.63 MB/sec
Elapsed Time    : 0h  7m  1s
Bad Sectors     : 0
SHA-1 Value     : f5f9f2903dcab895f36e270fb22a722e27918125
                : for 9105023488 bytes
``` |

Test Case DA-26-d2dd ILook IXimager Version 2.0, Feb 01 2006

```
                    Clearing computer memory...
                    Initializing...
                    Beginning Verify operation for 9105023488 bytes
                    Beginning Verify operation
                    Beginning Verify operation
                    Verify Complete
                    Verify was completed successfully.

                    Read            :  606.9 MB (606900616 bytes)
                    Written         :  0.000 MB (0 bytes)
                    Total Processed:  9.105 GB (9105023488 bytes)
                    Verify Speed    :  31.84 MB/sec
                    Elapsed Time    :  0h  4m 46s
                    Bad Sectors     :  0
                    SHA-1 Value     :  f5f9f2903dcab895f36e270fb22a722e27918125
                                    :  for 9105023488 bytes
                    Clearing computer memory...
                    Initializing...
                    Beginning Verify operation for 9105023488 bytes
                    Beginning Verify operation
                    Beginning Verify operation
                    Verify Complete
                    Verify was completed successfully.

                    Read            :  606.9 MB (606938395 bytes)
                    Written         :  0.000 MB (0 bytes)
                    Total Processed:  9.105 GB (9105023488 bytes)
                    Verify Speed    :  31.61 MB/sec
                    Elapsed Time    :  0h  4m 48s
                    Bad Sectors     :  0
                    SHA-1 Value     :  f5f9f2903dcab895f36e270fb22a722e27918125
                                    :  for 9105023488 bytes
                    Clearing computer memory...
```

Results:

Assertion & Expected Result	Actual Result
AM-03 Execution environment is XE.	as expected
AO-09 Tool converts image file format.	as expected
AO-23 Logged information is correct.	as expected

Analysis: Expected results achieved

5.2.73 DA-26-D2E

Test Case DA-26-D2E ILook IXimager Version 2.0, Feb 01 2006	
Description:	DA-26 Convert an image to an alternate image file format.
Assertions:	AM-03 The tool executes in execution environment XE. AO-09 If the tool converts a source image file from one format to a target image file in another format, the acquired data represented in the target image file is the same as the acquired data in the source image file. AO-23 If the tool logs any log significant information, the information is accurately recorded in the log file.
Tester Name:	Brl
Test Host:	JohnSteed
Test Date:	Tue May 16 11:06:27 2006
Drives:	src(4D-FU2) dst (4D-FU2) other (none)

Source Setup:	src hash: < F5F9F2903DCAB895F36E270FB22A722E27918125 >
	17783249 total sectors (9105023488 bytes)
	Model (QM39100TD-SCA) serial # (PCB=20-116711-06 HDAQM39100TD-SCA)
	  N Start LBA Length Start C/H/S End C/H/S boot Partition type
	  1 P 000000063 017751762 0000/001/01 1023/254/63 Boot 07 NTFS
	  2 P 000000000 000000000 0000/000/00 0000/000/00 00 empty entry
	  3 P 000000000 000000000 0000/000/00 0000/000/00 00 empty entry
	  4 P 000000000 000000000 0000/000/00 0000/000/00 00 empty entry
	  1 017751762 sectors 9088902144 bytes

Log Highlights:	IXImager Log file

	Test Case DA-26-D2E ILook IXimager Version 2.0, Feb 01 2006
| | ```
hda: 156301488 sectors (80026 MB) w/8192KiB Cache, CHS=9729/255/63,
UDMA(100)
SCSI device sda: 781443888 512-byte hdwr sectors (400099 MB)
User selected ILook Encrypted Image Format
Initializing...
Opened output file '/ILookImager/ILook.027/DA06SCSI001.asb'
Beginning Copy operation for 9105023488 bytes
Beginning Copy operation
Beginning Copy operation
Copy Complete
Copy was completed successfully.

Read            : 606.9 MB (606900616 bytes)
Written         : 609.1 MB (609122162 bytes)
Total Processed : 9.105 GB (9105023488 bytes)
Copy Speed      : 20.51 MB/sec
Elapsed Time    : 0h  7m 24s
Compression     : 93.31%
Bad Sectors     : 0
SHA-1 Value     : f5f9f2903dcab895f36e270fb22a722e27918125
                : for 9105023488 bytes
Clearing computer memory...
Initializing...
Beginning Verify operation for 9105023488 bytes
Beginning Verify operation
Beginning Verify operation
Verify Complete
Verify was completed successfully.

Read            : 606.9 MB (606900616 bytes)
Written         : 0.000 MB (0 bytes)
Total Processed : 9.105 GB (9105023488 bytes)
Verify Speed    : 31.72 MB/sec
Elapsed Time    : 0h  4m 47s
Bad Sectors     : 0
SHA-1 Value     : f5f9f2903dcab895f36e270fb22a722e27918125
                : for 9105023488 bytes
Clearing computer memory...
Initializing...
Beginning Verify operation for 9105023488 bytes
Beginning Verify operation
Beginning Verify operation
Verify Complete
Verify was completed successfully.

Read            : 609.1 MB (609122162 bytes)
Written         : 0.000 MB (0 bytes)
Total Processed : 9.105 GB (9105023488 bytes)
Verify Speed    : 30.25 MB/sec
Elapsed Time    : 0h  5m  1s
Bad Sectors     : 0
SHA-1 Value     : f5f9f2903dcab895f36e270fb22a722e27918125
                : for 9105023488 bytes
Clearing computer memory...
``` |
| Results: | |

Assertion & Expected Result	Actual Result
AM-03 Execution environment is XE.	as expected
AO-09 Tool converts image file format.	as expected
AO-23 Logged information is correct.	as expected

Analysis:	Expected results achieved

5.2.74 DA-26-D2R

	Test Case DA-26-D2R ILook IXimager Version 2.0, Feb 01 2006
Description:	DA-26 Convert an image to an alternate image file format.
Assertions:	AM-03 The tool executes in execution environment XE. AO-09 If the tool converts a source image file from one format to a target image file in another format, the acquired data represented in the target
```

Test Case DA-26-D2R ILook IXimager Version 2.0, Feb 01 2006	
	image file is the same as the acquired data in the source image file. AO-23 If the tool logs any log significant information, the information is accurately recorded in the log file.
Tester Name:	Brl
Test Host:	JohnSteed
Test Date:	Tue May 16 11:06:44 2006
Drives:	src(4D-FU2) dst (4D-FU2) other (none)
Source Setup:	src hash: < F5F9F2903DCAB895F36E270FB22A722E27918125 > 17783249 total sectors (9105023488 bytes) Model (QM39100TD-SCA) serial # (PCB=20-116711-06 HDAQM39100TD-SCA) N Start LBA Length Start C/H/S End C/H/S boot Partition type 1 P 000000063 017751762 0000/001/01 1023/254/63 Boot 07 NTFS 2 P 000000000 000000000 0000/000/00 0000/000/00 00 empty entry 3 P 000000000 000000000 0000/000/00 0000/000/00 00 empty entry 4 P 000000000 000000000 0000/000/00 0000/000/00 00 empty entry 1 017751762 sectors 9088902144 bytes
Log Highlights:	IXImager Log file hda: 156301488 sectors (80026 MB) w/8192KiB Cache, CHS=9729/255/63, UDMA(100) SCSI device sda: 781443888 512-byte hdwr sectors (400099 MB) User selected ILook Raw Image Format Initializing... Opened output file '/ILookImager/ILook.028/DA06SCSI001.asb' Beginning Copy operation for 9105023488 bytes Beginning Copy operation Beginning Copy operation Opened output file '/ILookImager/ILook.028/DA06SCSI002.asb' continuing at byte 648675328 Copy is being stored to /ILook.028/DA06SCSI002.asb Opened output file '/ILookImager/ILook.028/DA06SCSI003.asb' continuing at byte 1295384576 Copy is being stored to /ILook.028/DA06SCSI003.asb Opened output file '/ILookImager/ILook.028/DA06SCSI004.asb' continuing at byte 1942093824 Copy is being stored to /ILook.028/DA06SCSI004.asb Opened output file '/ILookImager/ILook.028/DA06SCSI005.asb' continuing at byte 2588803072 Copy is being stored to /ILook.028/DA06SCSI005.asb Opened output file '/ILookImager/ILook.028/DA06SCSI006.asb' continuing at byte 3235512320 Copy is being stored to /ILook.028/DA06SCSI006.asb Opened output file '/ILookImager/ILook.028/DA06SCSI007.asb' continuing at byte 3882221568 Copy is being stored to /ILook.028/DA06SCSI007.asb Opened output file '/ILookImager/ILook.028/DA06SCSI008.asb' continuing at byte 4528930816 Copy is being stored to /ILook.028/DA06SCSI008.asb Opened output file '/ILookImager/ILook.028/DA06SCSI009.asb' continuing at byte 5175640064 Copy is being stored to /ILook.028/DA06SCSI009.asb Opened output file '/ILookImager/ILook.028/DA06SCSI010.asb' continuing at byte 5822349312 Copy is being stored to /ILook.028/DA06SCSI010.asb Opened output file '/ILookImager/ILook.028/DA06SCSI011.asb' continuing at byte 6469058560 Copy is being stored to /ILook.028/DA06SCSI011.asb Opened output file '/ILookImager/ILook.028/DA06SCSI012.asb' continuing at byte 7115767808 Copy is being stored to /ILook.028/DA06SCSI012.asb Opened output file '/ILookImager/ILook.028/DA06SCSI013.asb' continuing at byte 7762477056 Copy is being stored to /ILook.028/DA06SCSI013.asb Opened output file '/ILookImager/ILook.028/DA06SCSI014.asb' continuing at byte 8409186304 Copy is being stored to /ILook.028/DA06SCSI014.asb Opened output file '/ILookImager/ILook.028/DA06SCSI015.asb' continuing at byte 9055895552 Copy is being stored to /ILook.028/DA06SCSI015.asb Copy Complete Copy was completed successfully.

Test Case DA-26-D2R ILook IXimager Version 2.0, Feb 01 2006

```
Read             : 606.9 MB (606900616 bytes)
Written          : 9.123 GB (9122743904 bytes)
Total Processed: 9.105 GB (9105023488 bytes)
Copy Speed       : 10.29 MB/sec
Elapsed Time     : 0h 14m 45s
Bad Sectors      : 0
SHA-1 Value      : f5f9f2903dcab895f36e270fb22a722e27918125
                 : for 9105023488 bytes
Clearing computer memory...
Initializing...
Beginning Verify operation for 9105023488 bytes
Beginning Verify operation
Beginning Verify operation
Verify Complete
Verify was completed successfully.

Read             : 606.9 MB (606900616 bytes)
Written          : 0.000 MB (0 bytes)
Total Processed: 9.105 GB (9105023488 bytes)
Verify Speed     : 31.72 MB/sec
Elapsed Time     : 0h  4m 47s
Bad Sectors      : 0
SHA-1 Value      : f5f9f2903dcab895f36e270fb22a722e27918125
                 : for 9105023488 bytes
Clearing computer memory...
Initializing...
Beginning Verify operation for 9105023488 bytes
Beginning Verify operation
Beginning Verify operation
Opened input file '/ILookImager/ILook.028/DA06SCSI002.asb'
continuing at byte 646709248
Calculating SHA-1 hash of /ILook.028/DA06SCSI002.asb
Opened input file '/ILookImager/ILook.028/DA06SCSI003.asb'
continuing at byte 1293418496
Calculating SHA-1 hash of /ILook.028/DA06SCSI003.asb
Opened input file '/ILookImager/ILook.028/DA06SCSI004.asb'
continuing at byte 1940127744
Calculating SHA-1 hash of /ILook.028/DA06SCSI004.asb
Opened input file '/ILookImager/ILook.028/DA06SCSI005.asb'
continuing at byte 2586836992
Calculating SHA-1 hash of /ILook.028/DA06SCSI005.asb
Opened input file '/ILookImager/ILook.028/DA06SCSI006.asb'
continuing at byte 3233546240
Calculating SHA-1 hash of /ILook.028/DA06SCSI006.asb
Opened input file '/ILookImager/ILook.028/DA06SCSI007.asb'
continuing at byte 3880255488
Calculating SHA-1 hash of /ILook.028/DA06SCSI007.asb
Opened input file '/ILookImager/ILook.028/DA06SCSI008.asb'
continuing at byte 4526964736
Calculating SHA-1 hash of /ILook.028/DA06SCSI008.asb
Opened input file '/ILookImager/ILook.028/DA06SCSI009.asb'
continuing at byte 5173673984
Calculating SHA-1 hash of /ILook.028/DA06SCSI009.asb
Opened input file '/ILookImager/ILook.028/DA06SCSI010.asb'
continuing at byte 5820383232
Calculating SHA-1 hash of /ILook.028/DA06SCSI010.asb
Opened input file '/ILookImager/ILook.028/DA06SCSI011.asb'
continuing at byte 6467092480
Calculating SHA-1 hash of /ILook.028/DA06SCSI011.asb
Opened input file '/ILookImager/ILook.028/DA06SCSI012.asb'
continuing at byte 7113801728
Calculating SHA-1 hash of /ILook.028/DA06SCSI012.asb
Opened input file '/ILookImager/ILook.028/DA06SCSI013.asb'
continuing at byte 7760510976
Calculating SHA-1 hash of /ILook.028/DA06SCSI013.asb
Opened input file '/ILookImager/ILook.028/DA06SCSI014.asb'
continuing at byte 8407220224
Calculating SHA-1 hash of /ILook.028/DA06SCSI014.asb
Opened input file '/ILookImager/ILook.028/DA06SCSI015.asb'
continuing at byte 9053929472
Calculating SHA-1 hash of /ILook.028/DA06SCSI015.asb
Verify Complete
```

Test Case DA-26-D2R ILook IXimager Version 2.0, Feb 01 2006	
	Verify was completed successfully. Read : 9.123 GB (9122743904 bytes) Written : 0.000 MB (0 bytes) Total Processed: 9.105 GB (9105023488 bytes) Verify Speed : 12.00 MB/sec Elapsed Time : 0h 12m 39s Bad Sectors : 0 SHA-1 Value : f5f9f2903dcab895f36e270fb22a722e27918125 : for 9105023488 bytes Clearing computer memory...
Results:	<table><tr><th>Assertion & Expected Result</th><th>Actual Result</th></tr><tr><td>AM-03 Execution environment is XE.</td><td>as expected</td></tr><tr><td>AO-09 Tool converts image file format.</td><td>as expected</td></tr><tr><td>AO-23 Logged information is correct.</td><td>as expected</td></tr></table>
Analysis:	Expected results achieved

5.2.75 DA-26-e2d

Test Case DA-26-e2d ILook IXimager Version 2.0, Feb 01 2006	
Description:	DA-26 Convert an image to an alternate image file format.
Assertions:	AM-03 The tool executes in execution environment XE. AO-09 If the tool converts a source image file from one format to a target image file in another format, the acquired data represented in the target image file is the same as the acquired data in the source image file. AO-23 If the tool logs any log significant information, the information is accurately recorded in the log file.
Tester Name:	Brl
Test Host:	JohnSteed
Test Date:	Tue May 16 11:07:04 2006
Drives:	src(4D-FU2) dst (4D-FU2) other (none)
Source Setup:	src hash: < F5F9F2903DCAB895F36E270FB22A722E27918125 > 17783249 total sectors (9105023488 bytes) Model (QM39100TD-SCA) serial # (PCB=20-116711-06 HDAQM39100TD-SCA) N Start LBA Length Start C/H/S End C/H/S boot Partition type 1 P 000000063 017751762 0000/001/01 1023/254/63 Boot 07 NTFS 2 P 000000000 000000000 0000/000/00 0000/000/00 00 empty entry 3 P 000000000 000000000 0000/000/00 0000/000/00 00 empty entry 4 P 000000000 000000000 0000/000/00 0000/000/00 00 empty entry 1 017751762 sectors 9088902144 bytes
Log Highlights:	IXImager Log file hda: 156301488 sectors (80026 MB) w/8192KiB Cache, CHS=9729/255/63, UDMA(100) SCSI device sda: 781443888 512-byte hdwr sectors (400099 MB) User selected ILook Default Image Format Initializing... Opened output file '/ILookImager/ILook.033/DA10ENCRYPTED001.asb' Beginning Copy operation for 9105023488 bytes Beginning Copy operation Beginning Copy operation Copy Complete Copy was completed successfully. Read : 609.1 MB (609137424 bytes) Written : 606.9 MB (606897233 bytes) Total Processed: 9.105 GB (9105023488 bytes) Copy Speed : 20.41 MB/sec Elapsed Time : 0h 7m 26s Compression : 93.33% Bad Sectors : 0 SHA-1 Value : f5f9f2903dcab895f36e270fb22a722e27918125 : for 9105023488 bytes Clearing computer memory...

```
Test Case DA-26-e2d ILook IXimager Version 2.0, Feb 01 2006
```
	Initializing...
	Beginning Verify operation for 9105023488 bytes
	Beginning Verify operation
	Beginning Verify operation
	Verify Complete
	Verify was completed successfully.
	
	Read : 609.1 MB (609137424 bytes)
	Written : 0.000 MB (0 bytes)
	Total Processed : 9.105 GB (9105023488 bytes)
	Verify Speed : 29.85 MB/sec
	Elapsed Time : 0h 5m 5s
	Bad Sectors : 0
	SHA-1 Value : f5f9f2903dcab895f36e270fb22a722e27918125
	                : for 9105023488 bytes
	Clearing computer memory...
	Initializing...
	Beginning Verify operation for 9105023488 bytes
	Beginning Verify operation
	Beginning Verify operation
	Verify Complete
	Verify was completed successfully.
	
	Read : 606.9 MB (606897233 bytes)
	Written : 0.000 MB (0 bytes)
	Total Processed : 9.105 GB (9105023488 bytes)
	Verify Speed : 31.84 MB/sec
	Elapsed Time : 0h 4m 46s
	Bad Sectors : 0
	SHA-1 Value : f5f9f2903dcab895f36e270fb22a722e27918125
	                : for 9105023488 bytes
	Clearing computer memory...

Results:	<table><tr><th>Assertion & Expected Result</th><th>Actual Result</th></tr><tr><td>AM-03 Execution environment is XE.</td><td>as expected</td></tr><tr><td>AO-09 Tool converts image file format.</td><td>as expected</td></tr><tr><td>AO-23 Logged information is correct.</td><td>as expected</td></tr></table>
Analysis:	Expected results achieved

5.2.76 DA-26-r2d

```
Test Case DA-26-r2d ILook IXimager Version 2.0, Feb 01 2006
```
Description:	DA-26 Convert an image to an alternate image file format.
Assertions:	AM-03 The tool executes in execution environment XE. AO-09 If the tool converts a source image file from one format to a target image file in another format, the acquired data represented in the target image file is the same as the acquired data in the source image file. AO-23 If the tool logs any log significant information, the information is accurately recorded in the log file.
Tester Name:	Brl
Test Host:	JohnSteed
Test Date:	Tue May 16 11:07:39 2006
Drives:	src(4D-FU2) dst (4D-FU2) other (none)

Source Setup:	src hash: < F5F9F2903DCAB895F36E270FB22A722E27918125 >
	17783249 total sectors (9105023488 bytes)
	Model (QM39100TD-SCA) serial # (PCB=20-116711-06 HDAQM39100TD-SCA)
	  N Start LBA Length Start C/H/S End C/H/S boot Partition type
	  1 P 000000063 017751762 0000/001/01 1023/254/63 Boot 07 NTFS
	  2 P 000000000 000000000 0000/000/00 0000/000/00 00 empty entry
	  3 P 000000000 000000000 0000/000/00 0000/000/00 00 empty entry
	  4 P 000000000 000000000 0000/000/00 0000/000/00 00 empty entry
	  1 017751762 sectors 9088902144 bytes

Log Highlights:	IXImager Log file hda: 156301488 sectors (80026 MB) w/8192KiB Cache, CHS=9729/255/63,

```
Test Case DA-26-r2d ILook IXimager Version 2.0, Feb 01 2006
                UDMA(100)
                SCSI device sda: 781443888 512-byte hdwr sectors (400099 MB)
                User selected ILook Default Image Format
                Initializing...
                Opened output file '/ILookImager/ILook.034/DA10RAW001.asb'
                Beginning Copy operation for 9105023488 bytes
                Beginning Copy operation
                Beginning Copy operation
                Opened input file '/ILookImager/ILook.022/DA10RAW002.asb'
                continuing at byte 646709248
                Making a copy of /ILook.022/DA10RAW002.asb
                Opened input file '/ILookImager/ILook.022/DA10RAW003.asb'
                continuing at byte 1293418496
                Making a copy of /ILook.022/DA10RAW003.asb
                Opened input file '/ILookImager/ILook.022/DA10RAW004.asb'
                continuing at byte 1940127744
                Making a copy of /ILook.022/DA10RAW004.asb
                Opened input file '/ILookImager/ILook.022/DA10RAW005.asb'
                continuing at byte 2586836992
                Making a copy of /ILook.022/DA10RAW005.asb
                Opened input file '/ILookImager/ILook.022/DA10RAW006.asb'
                continuing at byte 3233546240
                Making a copy of /ILook.022/DA10RAW006.asb
                Opened input file '/ILookImager/ILook.022/DA10RAW007.asb'
                continuing at byte 3880255488
                Making a copy of /ILook.022/DA10RAW007.asb
                Opened input file '/ILookImager/ILook.022/DA10RAW008.asb'
                continuing at byte 4526964736
                Making a copy of /ILook.022/DA10RAW008.asb
                Opened input file '/ILookImager/ILook.022/DA10RAW009.asb'
                continuing at byte 5173673984
                Making a copy of /ILook.022/DA10RAW009.asb
                Opened input file '/ILookImager/ILook.022/DA10RAW010.asb'
                continuing at byte 5820383232
                Making a copy of /ILook.022/DA10RAW010.asb
                Opened input file '/ILookImager/ILook.022/DA10RAW011.asb'
                continuing at byte 6467092480
                Making a copy of /ILook.022/DA10RAW011.asb
                Opened input file '/ILookImager/ILook.022/DA10RAW012.asb'
                continuing at byte 7113801728
                Making a copy of /ILook.022/DA10RAW012.asb
                Opened input file '/ILookImager/ILook.022/DA10RAW013.asb'
                continuing at byte 7760510976
                Making a copy of /ILook.022/DA10RAW013.asb
                Opened input file '/ILookImager/ILook.022/DA10RAW014.asb'
                continuing at byte 8407220224
                Making a copy of /ILook.022/DA10RAW014.asb
                Opened input file '/ILookImager/ILook.022/DA10RAW015.asb'
                continuing at byte 9053929472
                Making a copy of /ILook.022/DA10RAW015.asb
                Copy Complete
                Copy was completed successfully.

                Read           : 9.123 GB (9122743904 bytes)
                Written        : 606.9 MB (606936490 bytes)
                Total Processed: 9.105 GB (9105023488 bytes)
                Copy Speed     : 9.188 MB/sec
                Elapsed Time   : 0h 16m 31s
                Compression    : 93.33%
                Bad Sectors    : 0
                SHA-1 Value    : f5f9f2903dcab895f36e270fb22a722e27918125
                               : for 9105023488 bytes
                Clearing computer memory...
                Initializing...
                Beginning Verify operation for 9105023488 bytes
                Beginning Verify operation
                Beginning Verify operation
                Opened input file '/ILookImager/ILook.022/DA10RAW002.asb'
                continuing at byte 646709248
                Calculating SHA-1 hash of /ILook.022/DA10RAW002.asb
                Opened input file '/ILookImager/ILook.022/DA10RAW003.asb'
                continuing at byte 1293418496
                Calculating SHA-1 hash of /ILook.022/DA10RAW003.asb
```

Test Case DA-26-r2d ILook IXimager Version 2.0, Feb 01 2006

```
Opened input file '/ILookImager/ILook.022/DA10RAW004.asb'
continuing at byte 1940127744
Calculating SHA-1 hash of /ILook.022/DA10RAW004.asb
Opened input file '/ILookImager/ILook.022/DA10RAW005.asb'
continuing at byte 2586836992
Calculating SHA-1 hash of /ILook.022/DA10RAW005.asb
Opened input file '/ILookImager/ILook.022/DA10RAW006.asb'
continuing at byte 3233546240
Calculating SHA-1 hash of /ILook.022/DA10RAW006.asb
Opened input file '/ILookImager/ILook.022/DA10RAW007.asb'
continuing at byte 3880255488
Calculating SHA-1 hash of /ILook.022/DA10RAW007.asb
Opened input file '/ILookImager/ILook.022/DA10RAW008.asb'
continuing at byte 4526964736
Calculating SHA-1 hash of /ILook.022/DA10RAW008.asb
Opened input file '/ILookImager/ILook.022/DA10RAW009.asb'
continuing at byte 5173673984
Calculating SHA-1 hash of /ILook.022/DA10RAW009.asb
Opened input file '/ILookImager/ILook.022/DA10RAW010.asb'
continuing at byte 5820383232
Calculating SHA-1 hash of /ILook.022/DA10RAW010.asb
Opened input file '/ILookImager/ILook.022/DA10RAW011.asb'
continuing at byte 6467092480
Calculating SHA-1 hash of /ILook.022/DA10RAW011.asb
Opened input file '/ILookImager/ILook.022/DA10RAW012.asb'
continuing at byte 7113801728
Calculating SHA-1 hash of /ILook.022/DA10RAW012.asb
Opened input file '/ILookImager/ILook.022/DA10RAW013.asb'
continuing at byte 7760510976
Calculating SHA-1 hash of /ILook.022/DA10RAW013.asb
Opened input file '/ILookImager/ILook.022/DA10RAW014.asb'
continuing at byte 8407220224
Calculating SHA-1 hash of /ILook.022/DA10RAW014.asb
Opened input file '/ILookImager/ILook.022/DA10RAW015.asb'
continuing at byte 9053929472
Calculating SHA-1 hash of /ILook.022/DA10RAW015.asb
Verify Complete
Verify was completed successfully.

Read            :  9.123 GB (9122743904 bytes)
Written         :  0.000 MB (0 bytes)
Total Processed:  9.105 GB (9105023488 bytes)
Verify Speed    :  12.04 MB/sec
Elapsed Time    :  0h 12m 36s
Bad Sectors     :  0
SHA-1 Value     :  f5f9f2903dcab895f36e270fb22a722e27918125
                :  for 9105023488 bytes
Clearing computer memory...
Initializing...
Beginning Verify operation for 9105023488 bytes
Beginning Verify operation
Beginning Verify operation
Verify Complete
Verify was completed successfully.

Read            :  606.9 MB (606936490 bytes)
Written         :  0.000 MB (0 bytes)
Total Processed:  9.105 GB (9105023488 bytes)
Verify Speed    :  31.72 MB/sec
Elapsed Time    :  0h  4m 47s
Bad Sectors     :  0
SHA-1 Value     :  f5f9f2903dcab895f36e270fb22a722e27918125
                :  for 9105023488 bytes
Clearing computer memory...
```

Results:	Assertion & Expected Result	Actual Result
	AM-03 Execution environment is XE.	as expected
	AO-09 Tool converts image file format.	as expected
	AO-23 Logged information is correct.	as expected

Analysis:	Expected results achieved

About the National Institute of Justice

NIJ is the research, development, and evaluation agency of the U.S. Department of Justice. NIJ's mission is to advance scientific research, development, and evaluation to enhance the administration of justice and public safety. NIJ's principal authorities are derived from the Omnibus Crime Control and Safe Streets Act of 1968, as amended (see 42 U.S.C. §§ 3721–3723).

The NIJ Director is appointed by the President and confirmed by the Senate. The Director establishes the Institute's objectives, guided by the priorities of the Office of Justice Programs, the U.S. Department of Justice, and the needs of the field. The Institute actively solicits the views of criminal justice and other professionals and researchers to inform its search for the knowledge and tools to guide policy and practice.

Strategic Goals

NIJ has seven strategic goals grouped into three categories:

Creating relevant knowledge and tools

1. Partner with State and local practitioners and policymakers to identify social science research and technology needs.
2. Create scientific, relevant, and reliable knowledge—with a particular emphasis on terrorism, violent crime, drugs and crime, cost-effectiveness, and community-based efforts—to enhance the administration of justice and public safety.
3. Develop affordable and effective tools and technologies to enhance the administration of justice and public safety.

Dissemination

4. Disseminate relevant knowledge and information to practitioners and policymakers in an understandable, timely, and concise manner.
5. Act as an honest broker to identify the information, tools, and technologies that respond to the needs of stakeholders.

Agency management

6. Practice fairness and openness in the research and development process.
7. Ensure professionalism, excellence, accountability, cost-effectiveness, and integrity in the management and conduct of NIJ activities and programs.

Program Areas

In addressing these strategic challenges, the Institute is involved in the following program areas: crime control and prevention, including policing; drugs and crime; justice systems and offender behavior, including corrections; violence and victimization; communications and information technologies; critical incident response; investigative and forensic sciences, including DNA; less-than-lethal technologies; officer protection; education and training technologies; testing and standards; technology assistance to law enforcement and corrections agencies; field testing of promising programs; and international crime control.

In addition to sponsoring research and development and technology assistance, NIJ evaluates programs, policies, and technologies. NIJ communicates its research and evaluation findings through conferences and print and electronic media.

To find out more about the National Institute of Justice, please visit:

http://www.ojp.usdoj.gov/nij

or contact:

National Criminal Justice
 Reference Service
P.O. Box 6000
Rockville, MD 20849–6000
800–851–3420
e-mail: *askncjrs@ncjrs.org*